M000204654

Sponsored by:

SUPREME PRINTING LTD.
Unit 104 , 1915 - 27 Ave N.E.
Calgary AB T2E 7E4
Tel.: 403-277-7779
info@SupremePrinting.ca
www.SupremePrinting.ca

Thank you Sam at Supreme, for supporting
printing costs, and recognizing the importance
of elevating women's confidence with
copies being shared with women's shelters,
foundations and not-for-profit groups.

elevate &
inspire others!

Yvonne

Words,
Women & Wisdom™

The Modern Art of Confident Conversations.

For the woman who wants to elevate her voice.

Rediscover your inner confidence

and take a stand in life and business

by using powerful language — in modern ways.

EARLY PRAISE AND COMMENTS

"Written in a conversational, almost confiding tone this guidebook offers a somewhat fresh perspective to women everywhere, who are looking to increase their authority and take a stand for themselves in life and business. If you want to make an impact and fulfill your potential in life and business, this is a MUST read. It's the book we've all been waiting for." — *Jayne Warrilow, Author The 10 Day Coaches MBA, Founder of Coaches Business School*

"This is a time of massive global change & individual transformation. And I believe women have the power to inspire change that's good for everyone. Yvonne Silver's book offers a treasure trove of mind-shifting insights and practical guidance that will quickly & easily elevate influence, conversation, and confidence. I'm recommending this powerful book of powerful words to all my clients. Whether you call it your library or your toolbox, make sure this book is in there."
— *Ben Gioia, Helping Kick-Ass, Heart-Based Women Change The World, InfluenceWithAHeart.com*

"Missing from the curriculum! I wish someone had taught me years ago all the important messages that Yvonne conveys in this book. As women step more and more into their rightful places in society, the knowledge gained from this book will help get them there faster and easier. My very best wishes for your book's success!"
— *Renee Paser-Paull, President, Soaring Pathways (Changing survivors into thrivers, by transforming sexual trauma)*

"I have had the pleasure to work with and be friends with Yvonne for over a decade and have watched her grow and FLOURISH in her business ventures. Reading "Words, Women & Wisdom - The Modern Art of Confident Conversations" is like speaking with her across the table as she shares her personal experiences and wisdom garnered over twenty-five years of entrepreneurial business success; from sales, to an HR leader, and then as a professional

coach and mentor. Yvonne's writing style is conversational and makes it easy for women to learn how to create greater success and happiness in their professional and personal lives through more confident conversation!"
— *Linda L. Matthie, Entrepreneur/Consultant/Author, MentorCloud, Inc.*

"At a time when it seems that people in general are reducing their vocabulary to meaningless expletives, here comes Yvonne, with a book that provides an insight into and road map, the destination of which is to demonstrate how, using the right word, in the right situation can bring the right solution for those who dare to learn and speak up . . ."
— *Jo Ackerman, Director, Fusion Therapy Services Ltd.*

"In "Words, Women & Wisdom: The Modern Art of Confident Conversations," Yvonne E.L. Silver combines her own professional and personal expertise with research into an action producing guide book for women to confidently step into their full potential by paying attention to the conversations they have with themselves and others."
— *Marilyn O'Hearne, MA, MCC, Potential, Prosperity & Peace Unlocking Coach and author of "Breaking Free from Bias: Preventing Costly Complaints, Conflict and Talent Loss.*

"To care for yourself is living from commitment. To care with others is living from purpose. And, to express your commitment and purpose is about presence.
Yvonne Silver offers women insights and activities to live from presence. Using a mix of personal experiences and the results of others, she encourages the use of confident conversations to breathe life into being for the world. That is, being naturally YOU, to flourish in your life as you nurture your relationships."
— *Dr. Stephen Hobbs, Business/Life Author and Founder of WELLth Movement*

Make an impact, make a difference - for other women too.

"For every book purchased, I am committed to donating one copy of this book to a women's shelter, not-for-profit or foundation, honoring a Buy One, Give One — B1G1 social enterprise model.

Please consider purchasing an extra copy for a girlfriend, work colleague, sister, mother or student who would benefit from having more confidence, as every book purchased makes a huge difference."

Warmly, Yvonne

Words, Women & Wisdom™

The Modern Art of Confident Conversations.

For the woman who wants to elevate her voice.

By Yvonne E.L. Silver

2018
Women and Wisdom Media

Words, Women & Wisdom
The Modern Art of Confident Conversations

Published by Yvonne E.L. Silver
In Association with Women & Wisdom Media

First Printing: October 2018
Edition 000.000.000.001

Printed and bound in Canada

Copyright © 2018 by Yvonne E.L. Silver
All rights reserved.

This book may not be reproduced in whole or in part by any means without express
written permission from the author, save short extracts for review purposes.
Such extracts should not exceed 200 words.

For more information, go to WordsWomenAndWisdom.com
Contact at: Admin@WordsWomenAndWisdom.com
In Association with Women & Wisdom Media — Calgary, Alberta, Canada

Editor: Naomi Lewis

Cover by Rebeca Covers
Book Design by Red Spot Books

ISBN: 978-1-9994074-0-7 (paperback)
ISBN: 978-1-9994074-1-4 (e-book)
ISBN: 978-1-9994074-2-1 (audio book)

Disclaimer:

Due to the dynamic nature of the Internet, any web addresses or links
mentioned in this book may change without notice. The author has
included the most up-to-date information available as of time of
publication.
The material, ideas, and content in this book cannot substitute for
professional advice, and individualized professional coaching
conversations are encouraged as an extension of this content. The
author shares stories to the best of her recollection or based on
transcriptions of recorded interviews.

Table of Contents

Chapter Seven: Powerful Words at Work — Be Heard!   . . . 224

Chapter Eight: When No Words Are Required   . . . 269

DEDICATION

To my mother Peggy, my original Mentor, who taught me the power of words to elevate or deflate in a heartbeat.

To you, the reader, for being willing to explore how to use more confident language with your feminine yet assertive energy. To request what you want in a win-win way that honours who you are while expressing your needs clearly and assertively. As each airline safety demonstration shares, you must put your own oxygen mask on first, as ONLY then can you help others do the same. Slip it on with ease and grace, and show others how to treat you the way you want to be treated.

Confident conversations happen when you begin with a positive intention and the knowledge that you can often shift the outcome by changing just one word …

Preface

Ladies — it's time! This book is for women who want to feel more confident. When women feel confident in their relationships, they are stronger role models for their children and their career and family thrives. Women can help evolve a powerful nurturing ripple effect for others, especially other women.

Where business is led by women, we infuse our feminine energy, nurturing collaboration and make heart-based decisions. Our focus is long-term sustainability and thoughtful impact, creating a better world our children will be proud to inherit. Yet the fast pace of our economy (as data shows, still led by a majority of male executives and board members) is driven by short-term monetary goals vs. long-term vision for creating a better world. It's time for change. It's time to bring these two disparities together.

I believe women have a powerful role to play as leaders —

leaders of our own lives first, our families second, and our

communities third.

When women have confident conversations — are truly heard — collaboration and co-operation flourishes. Confident women are promoted, receive salary increases, and secure promotions. I want YOU to step into your maximum potential and your highest earning power, by using more powerful language and having more confident conversations. With the social media explosion following the Harvey Weinstein allegations, women are no longer willing to be quiet and subservient bystanders of their lives. It is time for women to be heard and respected. Using more confident and effective language is a beginning.

Confidence comes from deep within, as our words reflect what we feel inside, and how our grounded energy and inner knowing shines through in our external communications. Let's meet the world where it is right now, with the elevated social media focus on treating women more fairly and respectfully. What kind of beautiful shift occurs in this perfect storm of events?

ACKNOWLEDGEMENTS

There are many people who I am grateful to have in my life, who have impacted creating this book and influenced the content, including:

Alex — my special-needs son (age twenty-three at time of writing), who teaches me patience and persistence — who never gives up on an idea or a dream, and lives life with a passionate and generous heart. The brown leather bracelet he gave me on Mother's Day 2014 inscribed with delicate silver lettering, highlighted specific words which I needed to draw strength from at that time. That beautiful gift was a powerful catalyst for my own healing journey (from being driven and burning out to flourishing with ease and flow) and was the impetus for writing this book, as I recognized incredible power that words can have.

John — my husband, who has given his unwavering support for completing this book, dedicated himself to keeping the home fires burning and the lights on at home, while I journeyed into the unknown. He provides love and stability with a mix of music and fun, despite the unclear impact this book may have, to change and enrich our lives, and enhance the lives of many women globally.

Jayne Warrilow — my coach, who opened my eyes to the world of energetic resonance, and continues to support my evolution. Jayne encourages me to step up to a bigger role of teacher and "uplift the spirit of humanity" by sharing my experiences with compassion, creativity, awareness, and increased consciousness.

Rita Bozi — **energy healer extraordinaire**, who lovingly guides me to my own authentic centre, peeling back the layers of hurt and aggressive energy to find the assertive feminine energy within, and helping me to heal the traumatic events of my early life.

Dixie Bennett — **reiki master and angelic being**, who teaches me the power of the unseen: healing reiki energy and love, the energy of crystals, vibrational elevation techniques, tools and how to release stuck energy showing up in my body as pain. Your gentle yet powerful and wise light shines brightly in the world.

My female clients and protégées, who are willing to dig deeply to find their own truths, while helping me refine many of these language concepts. I continue to learn from them, while helping them to achieve their big goals and dreams.

My Mother and Father — who taught me, albeit unwittingly perhaps, so many childhood lessons which have shaped my life experiences and this book content. *Dad — I forgive you for your words said in anger...*

Numerous spiritual and transformational teachers, including: **Oprah Winfrey** — who continuously expands my horizons by gathering and disseminating some of the greatest spiritual lessons, through transformational teachers showcased through the OWN television network (and sharing her favourite books and empowerment programs). Thank you to **T. Harv Eker** (Author of The Millionaire Mind and Quantum Leap workshops), **Jack Canfield** (Author of The Success Principles and coaching program) and **Satyen Raja** (Founder, Warrior Sage programs).

My influential women friends, colleagues and interview guests, many of who gladly shared their comments and word examples for the interviews supporting the book launch. *Thank you for believing in the vision that this book is needed in the world.* My guests interviewed for the pre-launch series included best-selling authors, award winning speakers, business founders and CEOs, a national president, a regional VP, a seasoned journalist and podcaster, a global media strategist, an image consultant and a self-care and embodiment coach. Thank you: *Teresa de Grosbois, Melinda Wittstock, Tasha Giroux, Marci Shimoff, Jenny Gulamani-Abdulla, Monica Kretschmer, Karen McGregor, Catherine Brownlee, Leslie Davies, Lisa Mundell-*

Lawrence, Christina Marlett, Patty Farmer, Brigitte Lessard-Deyell and Dr. Dahlia Mostafa, Andrea Iervella, and Alison Donaghey for sharing your wisdom and contributing to this book.

My dear friends and colleagues who have cheered me on and honoured the space I needed to write and finish this book — *thank you for your patience* — you know who you are :)

My supporters, sponsors and contributors — Thank you to those who committed early to help give this book the wings it needed to gain lift-off, leading to sharing it with thousands of women who are ready to expand.

The editing and production team Naomi Lewis and Renée Bennett for helping take my vision from an idea to reality, a published book.

To you, the reader — for being willing to explore how to use more confident language, with your feminine yet assertive energy. To request what you want, in a win-win way that honours who you are, while expressing your needs clearly and assertively. As each airline safety demonstration shares, you must put your own oxygen mask on first, as ONLY then can you help others to do the same. Slip it on with ease and grace, and show others how to treat you the way you want to be treated. Confident conversations happen when you begin with a positive intention, and the knowledge that you can often shift the outcome by changing just *one word*...

Please buy an extra copy of this book and gift it to another woman who could benefit from having more confidence and more confident conversations.

For every copy sold, one copy will be donated to a women's shelter, foundation, or not-for-profit.

INTRODUCTION

Women and Social Media

The world of business today — On a global level, the United Nations identified seventeen sustainable development goals, including gender equality as number five.[1] Gender equality is a lofty goal to reach, as is workplace parity, based on the current number of executive positions being held by women. At Catalyst (a research firm collecting data on women's topics for over 50 years) research shows women hold just 21.2 percent of the board seats in S&P (Standard and Poor) companies in 2017, and 26.5 percent in executive or senior level roles from a total of 44.7 percent of employees. How could equality in wages, respect in the workplace and confidence rise for women if that ratio was 50.0 percent of women holding leadership roles?

How can you be more confident?

I teach women to flourish in business. As a professional executive coach, I help women elevate their voices and have more confident conversations — to ask for what they really want **confidently**, and to achieve it. I combine my techniques learned over twenty-five years of high-growth business success, first in sales roles and later as a senior human resources (HR) leader working with high growth start-ups, and then as a professional coach and mentor. I have guided hundreds of sales conversations, interviewed and hired over six thousand people, and asked thousands of coaching questions to help people explore how to develop purposeful and fulfilling lives. In the past decade working specifically with professional women and female entrepreneurs, I have been asked one question more times than any other topic. *"How can I be more confident?"*

In January 2017, the idea for this book blossomed as I reflected on my results as a professional coach, supporting women and entrepreneurs. Over and over I had similar conversations with hundreds of women in business who were looking for new approaches to ask for what they really wanted, and to be heard. I saw a pattern with the words cropping up that diminished the power of women's energy. There were several concepts I had learned personally and shared which consistently helped my female clients (and protégées) elevate their confidence. The words and word concepts highlighted in this book are a culmination of insights gathered over twenty-five years of helping people find a place of alignment — living confidently and purposefully. It began with an appreciation of how living purposefully and resiliently intersects with positive energy and psychology, and how confident language emerges from high self-awareness combined with honesty and integrity.

Many of those years included supporting job-seekers looking for a workplace to connect their passions, express their full creativity, and find an environment which valued their contribution. In 2010, after taking an executive coaching certification, this fulfilling work has evolved to helping women in particular find clarity and purpose, and step into the strongest versions of themselves as female professionals, entrepreneurs, and corporate leaders. Throughout this book I share many stories to bring the concepts to life, combined with insights shared by my clients and several of the confident and influential women I have met on my journey.

This book was already almost eighty percent written before the events of fall 2017 exploded in the media, exposing the injustices of many working situations women experience, creating a perfect storm and time for this book to be born. The content provides practical approaches to support women in speaking up, asking for what they really want, encouraging others to engage in collaborative conversations (a dialogue rather than a monologue) for win-win outcomes. Weak words and poor voice intonation rob us of our power. This book is designed to raise your awareness about specific words to add and words to delete, a practical guide, with "Action Steps" included in each section.

Once a young girl living with oppression myself, I have taken years to fully step into my own confidence in a way that is assertive vs. aggressive. I have extensively honed my language skills and have immersed myself over the past twenty years with many of the world's most respected transformational teachers, including Jack Canfield, T. Harv Eker, and Jayne Warrilow. An avid reader and student, I have absorbed hundreds of books and hours of courses and TED Talks, combined with developing daily spiritual practices — uncovering my purpose and evolving my own confidence, while refining my skills as a speaker, mentor, and coach. This book contains the key tools and encouragement to practise using powerful language and confident conversations to enable your dreams to flourish too, with clarity and proven concepts supported by research and transformational teachings.

Ladies, it's time for change!

The world is more ready today for confident and

powerful women

to step forth than it has ever been. It's your time!

Fall 2017 — Historical events occurred

On Thursday October 5, 2017, *The New York Times* published a story detailing decades of allegations of sexual harassment against Harvey Weinstein, an American film producer. In the story, actresses Rose McGowan and Ashley Judd were among the many women who came forward to speak. Women who had for years been given the choice of tolerating sexual advances or facing limitations on their career advancement now stepped forth.

On January 7, 2018 at the 75th Golden Globe Awards, Hollywood celebrities gathered for their annual industry celebration while clearly stating that the harassment of women would no longer be tolerated. The culture of silence in order to get ahead, and of men who abused their seniority and power, was over. Many women in the industry who had been victims of harassment, or who had friends and colleagues who had been mistreated, banded together in black gowns showing solidarity, signalling change was long overdue. Oprah Winfrey, a strong example herself of living the "American Dream", spoke of the need for change. This series of recent events, highlighted with a platform of global awareness, fostered public outrage and offered a powerful mindset shift, which is yours to leverage if you choose. It's time for us to develop fair, inclusive working environments.

"I want all of the girls watching here now to know that a new day is on the horizon. And when that new day finally dawns, it will be because of a lot of magnificent women, many of whom are right here in this room tonight, and some pretty phenomenal men, fighting hard to make sure that they become the leaders who take us to the time when nobody ever has to say, "Me too," again."

Oprah Winfrey, OWN TV Network, speech while accepting the
Cecil B. de Mille award at the Golden Globe Awards
January 7, 2018

Since the complaints first surfaced, there are two initiatives in particular garnering public attention and support — the Time's Up Legal Defense Fund and the #MeToo movement. A group of three hundred women in the entertainment industry working to resolve the systemic power imbalances that have kept under-represented groups from reaching their full potential, have started a legal defense fund for sexual harassment claims.[2] The Time's Up Legal Defense Fund, spearheaded by Tina Tchen and Roberta Kaplan, will help individuals who experience sexual misconduct, including assault, abuse or harassment, find legal representation. Prior to its formal launch, Time's Up had raised more than thirteen million dollars from over two hundred donors. The media has become an ally for fairness and good conscience in many instances.

Your voice is powerful.

Your words are powerful.

When women have more confidence to speak up earlier in a chain of events and have assertive language concepts to ask for what they want and get it, fewer of these injustices will occur or be aired on social media. Based on my own childhood (shared later in this book) I saw firsthand how a woman's confidence can be drained by not speaking up, by not being heard.

A number of historical events have impacted the evolution of women. It took strong voices and courage to fight for being accepted to have a vote in politics and to gain the right to work outside the home. Change takes time. It takes more women speaking up, more ladies holding board, leadership and parliamentary positions to demonstrate our capability to lead, with more voices continuing to demand workplace equality and fairness.

Erasing the lack of equality has been an area of focus for almost ninety years for one women's organization in particular. The International Federation of Business and Professional Women (BPW) is one of the longest standing and most active women's advocacy groups globally, and has held consultative status at the United Nations Economic and Social Council (ECOSOC) since 1947.[3] The organization was founded in 1930 by Dr. Lena Madesin Phillips, a lawyer and clubwoman who was herself an example of leadership, having graduated top of her class from the University of Kentucky in 1917, the first woman to graduate with full honors from that institution.

Every woman can take a leadership role in advancing empowerment for women. In Canada where I live with my family, I proudly serve as an active member of BPW as mentorship chair in Calgary (2016-2018) continuing the focus of women's empowerment and advancement. As an active member I chair the Canadian Business Chicks Mentorship Program (2017-present), and also serve on the board for The Nest Foundation, supporting women rebuilding their lives through education. Through my own organizations "Flourish — with Yvonne Silver" and "Women & Wisdom Media," I passionately help women elevate their confidence, facilitating and hosting women's empowerment initiatives.

The *Modern Art of Confident Conversations* is not a history book, yet it is important to acknowledge how we came to the commonly accepted norms determining how women are treated today by understanding the overall context. When we notice and acknowledge the language we are using, we have more finely tuned awareness and choice to change our words for powerful and assertive language.

Feminism and the Women's Movement

From Adam and Eve in the Garden of Eden — where life was a simple harmonious balance of nature — to leading the homestead and family life, now women are mobilizing to showcase our contributions in today's more complex commercial world while seeking equality.

There are several key realizations in history leading to an uprising of women which are often grouped together under the term *feminism* (named as word of the year for 2017 by Mirriam-Webster Dictionary). The word dates back to 1851, a "state of being feminine." In the sense of "advocacy of women's rights" it dates to 1895 (Online Etymology Dictionary). According to Wikipedia, the feminist movement (also known as Women's Liberation, Women's Rights, Women's Suffrage, and the Women's Movement) refers to a series of political campaigns for reforms on issues such as reproductive rights, domestic violence, maternity leave, equal pay, women's suffrage, sexual harassment, and sexual violence, all of which fall under the label of feminism and the feminist movement. The movement's priorities vary among nations and communities and range from opposition to female genital mutilation in one country to opposition to breaking the corporate glass ceiling in another. [4]

Feminism in parts of the western world has seen three main waves of change:

First-wave feminism (from the 1830's)

Activity was oriented around the station of middle or upper-class white women and involved suffrage (the right to have a political vote) and political equality. The wave formally began at the Seneca Falls Convention in New York on July 19 and 20, 1848, when three hundred men and women rallied to the cause of equality for women, followed by a series of annual National Women's Rights Conventions in Worcester, Massachusetts. Elizabeth Cady Stanton drafted the Seneca Falls Declaration outlining the new movement's ideology and political strategies. [3]

With a younger history of Confederation, Canada has made significant strides regarding equality for women. Canada was founded in 1867 as a union of the British colonies, gaining independence from the United Kingdom in 1982. In Alberta, Western Canada, five women known as the "*Famous Five*" were petitioners in the ground-breaking Persons Case, brought before the Supreme Court of Canada in 1927. Led by Judge Emily Murphy, the "Famous Five" group included Henrietta Muir Edwards, Nellie McClung, Louise Crummy McKinney and Irene Parlby, who had years of active work in various campaigns for women's rights dating back to the 1880s and 1890s.[5]

Second-wave feminism (1960's–1990's)

With a focus on social and cultural inequalities, this wave brought in women of colour and women from other developing nations that were seeking solidarity between members of a group, or between classes or peoples. Coming off the heels of women supporting the Second World War effort, the second wave of feminism focused on the workplace, sexuality, family, and reproductive rights.

The ratification of the US Equal Rights Amendment, first proposed in 1923, was passed by the US Senate in 1972.[6] In Canada, one of the first major steps toward equality between women and men in the workforce was the passing of the *Fair Employment Practices Act and the Female Employees Fair Remuneration Act in Ontario* in 1951, to grant women equal pay for work of equal value.[7]

Third-wave feminism began in the mid-90's

Political activity that continues to address financial, social and cultural inequalities, and includes renewed campaigning for greater influence of women in politics and media — including women's reproductive rights, such as the right to abortion.[6] The girls of the third wave stepped onto the stage as strong and empowered, abstaining from victimization. They defined feminine beauty for themselves as subjects not as sex objects, with re-adoption of our feminine differences with lip-stick, high-heels, and cleavage proudly exposed by low cut necklines — no longer willing to wear suits and dress like men, as often seen in the first two phases of the movement when male oppression existed.

Words and information are powerful...

Fourth wave?

Recent events (early 2010s), suggests there may be a fourth wave characterized, in part, by new media platforms, which is now being widely experienced as social media spreading messages that offer hope for change. With over 1.6 billion households (89 percent) of all homes globally having one television set[8] (and 61 percent watching television) combined with the rise of internet usage, live streaming and Facebook, spreading ideas and information has become easier.

On March 11, 2013, International Women's Day, chief operating officer of Facebook Sheryl Sandberg published her book *Lean In: Women, Work, and the Will to Lead.* In 2017, the evolving Lean In organization partnered with McKinsey & Company to research 222 companies employing twelve million staff, to provide data for the report *Women in the Workplace 2017.*

Despite the progress made over the years of various women's movements, the report finds we still have a long way to go, as women hold just 21 percent of senior vice president roles, which are the talent pipeline to CEO positions. "Progress continues to be slow, with women underrepresented at all levels in corporate America despite earning more college degrees than men for the past 30 years. An equitable workplace allows the best talent to rise to the top regardless of gender, race, ethnicity, background or beliefs" the report summarizes.

One of the report's recommended "5 steps women can take to achieve better outcomes" in salary negotiation is to "ASK for a raise," as the data showed that just 23 percent was the highest statistic of women who asked for one (across four races and ethnicities). The other four recommendations included: specifying an amount, preparing, making your best pitch and soliciting manager support.[9] In Chapter Seven — "Powerful Words at Work — Be Heard!" *(Section 7.4)* I include examples of asking for a raise, based on my roles as a department manager, HR director, and as an executive coach.

It is important to celebrate our progress and successes. The annual Women of Inspiration celebration in Canada recognizes the accomplishments of women in over ten categories, as well as Women's Executive Network (WXN) annual Top 100 Most Powerful Women and annual listing of the Women of Influence Top 25 — to name a few groups acknowledging women making a difference. Women supporting women is a powerful concept! I was proud to be recognized with a Women of Inspiration Award for my contribution to empowering women through the mentorship programs I design and chair, in September 2018.

How can you take action in
the Women's Empowerment movement?

At the United Nations Global Compact on March 8, 2010 (International Women's Day) the Women's Empowerment Principles — Equality Means Business initiative was launched. The empowerment principles suggest seven steps for companies to take to empower women in the workplace.

The 7 *Women's Empowerment Principles* are:

1. Establish high-level corporate leadership for gender equality.
2. Treat all women and men fairly at work — respect and support human rights and non-discrimination.
3. Ensure the health, safety and well-being of all women and men workers.
4. Promote education, training and professional development for women.
5. Implement enterprise development, supply chain and marketing practices that empower women.
6. Promote equality through community initiatives and advocacy.
7. Measure and publicly report on progress to achieve gender equality.[10]

Are you willing to share these principles for discussion and action in your organization? Does your organization have a Women's Resource Centre to build collaboration and share knowledge, tools and information to help more women attain leadership positions?

What's my story, and why do I care about Women's Equality?

CRASH! Another plate slipped out of my mum's hands, falling to the linoleum kitchen floor of our modest home in N.W. London. I instantly thought, "There goes another set of dishes that is now incomplete, mismatched and not presentable when we have visitors or company coming by." As a stay-at-home mum, my mother was extremely house-proud, ensuring that our house was neat and tidy and having a set of matching dishes was important for her sense of pride. Yet we didn't have a complete matching set, ever, as long as I can remember.

Living in a household where a constant flow of negative language from my father slowly drained the confidence from my mum created a painful childhood. I saw her shattered nerves on a regular basis, as she periodically dropped dishes or drinking glasses. She slowly became an empty shell of the vibrant woman she had once been, exhausted by the constant criticism and comments from her husband questioning her abilities. She had been an adventurous young woman who learned how to drive at the earliest legal age possible (age seventeen in England) and was an independent working professional until she married my father. From the wedding photographs, she seemed excited to be married at age thirty-six, and looked forward to finally starting a family of her own. The Second World War, raging in over thirty countries from 1939 to 1945, had an impact on so many young women looking to marry.

My father was grazed on the temple by a bullet during a vicious battle in Dunkirk and was scarred for life by the experience. After seeing the tragedy and horror of war he returned home with thousands of other men, without having the psychological support that many soldiers needed to deal with their post-traumatic stress disorder (PTSD).

Slowly, his cutting remarks and critical comments, which showed up as violence and disrespect, wicked away the strength inside my mum and contributed to her being extremely nervous, sapping her confidence, and her body moved from attractively slim to incredibly thin. As a teenage girl, I saw this and vowed that I would never let a man destroy my confidence or take away my independence — and *freedom* became a word I highly valued.

Words — are so powerful.

My fascination with words began a long time ago, whether they appeared in a handwritten note, or were spoken verbally, whether printed in a novel or a reference book or sung with joy and passion — words are so powerful. I believe that words carry an energy that connects us, like the threads of a patchwork quilt that connect each unique and interesting piece with another — creating a glorious tapestry of life.

Words — are so powerful.

As I discovered through my own life journey, there are critical links between our use of words and our actions, our language and our behaviour, our mindset and our success in life. There are links between positive psychology and personal development and growth — motivated by encouraging words. Positive self-talk can bolster confidence and negative self-talk can create doubt. External bragging can push people away when comments echo with a self-centered focus. Words describing a common cause can bring us together with a rallying cry.

Words running through our heads from an upsetting conversation can distract us for hours — a cross word from a loved one can cause intense heartache for days, while words from a song embed individual verses in our soul for years, and poetry can trigger a lump in our throats.

Words — are so powerful.

My hope is that you deepen your appreciation for the power of your words, becoming more conscious of how you use specific words — both with yourself and with others around you. Your closest relationships — with your spouse and children, your extended family and your friends — are most impacted by your words. Positively or negatively — showing how you feel, what you are thinking, excitement or sadness, confusion or anger, piquing curiosity or when you need comfort.

Often, you share your thoughts with the people closest to you, yet they are powerless to make any changes to annoying situations, especially those at work. They may become sounding boards or even "punching bags" for venting frustration upon, as my mum became. Stop venting and take action, making the changes you want to see happen.

Words — are so powerful.

By becoming aware of your individual words first, then practising the conversational approaches shared in this book you can expand your power in a positive and concise way. This powerful book is about *HOW* to leverage your words, with brief definitions for each word showcased. Note down any unfamiliar words you come across in the back of this book and research the meaning for clarity and to expand your reading vocabulary.

Consider your intention and your tone. Notice how your words connect to your body language — and how a whole-body connection feels more authentic. A few words said in anger can create weeks of heartache to resolve, hence awareness and taking a few deep breaths matters (more on the power pause concept is shared later). I know from my own young experiences, a few words said in anger by a parent can impact your confidence for years. Please — if you are a parent especially — pay attention to your words!

Why is this book an important gift especially for women?

Women are raising their visibility and authority in the world, especially in business, although progress is slow. By using powerful language, demonstrating confidence, and leveraging the natural competencies you have as a collaborator, you too can create an inclusive work environment built for the long term. This book is written for all women wanting to increase their confident conversations overall, not written specifically for the female leader. By using powerful questions and building trust, women can achieve larger sales and develop deeper customer relationships, impacting retention and business profitability overall. Becoming a more articulate and authentic female leader, capable of empowering and delegating effectively to staff, will foster consideration for more senior roles, based on demonstrating competence and a caring leadership style.

I believe women need to showcase clearly why they are applying for a senior role, and why they are THE best candidate for the position, not simply be selected to fill a quota or a mandated diversity initiative. The Peterson Institute for International Economics conducted a survey of nearly twenty-two thousand firms globally in 2014. Findings showed that almost sixty percent of these firms had no female board members, just over half had no female C-suite executives, and fewer than five percent had a female CEO. There was considerable variation among countries: Norway, Latvia, Slovenia, and Bulgaria had at least twenty percent female representation in board members and senior executives; only two percent of Japanese board members and two and a half percent of Japanese C-suite executives were women.[11]

There was similar variation across sectors. Financial services, health care, utilities, and telecommunications were relatively welcoming to female leadership, while fewer women were found at the top in basic materials, technology, energy, and industrial sectors. The profitable firms in the study sample (average net margin of 6.4 percent) showed that moving from having no women in corporate leadership (the CEO, the board, and other C-suite positions) to having a thirty percent female share is associated with a one percentage point increase in net margin— which translates to a fifteen percent increase in profitability for a typical firm.

The Peterson Institute also concluded that there are two channels through which more female senior leaders could contribute to superior firm performance with increased skill diversity within top management, which increases effectiveness in monitoring staff performance and less gender discrimination throughout the management ranks. This helps to recruit, promote, and retain talent.

Further comments by the Catalyst Group in 2011 indicated that Fortune 500 companies with the highest proportion of women on their boards performed significantly better than firms with the lowest proportion. [12] McKinsey & Company's global study of more than 1000 companies in twelve countries found that organizations in the top quartile of gender diversity among executive leadership teams were more likely to outperform on profitability (21%) and value creation (27%).[13] Organizations in the top quartile for ethnic/cultural diversity were more likely to achieve above-average profitability—33% more likely for diverse executive teams and 43% more likely for diverse boards. Other research on US firms finds that mixed-gender boards outperform all-male boards.[14] The HFRI Women Index has returned 4.4 per cent over the past five years, compared with a 4.2 per cent return for the HFRI Fund Weighted Composite Index, a broader gauge of hedge funds across all strategies and genders. The figures support research by Rothstein Kass, the accounting firm, in 2012 and earlier academic studies that found hedge funds run by women outperform those managed by men.[15]

Women are generally natural nurturers and collaborators, caring that everyone has a say, and enjoying using win-win approaches to involve and engage staff and to build authentic and long-term relationships with customers and vendors. Strong authentic feminine leadership starts with self-awareness of one's own abilities and understanding how to achieve outcomes through working together with others and leveraging the power of "we". It is followed by using language more effectively to ask collaborative and inclusive questions, showing respect to others, earning their respect by being observed treating others fairly. Leadership is a mindset not a title.

**You don't need everyone to like you,
but they do have to *respect* you.**

I conducted a series of interviews with influential and powerful women, from corporate leaders to speakers and authors to women working to advance women's empowerment, to seek out words they had noticed which either helped to build women's confidence or deplete it. Several interesting nuggets of wisdom emerged and many of those words and word concepts are included in this book to supplement my own insights.

The words varied from simple yet uncommon ways to use language, to specific words not commonly used in conversation such as *meritocracy* and *pluralism* — used to advance the equality of women in the workplace. Jenny Gulamani-Abdulla — BPW Canada President (2016-2018) shared her perspective:

> "Meritocracy encompasses a feeling of power in your ability, in your competence and talents, as merit goes beyond your intelligence and education to how you leverage your key principles, values, and knowledge. Immediately your confidence is boosted when you know deeply you are competent and can stand on an equal footing with others. Canada is a meritocratic society not an aristocratic society, it is about *what* you know and demonstrating competence. We need to go beyond diversity and move into pluralism — accepting and embracing that we are all unique so that we stop focussing on conflicting viewpoints and accept our identity and accept others. To have a shared sense of pride, when you accept yourself no matter how different you are than others — you no longer doubt yourself, which boosts your confidence."[16]

Sometimes no words are even required, as body language can speak volumes (see Chapter Eight). Confidence builds by achieving goals despite adversity, and also by asking powerful and insightful questions which demonstrate your knowledge. The person asking the questions in the conversation is the person who can guide the direction — create an open environment to build trust and show curiosity — while demonstrating wisdom and an understanding of industry trends.

How change happens…

As a seasoned executive coach, I know that change happens faster when my client generates her own solutions, then makes a commitment based on the activities she has chosen to act upon.

The faster she takes action after making a decision, the quicker her brain will rewire itself to accommodate the new learning. Neuroscience continues to provide us with research results to show what happens when action is taken with a desire to make a positive change.

"Neuroplasticity," also called brain plasticity, is the process in which your brain's neural synapses and pathways are altered as an effect of environmental, behavioural, and neural changes. Neuroplasticity is the brain's ability to reorganize itself by forming new neural connections throughout life and allows the neurons (nerve cells) in the brain to compensate for injury and disease, and to adjust their activities in response to new situations or to changes in their environment. If someone suffers a brain injury, neuroplasticity allows the brain to "rewire" itself to restore or maximize brain functioning by rebuilding neural circuits and allowing an uninjured part of the brain to take over the function of the damaged part. [17]

Neuroplasticity also occurs hand-in-hand with synaptic pruning, which is the brain's way of deleting neural connections that are no longer necessary or useful, and strengthening the necessary ones. In much the same way, neurons that grow weak from underuse die off through the process of apoptosis, to fine-tune the brain for efficiency. Neuroplasticity also occurs when we stretch ourselves and learn something new, become mindful of habitual reactions to unpleasant emotions, or shift beliefs. We actually alter the neurochemistry and the structure of our brains by solving a problem ourselves, as the brain releases a rush of neurotransmitters like adrenaline. If action is taken within two to five days of learning something new, neuroplasticity occurs, similar to stretching out clay; once stretched, the brain's connections will not go back to their original shapes.

In my own coaching I have observed at the moment of insight (in coaching conversations called an "Aha moment") an adrenaline-like rush of insight occurs only if people are making connections themselves, and this rush of energy may be central to facilitating change. It helps fight against the internal and external forces trying to keep change from occurring, including the fear response of the amygdala, the part of our brain that alerts us to danger situations.

Personally, I love change, especially where travel to new places and meeting new people is part of my experience. Each year, I purposefully select one word to place focus on for the entire year. In 2016, it was *flourish* (the name of my business), and *adventure* in 2017, which led to travelling to nine different cities across North America and delivering seventeen varied talks, workshops, and keynotes.

In 2018, the word bubbling up in meditation was *expansion,* with *influence* and *connection* appearing as meaningful supportive words. By early February, I was invited to attend a Global Influence Summit, connecting with other transformational heart-centred entrepreneurs, authors and speakers, which was an easy decision to make as this invitation clearly aligned with my 2018 focus. The activities of *expansion* with *influence* and *connection* were all likely with meeting seasoned global influencers who were attending, and this trip led to developing some amazing connections. By mid-June an invitation to host my own radio show emerged.

Picking one word creates a powerful intention, as each of my decisions directly link back to one central focus, and help me explore "how does this support my goal of expansion?" As opportunities arise, it creates simplicity to say *yes* or *no* to each one when you have a focus word for the year. No more mind chatter, no more sleepless nights — a simple, easy decision made![18]

I believe that by leveraging just ONE word, you can change your life. This book contains forty words and word concepts that women can use in more powerful ways — so here is your first question for reflection and focus.

What is the ONE word that will be
the most impactful for you this year?

Why I wrote this book…

Being confident and believing in your own self-worth

is necessary to achieving your potential.

Sheryl Sandberg, author of *"Lean In: Women, Work, and*

the Will to Lead"

(Chief Operating Office, Facebook)

My greatest honour is to serve, to help women flourish in business. I support women professionals, leaders, and entrepreneurs to have the inner confidence to know how to ask for what they want, and to get it. When you ask with caring and authenticity, you gain respect from others. Avoid becoming a woman leader who is described as *bossy* or *bitchy*. By understanding the impact that a single word can create, you can move from being *aggressive* with your language to *assertive* — using your feminine energy — and excel in life with ease and grace.

Over the past twenty-five-plus years — first in sales, then increasingly more senior HR roles hosting numerous interviews, I have asked thousands of questions. During my years dedicated to coaching others, it has become even more evident how our daily language can create choices — often opening up surprising options. Words are my passion, and helping women gain more confidence using what I coined as "Verbal Agility" is my most meaningful work. An unanticipated side benefit in baring my soul and sharing my insights gathered over many years while writing this book is "soul cleansing" — a lovely cathartic bonus to emerge.

Your words matter!

Timing is everything. Bold women in the entertainment industry recently found the inner strength to put the spotlight on sexual misconduct and the need for change. The social media #MeToo movement has begun, triggering a powerful tidal wave of possibility, encouraging women in other industries to speak up and speak out. To step into using more powerful language, to support and encourage other women to find their inner strength and use their words assertively. Powerful words are your tools to step forward into new possibilities. In the ocean of information you receive over your lifetime, the pearls of wisdom here show how to leverage powerful words and language concepts. A rising tide raises all boats. As you raise your own confidence, please help other women rise up with the impact of your confidence ripples.

Here is one of my favourite quotes, even though it reflects the word *man*.

> Give a man a fish and you feed him for a day.
> Teach him how to fish
> and you feed him for a lifetime.
> Lao Tzu
> 600 - 470 BC

Women have the opportunity to change the face of business and impact social change when we use our words in powerful ways, to bring more empathy and emotional connection into the workplace. When women lead organizations or teams, we mostly lead in ways that nurture and encourage others. In my coaching, I have seen these differences as women start new business ventures and step into more responsibility and senior leadership roles. Women have the natural nurturing abilities to cultivate a different type of work environment, with a long-term mindset of collaboration, attention to detail, and creating positive relationship-building conversations.

By creating a collaborative, caring, and respectful workplace, the focus shifts from the short-term mindset of profit and more profit to a longer-term focus of impact, creating stability by building relationships that last. With a short-term focus, the behaviour needed to secure a quick sale at any cost trickles down through the organization, often led by the board of directors or executive whose primary focus is to deliver maximum value to shareholders in the shortest time possible.

In my previous senior HR roles, I saw this occur frequently where the Number One focus on profit was rewarded with short-term incentives, and compensation plans were built solely around this metric. Consider your own compensation: what results and behaviour are you compensated for, and how does that shape how you achieve those desired results?

When female leaders build a culture of collaboration with a mindset of long-term stability and can articulate a purposeful mission, everyone wins. Women naturally foster collaborative conversations, as we care *how* the work objectives are accomplished. We want to invite opinions before making decisions, to understand the impact of a new project or change in the environment. We want to appreciate how a proposed change will affect staff and clients and how it will strengthen the overall mission of the business. Clients who have strong caring relationships and are happy with service levels received are less likely to be distracted by lower pricing from a competitor.

When women leaders show they care, research shows that women are identified as "more likeable as leaders." [19] When women see the positive impact their words have when they step up and speak out, others begin treating them more respectfully, and as they feel valued, they show up more confidently.

Over my twenty-five-year career, I have lived in numerous cities, worked in four countries, and interviewed over six thousand people for jobs while working in HR, combined with my coaching, sales and consulting roles. I have asked a lot of questions — some to gather information, some to showcase an issue my service could resolve, some to provoke insight and to foster collaboration — or to share an opinion and then invite a new perspective. Can you share your perspective in the form of a question, fostering relationships naturally in the process? This book includes particular words to open up a conversation, to strengthen your inner resolve, to take a stand for how you wish to be treated — asserting yourself firmly — and elevating your confidence.

Being *assertive* is different from being *aggressive* — as it begins with your *intention* before you even speak. Using words in ways that help you achieve your desired outcome while still being respectful of others is an art. In this book, I will teach you this art. *The Art of Confident Conversations. . .* Words can be so very powerful, to build us up, or knock us down — to nourish our souls or to deflate them. Using assertive words effectively results in collaboration with others, respectfully engaging them with your vision for success, and seeing specific results — often faster — as the commitment is shared clearly.

You have control over your inner self-talk, and the words you choose to use. For some of you I hear the mind chatter kicking in right away (I hear you saying, "Really, you should be inside MY head, I have negative thoughts running through my head all the time. Once it takes over that little voice of doubt will not shut up!"). I know this inner dialogue well, because at one time it also clouded my head too. The negative words and critical comments yelled by my father caused me to withdraw, then add on layers of emotional protection (known as "armouring") to prevent his cutting remarks from hurting me.

That shield of armour I put on was like a mask, a layer that did protect me, yet also did not let anyone else in. My shield kept me safe; it also kept me buried behind it. While I kept "pushing" forward in life, I was fired up by negative energy (fuelled by my father's mean comments predicting my success level). My attitude was a rebellious "I will darn well prove you wrong!" To reach my achievements, I actually created an energy of resistance because I was pushing and pushing with the extra weight of a heavy shield layered on top. Pushing uphill for years and years is hard work!

I finally realized what I was doing when I began emotionally burning out from all the years of effort. I understood that I could take back my power by using more effective language to ask for what I really wanted. By asking in a different way, I began seeing others respond more positively, and I began to lower my shield. One day, I found that I no longer needed it at all. Words became a layer of comfort, like a warm snuggly blanket that I could wrap around myself when I felt chilled or in need of warmth. Powerful yet assertive language was the tool I discovered could help me in any situation, to feel heard, to feel respected, to share my opinions and see them received thoughtfully. When I stayed in an energy of curiosity, I remained open and transparent, like choosing a blanket as light as chiffon rather than needing a heavy shield.

Becoming more aware of the language and questions that I was using, deepening my listening skills over the course of hundreds of coaching conversations with managers, leaders and entrepreneurs, I learned many of the words that are commonly used, and those that deflate women's confidence. There are specific words women can use with more leverage, to energize and increase self-confidence. I learned the words that tripped me up, those that triggered an unexpected response from others and which words gave me a feeling of choice and control.

Most of the words explored are *verbs* (words expressing a state or action) and *nouns* (words naming the subject or object) which create concise and powerful sentences. Keep in mind that using *conjunctions* (connectors between words: *as*, *and*, *because*, *but*, *however*) highlights where women often over explain themselves. Using excessive pronouns (*I*, *you*, *he*, *this*, *who*, *what*) as replacements or substitutes for nouns and noun phrases, is often perceived as showing a lack of confidence, unless balanced with verbs and nouns.

By using more confident language, fruitful conversations result. You can SEE and FEEL the difference it makes when you know from how others treat you that you have been HEARD. Yes, truly HEARD and understood.

What is confidence, anyway?

con•fi•dence [kon-fi-duh ns] definition:

Noun:

1.   full trust; belief in the powers, trustworthiness, or reliability of a person or thing.
2.   belief in oneself and one's powers or abilities; self-confidence.[20]

How can you have full trust, belief in your own powers? I believe that confidence is an outcome, a state of mind, and therefore it can be cultivated. As babies trying to walk for the first time, or children learning how to ride a bike, we expect learning to be a process. Using powerful language is a skill that can be learned too, cultivated and leveraged in an assertive way.

How This Book Works

This book explores between five to seven words in each chapter, using examples, research, and stories from my own experience or my clients, with insights from confident female colleagues. An *ACTION STEP* follows each one, providing ways to practice and deepen your awareness and suggested use of each word, or word concept. The final chapter explores other ways we communicate, when no words are required. I recommend pairing it with a journal to capture your biggest learnings from the text and action steps.

The dance begins in the conversation, seeing how others respond to you,

and how they treat you differently, more respectfully,

with your new level of assertiveness.

Are you ready to learn the steps of the enhanced version of the "dance"

— the Modern Art of Confident Conversations?

After completing this book I welcome receiving your comments via email directly. I am curious to hear how your world changes after shifting your language to have more Confident Conversations.

Connect with me through my "Contact" page at www.WordsWomenAndWisdom.com or send me a message via LinkedIn or Facebook. My biography and contact information is included at the end of this book.

CHAPTER 1

Change Everyday Language That Trips Women Up!

Context is important, so here is my context for writing this book. In junior high school, my best exam result was earning a 92 percent in English Language. I loved reading, I loved writing, and I loved the creativity of language. Creativity and self-expression were concepts totally at odds with my reality — living under the iron fist of my father — as a child being taught that "children should be seen and not heard". Being "seen and not heard" — those early words left an impression, and not a kind and loving one. If you are a mother reading this, please consider how one or two phrases can so easily be absorbed by your children. Watch how they are acting after hearing particular phrases you use at home, and become very aware of their behaviour in response to your words, especially in their early personality forming years (under age six).

In the house where I grew up in England, language was not exactly my friend. I call it a house rather than a home, because it was a shelter from the elements, not a warm and inviting place that you were proud to bring your friends to visit. It was a shell of mixed emotions and competing energies. My father was traumatized, scarred by the horrors of experiencing war on the battlefields of Dunkirk in the Second World War. He was an angry man who was intolerant of others, and lived a solitary lifestyle, inviting few visitors into our house, so I escaped by visiting friends at their homes.

At an early age I loved to read, to let my imagination wander into fantasy. I used reading to escape my hostile environment, which was corralling my young creative mind. Today, I almost always have a book on my coffee table that I am in the middle of reading. When I am stressed (yes, I still feel it occasionally), I find myself diving into a new book. Mostly, my choices are nonfiction — as a way to put a degree of certainty back in my life, perhaps. For me, the written word is fact, it is truth. Reading brings me back to reality while stirring up creative new ideas.

From conversations with my coach and mentor Jayne Warrilow — an expert in energetic resonance — I learned that words contain either positive or negative energy. Warrilow shares in her book *The Secret Language of Resonance* that "words have energy." She encourages: "Allow the energy from your words to enter your experience, to gently swim around in your energy field. Feel the energy rippling through you setting into your intelligence, so that you enter into an active dialogue. You don't just have energy, you ARE energy."[21] Varying tone, pace, force, and volume all impact the way the same word is received with different emphasis or volume. (Try saying the word *why* for example, using varied volume, pace, tone, and force — it has a different energy in each situation.)

As I delved into becoming a certified reiki practitioner three years ago and began working firsthand (as well as remotely), using reiki energy for healing and removing energy blocks in the body, the concept of our words holding energy made more sense. When you feel a constriction in your throat for example, I learned that it is often stuck energy, which needs to dissipate and release to create flow, and allow you to breathe more deeply and fully. When you are confident, you breathe more deeply. When you are nervous, your breathing is shallower. Remember attending an interview? Or watching a horror movie and anticipating the heroine being attacked right before it happens? You likely held your breath altogether.

Watching well-known speakers including Tony Robbins preparing to speak at a motivational event, I appreciate the importance of breathing, and raising our vibrational energy, especially how he chooses to uplift himself as well as the audience as he bounds onto the stage. Recently at international speaker Karen McGregor's Rock the Stage speaker's success weekend, I learned the important mindset and energetic resonance preparation that is needed prior to delivering a great talk. An energy of resonance and authenticity creates a powerful wave of truth that emanates from the speaker on the stage, just as the printed word confirms truth when on a price sticker. Energetic resonance is believable, solid, we feel it and can experience a deep sense of simply "knowing" inside us.

Karen also shared the importance of being open to learning, and what hurt her before she became a successful speaker was saying to herself

> I know that already, I'm smart, I don't need help, I can figure it out. When I accepted that I needed help and was ready to learn from an expert it flowed much better, when I asked for support. "*I am*" is the most powerful starting phrase, especially when followed by serving the world with passion, power and integrity for example. Reminding ourselves that we have the capacity to give, while also transforming lives and making a good living. Keeping sentences short lands in our bodies and makes us feel more powerful, so ego has no room to creep in . . . The idea of having sacred space is so important as well, open space that is not cluttered — so that what we say comes from a clear vs. cluttered mind. The most powerful expressions of ourselves come when we are fully present.[22]

According to Samantha Olson of *Medical Daily*, women may have a stronger ability to make a successful intuitive decision because of our exceptional skills in reading other humans. Referencing a 2011 study published in the journal *Psychological Science,* she shares that

> our female ancestors needed to evaluate a situation quickly in order to tune in to their infant and their environment, for protection and survival. Their brains were trained with peak awareness because they were protecting a heart outside of their own bodies. Female brains therefore evolved to have a

larger composition and ability to organize chunks
of environmental information at a time, giving
them an edge on how to read people.[23]

It's time to bring your powerful awareness, energy and intuition
more purposefully to the forefront of business and to the steps of
government, to pave the way for more acceptance that business
requires collaboration and heart-based decision making. It's not
just about profits in business. The Millennials demographic (those
born between approximately 1980 and 1999) are demanding more
passion from their product vendors. Millennials value using
business for good, to create a positive impact on our planet too
(purpose, profit and planet). Leading business with a longer-term
focus for sustainability (vs. short-term "profit only" thinking)
creates excellent opportunities for women's natural relationship
nurturing abilities.

Business success measured by impact as well as pure
profit is an evolving concept, and the social enterprise movement
is gathering steam — which is divine timing for professional
women. Social enterprises have a greater social cause at their
centre, yet are still designed to operate at a profit (rather than a
legally registered not-for-profit group or charity hosting special
events to raise project monies, yet are primarily funded via
government grants and donations). Many women founders are
shifting to a social enterprise model, as it nurtures both their desire
to have a profitable business, as well as making an impact in
society.

Practise the concepts and words shared in this book in
your daily life, while bringing your authentic self to the
conversation. Practise with friends and family first, and learn how
to step into a new and more powerful you, then take this enhanced
assertiveness forth to other parts of your life. How you use specific
words in everyday situations will enable you to have a more
predictable response from others — and for you to have more
certainty about the outcome. When you are concisely asking for
what you want — using less words overall (while maintaining
strong eye contact) and asking more confidently, you will be quite
pleasantly surprised at how others treat you. If you don't stand up
for yourself and your opinions, *no one else will* — it is up to you.
Be willing to really be heard, and see the results you desire actually
occur.

I encourage you to focus your awareness on

ONE word in particular each week from this book.

Changing even ONE word, *can change your life*. By becoming more aware of when that specific word shows up, its definition, how it triggers or guides your behaviour, and the implications of its misuse — you will understand how you react when you hear it. By learning how to use words more powerfully, especially in the workplace, we create choices and bring more conscious leadership to the business arena.

I define conscious leadership as *an awareness of one's self, the world, and one's purpose within it*. As leaders who become more conscious, take personal responsibility, and lead others in a win-win model, you can bring new and effective solutions to business challenges. Solutions that foster purpose and profit, and benefit people and the planet. While you may not be leading an organization and determining the business strategy, or choosing the words for the marketing for your firm, you are the leader of your life! When you increase your intention using positive words and language, it becomes a dance with your conversation partner, a dance of movement and being in flow. When there is alignment between another person's words and intention, you feel it. The energy feels pure, honest and clean — transparent and clear.

By shifting your awareness, you can choose to make a change, choose to use an individual word in a different way, or choose to eliminate it altogether. You can observe how you react when you hear it, or how others react when it is said. You can choose to respond instead of react — with the awareness of what particular emotion that word is triggering for you. Does hearing a specific word trigger fear, uncertainty or doubt, anger or a lump in your throat? Or does it fill your heart with a stronger desire to rise to a challenge, to tackle an issue with renewed vigor or make your heart ache with compassion? By increasing your awareness, by feeling where in your body you are responding to the energy behind the word, you can learn how to use it more effectively, to your advantage. If you know that a specific word triggers you to cry for example, and that crying in public creates a feeling of shame for you, you can be prepared.[24]

Most often women benefit by giving ourselves the opportunity of taking a pause… By pausing, slowing down the conversation, using a prepared one-*line PAUSE STATEMENT* or a *PAUSE QUESTION*, we can create the delay needed to compose ourselves. Then we can *CHOOSE* how we want to respond (vs. reacting and perhaps regretting what is said, or our behaviour).

ACTION STEPS:

When you are in a happy or calm state of mind, create 3 sentences that you can use in situations that may arise in the future. Use language that aligns your personality and connects to your values, and adjust it to suit the circumstances (e.g.: whether at work or home, with your leader or your teenager). Before saying your POWER PAUSE STATEMENT or QUESTION, stop and take a deep breaths first. Here are a few examples:

1st sentence – for use to deflect back something that you disagree with, and need to think about before responding. (Example response*: "Hmmmm, that is an interesting viewpoint. Let me get back to you on that topic, as I would like to fully consider your view before making a decision".*) By adding "*hmmmm*" at the beginning of the sentence, although that is not a word from the dictionary, it sounds more real, as though you just thought now about how you are responding, vs. having a "prepared answer" – it sounds more spontaneous. *(See Chapter 7: Bringing*

Powerful Words to Work for more on when to sound spontaneous and when to sound decisive and clear – and how to do so.)

2nd sentence – to reply with when you are stunned that something so outrageous was even suggested, as it clearly is the opposite of what you value. (Example response: *"Wow - your comments are quite surprising to hear and I have a very different view. Let's book a time to fully consider how we can move forwards respecting both our values and long-term goals."*)

3rd sentence – to recognize the value of the conversation, yet give yourself some time to think about your response. (Example response*: "I can hear the importance to you of having resolution on this topic, and also I believe there are a few different options to consider. If we can meet to discuss this further tomorrow, is that soon enough for us to collaborate on this issue/idea?"*)

By preparing 3 sentences in advance of an emotionally charged situation arising, with words prepared while you are in a happy or confident energetic state, you will be more able to take control of the situation by pressing the *PAUSE* button. By creating an opportunity to catch your breath, *PAUSE*, and give yourself a window of time to respond to the issue or situation, *YOU* take back your power.

You almost always have a choice, to react or respond. If you *REACT* you will likely end up RE-ACTing the situation by having to go back and do it over again, in a different way, to achieve a desirable outcome. If however, you *PAUSE* and *RESPOND*, you can choose your options more carefully and confidently, and have a better overall outcome – or at least one that you have fully considered, and are aware of the consequences of taking this course of action. Focused breathing helps calm the body by slowing the heart rate, lowering blood pressure, and improving focus. Controlled breathing can override the fight, flight, or freeze response set off by the amygdala, and instead enable mindful behavior

As a professional coach, I know that making changes stick takes time. Neuroscience research has shown that when we learn something new, and make a new choice to act, if we act within two to five days, we have a higher likelihood of integrating a new habit and embedding the new behaviour. Do you like the results showing up in your life? If your answer is NO, then let's shift that to a YES — one week at a time. Increasing your awareness about words gives you a choice — a choice of the outcome — now that is a powerful shift!

You may have selected this book looking for word insights, and how to make a "quick fix" in your life, and if so, explore these words as they arise in your daily life, or triggering events. These forty words are explained with knowledge that gradually builds, so I encourage you to read the chapters in the order presented, to gain the maximum benefit. The words included in this book have been selected to help you in one of five ways:

1. *Everyday awareness* — how you use words and how others react or respond to you
2. *Taking back your power* — by using more effective words and conversation strategies
3. *Building influence with others* — engaging them with positive psychology and questions
4. *Expanding your resilience* — self-talk and managing the unexpected with powerful words
5. *Connecting and growing* — personally and professionally as you build respect from others.

The purpose of this book is not "perfection," as effective learning happens in layers. Just like a rose that gradually opens its petals to reveal the inner stigma, with increased awareness of how to use specific words and word concepts in a more powerful way, your increased assertiveness will unfold. Conversation with another person is like a smooth dance when done well — with reciprocal moves flowing easily in synchronicity with the music. By learning the dance moves of powerful conversations, your dance will gradually become more natural, elegant and confident. Become aware of your language and take action and practice more assertive approaches. (You have likely heard the expression especially in the world of sports: "practice makes perfect." Or consider this perspective: *perfect practice makes perfect...* Keep practicing the *right* technique — *Ref.: Ron Ristroph Tennis Instructor — Hamptons, New York.*)

Using a journal will help you to notice your insights and shifts, and observe the areas where you are having ease adapting, and those areas which are needing more focus. The dance begins in the conversation, seeing how others respond to you, and how they treat you differently (more respectfully) with your new level of assertiveness. Are you ready to learn the steps of the enhanced version of the "dance" — to develop the **Modern Art of Confident Conversations**? Let's begin with an often undervalued word.

1.1

Space

As a professional coach, I have learned some of the best ways to enhance self-development and help change to "stick," embedding a new habit. When I am working with my coaching clients, one of the first things we co-create are ideas to help them to reprioritize their calendar and make space. If there is no space in your world, you will continue rushing from activity to activity without being able to absorb and reflect on the ideas shared in this book. To become more confident, first you need to create some mental space in order to learn a new approach or technique, and have time to practise what has just been learned. Creating space is critical for integrating your new learning and increased awareness of how to use language in a different and more powerful way.

One early request is to evaluate their calendar usage, and create space for higher value activities. For example, a busy woman entrepreneur may have her own business to run, her children to parent, a household to organize, a spousal relationship to round out a fulfilled life (and numerous other things in her calendar to maintain a feeling of work-life balance). With a calendar full of events, much like the overstuffed closet, there is simply no space to add anything else, or transition time between activities. We each have twenty-four hours in every day — that is non-negotiable. However, each of us has a *choice* of how much of the time is spent on low-value items, or invested in joy-filled activities that fill up our soul cup, that nourish us, and bring happiness.

Why are so many people busy and living unfulfilled and unhappy lives? I believe it stems from a societal tug that in order to live in community with others, we must stay within certain norms in order to be socially accepted. If we live in a way that is too "different," many of our friends do not understand why we are straying from the normal path. Deep inside each of us has a need to be accepted and liked, so many women try to live in ways that "don't rock the boat," or in ways that others don't question. Way back in caveman and cavewoman days, if we hunted alone we would likely be eaten alive — yet if we chose to hunt in groups we were more successful. The value of living in community began a long time ago.

In the more recent writings of neurologist and psychologist Viktor Frankl — author of *Man's Search for Meaning*, after many years imprisoned in a concentration camp, with months to ponder what contributes to a meaningful life, he landed on three concepts. One concept is that in order for our lives to have meaning, we need to be "engaged with something greater than ourselves" — activities that serve our community.[25] We know that for prisoners who are being punished being placed in solitary confinement, one of the worst things that can be done to a human being — cuts them off from others, as people are social in nature. Women especially are nurturers, and our friendships and social circle are important for support. In the same way, "conscious leaders" create a business that operates for a greater good, that is purposeful and meaningful to society (fostering something greater than ourselves), and not solely based on operating for a profit.

Sure, others may request time in your calendar. It is critical to remember that only YOU have a choice how you use YOUR next twenty-four hours, in the most meaningful way. Yes — you may have your aging mother in the hospital, and CHOOSE to put her needs before your need for sleep — for a short period of time. However, when life often throws what appears initially to be a curveball your way, you have a choice if you are going to embrace it and learn from it, or let it knock you on the head, which hurts more than if you chose to reach out and catch it. Continuing to put your sleep as a second priority will eventually show consequences, as you become exhausted and your own health suffers. So often you are not really saving any time, you are just deferring the inevitable.

Creating space in your calendar will give you the opportunity to take action — to engage with each word reviewed in this book, and reflect and act on the Action Step after each word. Creating space will give you practice time, reflection and review

time. **Most importantly giving you time to honour yourself —
to begin putting yourself as a priority more frequently.
Practise this, which may be a new habit**, then celebrate moving
forwards to a new level of confidence — taking control back of
your time.

Creating space for new energy is important in our lives
and our environment. In our homes, in Feng Shui wisdom, having
space for energy to flow in easily creates new, fresh life.
According to my colleague Myrna Brown — Feng Shui expert —
"Feng Shui is about balancing the energy of a space, be it a room,
a home, or an office. The belief is when we live or spend time in a
harmonious, balanced environment we will succeed in life, AND
also have good fortune. Although it's been around for more than
three thousand years, only now is Feng Shui beginning to take off
and have a stronger presence in our homes and offices."[26]

Chi, or Feng Shui energy, is manifested in yin and yang
characteristics and in a variety of forms according to the Feng Shui
five elements theory. This energy has two main expressions: the
outward flow and the inward flow (in Chinese Medicine this is
known as Yin and Yang energy). The Yang is the expression of
our masculine energy, while the Yin is the expression of our
feminine energy. We need both energies in order to live in
harmony. (The five Feng Shui elements are Fire, Earth, Metal,
Water, and Wood.) In daily life, we also need to be aware which
energy we are using in different conversations.

Life energy, known as *Qi* or *Chi,* needs to flow in order to
foster new life. In Feng Shui, as in Chinese medicine, chi is the
term for the universal energy or the energy that permeates
everything around us. Qi is the central underlying principle in
traditional Chinese medicine and martial arts. This Feng Shui term
applies to the energy inside your body, as well the energy both
inside and outside any man-made structures.

To nurture a relationship, Yin energy will build and
collaborate to build a bond. However, if you wish to be more firm
in your decisions and take a powerful stand for something you
believe in, tapping into your Yang (or masculine) energy gives you
a stronger position. Knowing how to move between the two
energies is a subtle art. Sometimes you need to be more assertive
(note I say assertive rather than aggressive) and sometimes you
will need to be conscious of letting your partner lead, just like in

dancing. Using Yin and Yang energy is a dance of collaboration and reciprocity, an ebb and flow of life, just like the tides flowing.

In your work life, creating space in your calendar by completing unfinished business or tasks frees up your mind to take on new projects. This might sound obvious; however, consider for a moment all the mental chatter that happens when we have multiple projects on the go, all at varying stages of completion, all calling for attention to be finished. All that mental nattering in our mind takes up space!

In the best-selling book *The Power of Focus*, authors Jack Canfield, Mark Victor Hansen and Les Hewitt detail the importance of the concept of unfinished business.[27] Finish one project and see how much lighter you feel. Clean up a drawer in your home and discover how much more organized you feel, or clear a whole room in your home and see how your energy level rises. Clutter takes up physical space and blocks energy from flowing through the room. Your energy will feel cleaner when your rooms have more openness for energy to circulate.

Confident conversations happen when each person has their needs met, when each one leaves the conversation knowing they have been heard, and that their needs are considered, and the outcome of the discussion is fair and acceptable to both parties. Win-lose thinking is out, and win-win energy of collaboration — "we" energy — is in. An African proverb I heard years ago has stuck with me:

You can go fast by going alone,

or you can go further

by going with others.

In early 2015, I dived fully into the world of energetic resonance and reiki energy and healing, after feeling major pain in my shoulder. After my first visit to an energy healer, I learned the pain was being caused by an energy block in my shoulder, caused by tightly hanging on to an old belief that no longer served me. I was both surprised and curious to learn more about energy and how my body was harbouring such powerful learnings. I completed first and second level reiki training to add "certified reiki practitioner" to my skillset, and then took a year of mentorship with my reiki master — Dixie Bennett, to deepen my new knowledge. Reiki training showed me how important it is to have space for energy to freely flow from our toes to our crown (and in our home or office environment).

Reiki is a form of alternative medicine developed in 1922 by Japanese Buddhist Mikao Usui. Since originating in Japan, reiki has been adapted into varying cultural traditions across the world. Reiki practitioners use a technique called palm healing or hands-on healing through which a "universal energy" is transferred through the palms of the practitioner to the patient, in order to encourage emotional or physical healing.[28] Reiki is increasing in popularity in the Western world, and is a powerful Japanese technique for stress reduction and relaxation that also promotes healing. It is administered by a trained reiki practitioner, to align energy chakras (there are seven within the body) for deep relaxation. Reiki is based on the idea that an unseen "life force energy" flows through us and is what causes us to be alive . . . **More aligned chakras mean more energy, less stress, and becoming more grounded!**

ACTION STEPS:

Start making SPACE for higher quality activities in your life today! Clean out one drawer or section of your closet, and start removing energy blocks in your environment. Identify one thing that you can delete from your calendar, something that is not rewarding for you, or that someone else could do better than you do, which sucks up your time or frustrates you. Start saying no to this activity. For example, on reflection you might find that you spend three hours per week in meetings that are informative, yet the participants take forever to make a decision. Who can you arrange to gather the minutes of the meeting from, and then scan through only the Action Items and Decisions Made, and focus on the key items?

Perhaps you can negotiate with your spouse that instead of you taking your child to hockey practice twice a week, that you take that role once a week. Start looking at where you can create space in your calendar, and what you need to STOP doing in order to START using your time differently, use assertive language in a way that enables you to free up more of your calendar time.

1.2

No

This short yet powerful word is learned early in our lives. It is typically considered to be a negative word, although in life and business, *no* is an important word, which if used well can create a sense of control over your life as well as your time. If you waste time on things that bring you no joy, once that time is spent, it is gone forever.

Saying no is a powerful way to stand up for yourself, your values, your opinion, what you feel is important to you, and what or who you wish to engage with, or not. I recently attended a seminar with a professional coaching colleague, Shelley Hayes-MacDonald, who also teaches self-defence, and loved her T-shirt quote: "NO is a complete sentence." I agree! When we say *no* to something, there is generally no need to explain further. Women so often feel they need to explain why not — *you don't!*

In Mark Waldman's "NeuroTips for Money, Happiness & Success: 21 Productivity Tips for your Brain," he shares that "brain-scan research shows that even seeing the word *no* for less than a half second will release dozens of stress chemicals into your body and brain." [29] According to Barbara Fredrickson's research, described in her book *POSITIVITY*, she found that "you have to generate at least three positive thoughts for every negative thought and feeling you have, if you want to be successful in relationships or business."[30] Fredrickson had been studying positive emotions since the mid-1990's along with a few other psychologists. In 2005, she began a study called the Open Heart Study where she explored the effects of meditation on stress. As Dr. John Gottman discovered, when you push your positivity ratio to 5:1 or 7:1, your relationships become deeply satisfying.[31]

If you want to shift your positivity, as with anything you want to change, awareness is the starting point. If you are not conscious of needing to change, it is not even on your radar.

Begin tracking positive experiences for several days in a row, on a sticky note in your calendar or on your phone or computer — somewhere handy that you can make a note quickly. Create two columns, one on the left for positive events happening, and use the right column to note down when negative events happen. Track it for the day and see what your ratios are. How many positive experiences did you have during your day rather than negative ones? What can you do early on in the day to set the tone for a more positive experience? How can you continue to fuel those experiences during your day?

By working in an environment where your values are aligned with the values of your organization, and where your skills and passions align with purposeful work, you will have more opportunities to remain positive. When the underlying purpose of your work is clear, and the results achieved for your organization's clients or your team objectives show significant impact — the higher your positivity. If you are also working in a social enterprise organization where your outcomes are tracked against a social mission (such as cleaning up the ocean, helping provide clean water to people in an underdeveloped nation, helping abuse victims get back on their feet, feeding the homeless, and so on), your positive focus will be easier to maintain, as you see and feel the social good your work is creating.

For many years as a child, my Dad said *no* frequently to me and my sister. As an adventurous child, I found his lack of permission to try new things was very frustrating! I learned that it was better not to ask. I learned it was better to ask for forgiveness afterwards than to ask for permission in the first place. By not asking, I retained my power, my self-worth and my courage to try something — to explore it without restriction. I also scraped my knees a lot, fell out of trees, got into trouble with my Dad on many occasions, and by his standards I was rather a handful — or as he would say a trouble-maker. I believe women give up independence to someone else far too often, and I encourage you to find places in your life where you can start stepping up and just doing it instead of asking for permission from anyone else.

Saying *no* creates a space to say *yes* to something else that is in more alignment with your focus, your values, where you are heading, and what else you want to put in your calendar instead. It fosters focus and a sense of being grounded when you deflect requests from others. Saying *no* can be done in a way that does not offend or upset the other party — when you learn to put a few more words around it, so that *no* does not sound rude, harsh, or dismissive.

For example, when first building up your personal power, if you are not used to saying *no*, you may want to try using alternative language. Pose a question in response to the other person's request: "Thank you for thinking of me for that project. I am fairly booked up already right now, and if I cannot do that, what is *your* next option?" By deflecting the request back to the other person, you clearly state that the problem remains theirs to resolve, and you are not taking it on. You have also not given them a hard *no* at this point by refusing to do it, yet by pushing back you are also asserting yourself. The next time the same person has a request for you, they will often remember that you did not say *yes* right away and may even choose to approach someone else for help first.

Using this technique, I cut back over half the things others were asking me to do and saved hours of time. This approach also helps others think about their own accountability and plan their work time more effectively, as it is clear that I am not going to rescue them each time they need help. This technique works well for leaders also, to foster independence and encourage each staff member to consider several alternatives before approaching them, hence the frequently used business term "bring me solutions, don't bring me problems."

Sometimes a simple "No, thank you," is all that is needed. You are being assertive and also polite. In the case of an invitation to an evening event, you could also add, "I already have plans." You are not required to share what those plans are, which can then turn the conversation into sounding like an excuse. If I tell you what those plans are, you will likely start to evaluate whether or not my plans are more important than your event, and then make a decision about my friendship or my prioritizing. This starts unnecessarily complicating the conversation; a simple *no* is all that is required. Or, "No, that does not work for me this time." There is no need to say *I'm sorry* afterwards, either. Stay assertive and put your needs first!

As a compassionate person, saying *no* in many situations has been challenging for me, because I care, want to do an excellent job of whatever I did take on, and enjoy helping people. However, I learned that I could have much higher quality results when I took on fewer tasks — quality over quantity — which fit with my values, and allowed my creative juices to flow more easily with less stress.

With my dad saying *no* frequently, I also learned that if I gave him two choices that the likelihood of him saying *yes* to one of them increased my chances to 50 percent. If I felt I needed to ask him rather than simply going ahead, I would phrase it this way: *Can I do X? Or I could do Y instead? Which one would be better?* I later learned that this technique works well in a sales situation as well and increases the likelihood of receiving a *yes* to one of the two options, rather than simply asking a question which required a *yes* or *no* answer. "Which one works best for you? Would you like the red one or the blue one?*"* If you have an existing client, you might ask, "I can upgrade you with more for a minor charge, if that works for you?"

By phrasing it this way you imply that of course they would want to do this, as they receive more value and services.

My rebellious childhood streak grew in strength, fuelled by watching my mother lose her confidence. My meagre allowance (called *pocket money* in England) would not stretch to cover all the things that I wanted, so I first began working as a kid-preneur at age seven, when I offered to walk small dogs for an elderly neighbour who had hurt her leg. This first job gave me a way to purchase my own items without relying on my dad for money, which was my first step into independence. By not putting myself into a situation where I felt I needed approval or permission from my parents, I reduced hearing the word *no*, and stepped into saying *yes* more often in my life! I had my first taste of freedom.

Knowing that you can support yourself is a key to feeling inner strength and confidence, assured that you have the capability to rely on one person — yourself! Knowing that you are employable with a solid education, understanding your personal values, and knowing how you add value in the world all helps you to feel competent and able to make your own way successfully through life independently. If you choose a partner it is a choice for shared relationship pleasure and love, not because you *need* to be supported financially or emotionally. Regularly assess your personal accomplishments and keep track of your valuable contributions to the world, you might be very surprised at all your wins and how capable you have proven you are.

ACTION STEPS:

Buy a really attractive journal, with a cover that feels nice to touch, or the pattern (or phrase) on the cover makes you smile when you pick it up. Select one that feels special for you — as this journey you are taking into a stronger version of yourself, with an even stronger voice, is a special journey — it is your time.

Begin paying attention to when you use the word no. Check in with yourself, ask how different it FEELS when you take the step of stating a firm no — keeping a commitment to yourself, using your assertiveness, to taking a stand for something you do not wish to do. When you say no to one thing it creates space for something better to come along. Start noticing and recording in a journal what you have said yes to instead.

Make journal notes at the end of each day before bedtime on the different situations arising, your observations and how your behaviour shifts with the use of the word no and FEEL what happens to your self-esteem.

1.3

Yes

Yes is one of the most positive words I know, other than perhaps the word *joy*. *Yes* has a powerful energy of possibility in three letters. *Yes* — a commitment to move forward, to take action, to follow through, to get engaged with something, or to begin a fresh start. I find in our world of fast-paced activity that commitments are not always followed through, even though we initially said *yes* to something. Your word with a handshake was all that was required in commerce before extensive paper contracts, yet people actually following through on their commitments seems to be less frequent today. Women are so often judged on our competence, so we especially benefit from committing and following through on every promise we make.

When you say *yes*, only say it if you really mean it. Say *yes*, and give a firm commitment, give a promise. Only use the word when you are fully on board with an idea, when you know without a doubt that you will complete a task. Your word is your reputation, whether making a commitment to yourself or to someone else during a business transaction, and showcases trustworthiness, so others will see you as consistent and trustworthy rather than flaky and unreliable. Your integrity is key in business relationships, in leadership, as a parent, and essential for your own self-worth.

After all, if you keep setting goals, setting commitments and flaking out on them, what is the point of even starting something? The unfinished-business energy I talked about in the section on the word *space* shows up again here too. Seeing a half-finished project on your desk, almost taunting you, is mental clutter causing your brain to say, *Oh rats, I really must finish that!* More unnecessary mind chatter created . . . Choose fewer projects, pick more initiatives that nourish your soul, and get them finished. Even if it is something that you are assigned by your supervisor, find a benefit from accomplishing it (you have an opportunity to research something new, make a new connection as you collaborate to finish it), learn to power through the things you don't like with a short energy burst. Look for the small chink of positive energy, like a curtain that has a very small opening where it meets the window and a sliver of sunlight shines through — look for the sunlight in every situation.

Whenever someone asks you to do something, you almost always have a choice to say either *yes* or *no*. Under some circumstances, in countries where women are not recognized as full voting members of society (or if you are an under-age teenager) you may feel that you have no choice, and yet I assure you that you do. You always have a choice regarding how you look at the world, and whether you maintain your positive spirit and keep a cheerful attitude. You do have choices, and with each choice you make typically comes a consequence. For every action there is a reaction — that is the science of the universe. It may be a positive reward or it may be some form of negative response from which there is a life lesson. However, you can decide to make that choice with either a smile or a frown . . .

Listening to the story of journalist Amanda Lindhout when she spoke at two events I have attended, then reading her powerful book *A House in the Sky,* reminds me that we each choose our attitude and our disposition. Despite being kidnapped and held in captivity for fifteen months by Islamist insurgents in southern Somalia, kept in dark rooms continually in fear, being raped and mistreated, she found a small ray of sunshine. Listening to a bird singing outside her window was one small thing which enabled her to stay positive until her release. No matter where you are in your life, always look for the light.

Between stimulus and response there is a space. In that space is our power to choose our response. In our response lies our growth and our freedom.

- Viktor E. Frankl, neurologist and psychiatrist, Man's Search for Meaning.

Yes, I know that quote is from "man's" search, and yet I believe the concept of space and choice applies regardless of gender. In the film *Yes Man,* starring Jim Carrey, the main character decides to spice up his life by saying *yes* to everything showing up in his life. It creates some interesting experiences and results in quite a journey for him, with a stirring ending. I recommend watching it, then deciding if you want to take this approach too. If not, ease into this concept of finding things in each day that you can say *yes* to. Increase your choices through effective language to clearly say *yes,* or saying *no* politely. When you take a stand for yourself, other people will treat you differently. When you have powerful language concepts ready in your back pocket, you gather inner strength and increase your commitment to honour yourself first.

ACTION STEPS:

Starting today, only say a firm yes to things, events, projects, activities, or people that you know that you will be able to follow through on. If you are not one hundred percent sure that you have the knowledge, tools, resources, connections, money or excitement to complete whatever you are saying yes to, stop! Alternative options may include this sentence: "Hmmmm, I cannot commit to X right now; however, I can do Y instead." (Perhaps Y is a smaller piece, something you know you can do in the timeframe or can commit to completing.)

Now, most importantly, write it down or make sure you book time in your calendar (with extra time allowed in case something unplanned causes a time challenge) to ensure you deliver on your commitment as promised. If you feel the request is unreasonable, or not a good fit for your skills or available time, do not apologize, simply decline (see the section on no). If it is outside your skill-set (no one knows everything), let the person who is making the request know this. "Hmmm, I haven't had the opportunity to work on this type of project before. I am interested to learn more about this topic, so it may take me a little longer to do my research before completing this work. Is there flexibility on the completion timeline?" Setting clear expectations will build trust with the other person, especially if you know there is a variable completion time rather than a hard stop date.

1.4

Why

This word is so interesting! It promotes curiosity. When I have an understanding about how something works, or why it is done in a particular way, this provides powerful clarity. In Simon Sinek's well-known TED Talk — "Start with Why," the power of the word becomes evident. His YouTube videos [32] highlight that when organizations know *what* they do, they can clearly articulate this, and attract customers by showcasing the features and benefits of their product or service. When they know *how* they do something, they can speak about their differentiators and what makes their offering unique. When they know *why* they do it, their purpose, then they can really tap into both the minds and hearts of their employees, with clarity and understanding.

Clients engage at a much higher rate when they understand the purpose of the organization (above and beyond simply making a profit). Simon uses the example of how marketing with the technology giant Apple has proven that people don't buy "What you do," they buy "*Why* you do it" — when we communicate from the inside to the outside layers of the circle, people understand the context of our comments much faster.

The Golden Circle

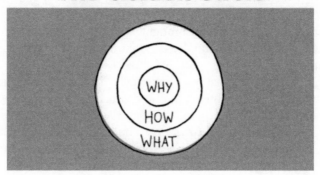

Ref: Simon Sinek

Knowing your values, knowing *why* you do what you do, what is pulling you to take this path, what you want to take a stand for, *why* you are driven to complete something, is important. As a mother when I heard my son Alex cry, I was compelled to soothe my baby and stop the crying. Why? Because the cry was like a siren in my head! Your baby's unique cry is not something a mother can ignore, women are simply not wired that way.

In the *Journal of Attached Parenting*, research shows that a baby whose parents have chosen to let them cry it out at night (to supposedly learn how to self-soothe and go to sleep by themselves) often later develops depression, anxiety disorders, stress-related illness and alcohol abuse — and are miserable children.[33] A child cries because he or she does not yet have the language skills to ask for what it wants. The infant brain is vulnerable to stress. During long bouts of crying, cortisol (a stress hormone) can reach toxic levels, activating pain circuits in the brain, causing an agonizing feeling of withdrawal of opioids (chemicals that promote positive feelings). Children who experience intense uncomforted distress can experience a shrunken hippocampus, the part of the brain involved with long-term memory and verbal reasoning. Our tissues hold energy, and this can cause illness or pain eventually. Stuck energy and outdated beliefs can get in the way of our success.

Author and metaphysical lecturer and teacher Louise Hay identifies numerous illnesses and their probable cause (and a new thought pattern to embrace to start breaking down that stuck energy) in her best-selling book *You Can Heal Your Life.*[34] If you have ever had a situation where you felt you had a lump in your throat and could not get your words out, it is unlikely you suddenly developed a sore throat. It is likely related to stuck energy that is trapped there after being brought up by an emotion, or a past memory of something unpleasant that happened when you spoke out previously.

Next time that you experience frustration with another person, take a deep breath and ask yourself, *what is the belief I have about this situation that is now surfacing for reflection, and is now triggering my frustration*? You may realize that what you experienced in how another person treated you, is something that *you* also do to others, and it's time to acknowledge this and make a change now that the actions are in your awareness . . . Things annoy you or frustrate you when you see that same behaviour in others. If it triggers a reaction in your body, pay attention and reflect at the end of the day in your journal on what happened. What was the situation right before you felt your emotions rose up? What was going on, what did someone around you do or say, and how did you respond? After the "heat" of the moment, take time to reflect what the possible learning is in that situation for you.

Understanding your core beliefs is an important step to knowing your *why*, and defining what you are willing to take a stand for. Also, knowing your character strengths (closely linked to our values) is a helpful way to make decisions in life, to forge a path in personal and energetic alignment, and help you to feel grounded and confident. Intrigued? Take ten to fifteen minutes to confirm your character strengths (closely aligned to values) by completing a free assessment online (The VIA Institute on Character) at: https://www.viacharacter.org/www/Character-Strengths-Survey [35] Click the gold button to begin the FREE assessment, and after answering a series of questions online, you will see your top twenty-four strengths show, for you to save and refer back to. I suggest cutting and pasting the results to a new document, if you choose not to upgrade to the paid report options. Print your results and use these to anchor your actions and decisions in life. Live these values in all that you do, and step into a higher level of alignment with your *Why*.

Use these strengths to decide which new jobs you might apply for, or organizations that have similar values to yours. Include your top descriptors in your application or resume "Career

Summary" statement and showcase these values in accomplishments described in a cover letter accompanying your resume or application. Working in HR and recruitment for many years, I always appreciated those candidates who took a few minutes to show me they had read about the company history, its *why*, and how their values aligned with our company culture and values. In a competitive job market, these small actions can make all the difference in whether or not you are selected for an interview.

I have noticed that often in everyday conversations asking *why* with others can also create tension (for instance inquiring *why* something was done in a certain manner.) When you ask *why* often others feel a need to justify their past actions or decisions, creating annoyance or anxiety. I know many women whose confidence disappears when they are criticized or feel they are being judged. They frequently feel a need to defend their logic, the reason they chose to complete the activity in that manner, and it either drains their confidence or causes them to get angry and defensive.

By asking, "Why did you do it that way?" you are asking the person to explain themselves, to clarify their approach, and it can sound judgemental in many situations. I recommend that you choose to use *why* sparingly, and first think about what you are going to do with that information . . . Why are you even asking? Is it to understand or to judge, or to appreciate and celebrate? Your choice will either engage the other person or may erode the relationship and push them away if they feel unfairly judged. Think carefully before using the word *why* . . .

ACTION STEPS:

*By adding a few additional words first, you can open an inclusive approach that will support a positive intention for your request, with more likelihood of a warm relationship following. Instead of **why** sounding like an inquisition, I recommend you say, "Hmmmm — this is interesting and I'm curious . . . Why was it done this way in the past?" Or even better could be, "How did we get to this point?" (Note I did not use the word you in the sentence, either. By keeping the question posed as a third-party question, it puts the focus on the action or situation rather than on the person who completed the action and their choice. This approach lessens the personal feeling of being judged for taking what may be perceived as an incorrect approach.)*

Recognize that when someone else is asking why, that it is not a criticism of you or your decision-making process, it is simply a request to understand. Any information they share after hearing your answer about why you did something, is simply feedback. Reframe the word criticism to feedback, an opportunity to do something even better next time, with new awareness or knowledge. Use feedback as your friend. You also have a choice whether or not to change your actions at all based on another's feedback. If you change your actions, you will see a different result of course. If you make no changes in your actions, there will be no change in the situation.

1.5

But

Another simple three-letter word, yet so powerful when understood and used in a manner that supports your conversation goal. There are so many ways to use it, and different meanings, (conjunction, preposition, adverb, noun, and idiom) it is important to use it cautiously, and to your advantage.

I love that dress on you, *but* it is a bit short to wear to work" — how would you feel hearing those words? You hear the first part (*I love that dress on you*) the compliment, and likely smile. Then the first half of the sentence would be completely dismissed by hearing the second part of the sentence (**but** *it is a bit short to wear to work*). When you bring the word *but* into your awareness, you will likely be surprised at how many sentences this little critical devil appears in.

Three letters that can turn a sentence into a judgement, into a threat or a warning, or cut the sentence into two pieces that are not related thoughts at all. (The words in the second half of the sentence are often the other person's opinion, yet not your truth.)

In researching for this book I found that *Pegasus NLP* has a clear way to describe the usage of the word *but*. "But negates whatever precedes it."[36] The word *but* negates or cancels out everything that goes before it. It is generally accepted as a signal that the really important part of the sentence is coming up next. When you use it, most people listening to you speak will give more attention and more weight to what you say *after* you say *but*. In a sentence or report, for example, the reader will often stop and go back to read the first part of the sentence, to confirm they are understanding what is being said. It can also cause confusion about the message you really wanted to share.

But, *however*, *nevertheless*, *still*, and *yet*, are words implying opposition to whatever idea or concept is being included in the rest of the sentence (with a possible concession coming after the word *but*). The word *but* marks an opposition or contrasting viewpoint, although it can be used in a very casual way: *We are going now, but we shall return*. As an alternative word to *but*, when the word *however* is used, it indicates a less marked opposition, yet still displays or introduces a second perspective to be compared with the first: We are going; however, we shall return. Consider the energy of the word *but* in this sentence — "We are going, but we shall return" — it sounds almost like a threat! And when we return, this bad thing will happen . . . Whereas, using the word *however* instead opens the energy of what will possibly happen when we return.

But, *like*, and *and* are common transitional words often used to begin a sentence. When used in the middle of a sentence as a coordinating conjunction such as *and* or *so*, it is not followed by a comma.

Upon reflection, *but* is a word that can be used in many different ways, so it is not surprising that the usage of the word has many different behavioural outcomes. Some behaviours may be a result that is intended, and some results show that the word was apparently misused or misunderstood. It is a conjunction, a verb, a preposition, and a noun — not surprising that this small word used since before the year 900, is a confusing one.[37]

I want to focus your attention on when *but* is used in the middle of a sentence, e.g.: "Mary, you did a great job on that project, but I would like to see you meet the deadline next time." If you are Mary, while you first heard a compliment, that *you did a great job*, because the word *but* was used in the middle of the sentence, it feels like it cuts the sentence into two parts. From Mary's perspective, the last thing she heard said was feedback on what the leader would like to see next time. Depending on how Mary grew up, she could hear that as feedback, or take it as a personal criticism. Working in HR, and listening to both managers as well as staff complaints, I have found that more people take feedback as a criticism and are frequently offended or upset by observations made regarding their results. Not many people enjoy performance reviews . . .

An alternative way to provide the same insight, and provide encouragement is to switch out the word *but* for *and*. Imagine you are Mary, and your leader told you: "Mary, you did a great job on that project, and I would like to see you meet the deadline next time" — how does this sentence now feel different? It feels more open to possibilities, giving gentle guidance. Yet it is still the same sentence with just one word placed differently, giving it a whole new feel. Words matter!

Try this approach using *and* with your children when giving feedback, and watch how they respond differently to your words. I believe that children are born with honesty and integrity, until life experiences may shape them otherwise. Using the word *but* with children can cause them to be afraid or shy — criticism will shut down a creative soul quickly, especially when it is given by a parent. As I was growing up, my father used *but* in many of his sentences, and I learned what it felt like to constantly be criticized. Nothing ever seemed good enough for him. I learned that I was not good enough.

Only now, after many years of deep inner reflection do I see another perspective. One friend had suggested it was possible that he pushed me because he saw so much potential in me, and that he wanted to stretch me and help me grow, to be my best. Yet, it did not feel like encouragement, it felt like he was always angry with how I completed something, and the result was not completed to his standards. As a child, feeling I was underperforming was a very painful experience. Girls especially like to please their fathers.

If you are a parent — pay special attention to your words!

In a recent interview I hosted with bestselling author Teresa de Grosbois (author of *Mass Influence: The Habits of the Highly Influential*) she shared more on the usage of the word *but*.

> If there is one skill we can learn, it is to recognize that we have a beautiful paradox in language. This exists in almost every culture . . . which is the distinction between the word *and* and the word *but*. The same person using the word *but* will interpret the word differently depending on whether they are saying it or hearing it. You may notice this, when we say the word *but*, we tend to mean "I agree with what you just said, *and* I am making a clarifying statement." When we hear the word *but*, we tend to hear only what was said after it. The word *but* just cancelled everything I first said, and now they are asserting a whole new point of view.
>
> If you can get sensitized to that, and start noticing that when you say *but*, it very obviously means I'm just making a clarifying point, and

when you hear *but*, it very obviously means that person just dismissed everything I just said — then you start getting sensitized to the fact that this paradox exists in language. It exists almost ubiquitously, whether you are talking about the English language, French, Spanish, and Asian languages have this issue too. Really start to notice that, and work to replace the word *but* with the word *and*. If you can start saying, 'I agree with what you just said, *and* we could also consider . . . ' it is a lot more powerful in communication, and you will have fewer communication break downs.[38]

ACTION STEP:

Notice how you use the word but *in your daily life. Observe how others respond to it. Notice when you know you said it, and perhaps stop yourself and just let the sentence hang, and let the other person finish it with their idea or conclusion. Engage with others in a two-way dialogue, not just a one-way monologue. Invite conversation, engage with others, and see what ideas emerge. Bring people into the conversation rather than pushing them out of it by using the critical word* but.

Share with others when you notice them saying but, *and how you are interpreting their words. Check in with them to inquire if they were aware they even used the word* but *in the middle of their sentence and share how it impacted you when you heard it. Let's use this focus to create a positive ripple effect in our conversations with others — let's share our learnings!*

1.6

You

You — three letters, packing a powerful punch! This word is so often used by one person to another, and often even a compliment can sound like a criticism. Often the word *you* is followed by "did something that I don't like," or "should have done this." As a coach, I often hear recently promoted leaders using *you* with disregard, which creates issues with their staff (especially those who were peers and are now staff they have to manage).

As an adventurous teenager growing up in England, I went out with my friends in the evening, often coming home late and wearily dropping my clothes on my bed. In the morning, after a late wake up, I found my mum had already come in and picked up my clothes to wash. However, her voice still rings in my head "Yvonne, why didn't you put away your clothes, why are you so untidy!" Not only was the word *you* in that sentence, she also used the word *why*, suggesting an accusatory tone . . . Put the two together, and this adds up in the teenage brain to a whole lot of criticism — not a great way to start my day!

When you want to build collaboration with another person, whether a temperamental teenager or a new team member, try using *we* instead. Build a collaborative energy first. Then move to using *you* when giving a specific directive outlining what the other person is responsible for. Help them to understand *why* they are completing the task, and how this individual task fits into the bigger organizational goal or larger departmental initiative (or how it ultimately impacts a client). "We are expected to complete this outcome in a timely manner. Mary, your responsibility will be keeping the project plan up-to-date, in order to meet the promised client delivery date." Using *we* builds more collaboration, rather than jumping right into "Mary, *you* will be responsible for keeping the project plan up to date." State the context first, then the content, to help others understand *why* something is important.

As Daniel Pink shares in his book *DRIVE: The Surprising Truth About What Really Motivates Us,* his research has shown that people are motivated by three things: autonomy, mastery and purpose.[39] By outlining the accountability of the whole team, and how the bigger group can make an impact, one person's individual contribution becomes more purposeful. Each person can see how their small cog contributes to the greater wheel turning, which gives more meaning and importance to a smaller task. In many of the HR job satisfaction surveys I reviewed over the years, employees identified "interesting and challenging work" as either number one or number two on their list (with "higher pay" being mentioned when they were not engaged in interesting and challenging work, and felt that a short term financial motivator would offset their feeling of doing "less than interesting" work.)

ACTION STEP:

*Begin listening to when the word **you** is used, notice how you feel when hearing it, and notice how others respond. Try using **we** instead, then move to using you when giving a specific request to another person, to clearly outline what their direct responsibility includes.*

Often the word you is followed with "always . . .," which can sound as though you are disbelieving that the other person feels their behaviour is an issue, or that they cannot make a positive change. Switch that phrase to include a positive ending: "When you do X (whatever the action is) I feel Y (upset, annoyed, sad, etc.), and what I would prefer to see instead is Z (state the alternative desired behaviour). Then solidify why: "This shift is important for our relationship to flourish, so I hope you will consider this request moving forwards."

Chapter Two: Asking For What You Want,

And Getting It!

Hello, fear. Thank you for being here.
You're my indication that I'm doing
what I need to do.

— Cheryl Strayed, Author: "Brave Enough"

2.1

Please

Such an interesting word! As children we are taught that having good manners will support acceptance in the world, and we should always say *please* and *thank you* when interacting with others. However, by asking for permission, women invariably end up often (unintentionally) giving away our power.

Frequently, in practical terms, it is not the word *please* that gets us into trouble; it is the fact that we asked in the first place. When we ask to do something, we give away our personal power. When working for my previous leader, I realized that I was doing this when I asked if I could arrange a group workshop on a particular topic. By asking, I reduced my chances of success by 50 percent, because she may say *no*. When she did start saying *no* to many of my requests, my rebellious nature kicked in, and I started taking action, and instead asking for forgiveness (if I needed to) afterwards. This approach kept my creativity flowing, kept my personal sense of confidence and inner power intact, and often the successful outcome from my actions spoke for themselves. With the positive results clear, she could see that while my approach may have been a little unconventional (and not the way she would have done it), and it worked well and had an impactful outcome.

If you are the leader of an organization or team, it helps to balance using the word *please* when making a requests of others. Including the word in your leadership style will demonstrate that you are polite yet warm, caring and respectful. However, when giving a directive that is nonnegotiable, leave the word *please* out of the sentence. In the case of a fire drill, you need everyone to listen to you and do exactly what you ask, and do it right away, as their safety is at stake! There are specific instructions that everyone needs to hear, in order to depart the building safely and quickly. No extra words are required. This is the drill process, and everyone must follow it for their own safety, it is not a discussion or debate, it is a directive: "Fire code requires following these instructions now." This approach demonstrates clear leadership. Appreciate when to involve your team and foster their ideas and questions, when to build collaboration through questions and when to give clear and concise direction.

Pay attention to when you use the word *please*. Used at the beginning of the sentence, it states your request in a polite manner. Using *please* at the end of the sentence often sounds like you are begging or making an apology for your request (*oh, please, please, please* — much like a young child might sound). Using it in the context of "May it please the court," almost sounds condescending, so watch how you use the word, and ensure that you are really conveying your intention.

ACTION STEP:

Pay attention to when you use the word please, *if your intention is to invite conversation, or if you actually need the other person to take your instructions and simply comply without any discussion. (If you have three teenagers who need to get ready for school in the morning, I would generally still say* please *with almost every request, as young adults — with crazy hormones and insatiable need for sleep — benefit from extra encouragement and nurturing.) Step into a greater level of confidence. Take action, and ask for forgiveness afterwards, if needed!*

2.2

Perhaps

When working with others, I want to create collaboration, connection, and explore possibilities, therefore I focus on asking more than telling. *Perhaps* is a word that I use fairly often. *Perhaps* demonstrates that you are open to hear more, to explore alternatives that someone is offering you, or that you are willing to consider a different way or perspective. As a coach, I may ask, "Perhaps there is another way; what else are you willing to explore?"

When I am leading a project, if someone is hesitant in committing to an activity, I may ask if we can try XYZ *perhaps*, as an invitation, a way to move the conversation forwards while still staying in an energy of possibility. *Perhaps* is a gentle inquiry, using the word *perhaps* shows a willingness to explore, to look at all ideas and options before choosing one. In everyday conversation, the word *perhaps* is often used after an activity has taken place, as a way to explore points of view and challenge if this was correct, or the best choice; for example, *"*Perhaps Charlie would have been able to climb the mountain, if X." Using the word *perhaps* keeps the door open to possibility, when used before an activity or after an event — to pose a question and stay in the energy of expansion and discussion, of choices . . .

When you want to encourage another person, using *perhaps* shows your support, that you are working with them to discover a way to complete something. It is an especially valuable word to use with young children, to foster exploration, creativity, and determination. As a leader, it can also be equally as effective to draw out new potential solutions from your team members, and to show them that you are still open to new options that may be an even better fit. When you tell one of your team to take action in a specific way to accomplish a task, you are being directive. However, when you give them the outcome or objective you want them to complete and let them figure out how they will best complete it, they are often more excited about completing the task, as they choose how to do so.

As a female leader, it is important to understand when to use *perhaps* and when to leave it out of the sentence. Inclusive, caring, and decisive leaders are respected. Your words show your commitment to moving forwards after hearing their input too, and shows strength that your team can count on you to lead them effectively. If you are still considering options, keep the word *perhaps* in the sentence. Once you have decided on your course of action, take the lead by being decisive and clear. Move the conversation from exploring to action steps, clearly letting your team know that the time for discussion is past. "Thank you all for sharing your ideas and exploring options that helped me understand what is at stake and the impact of taking one approach over another. As the leader for this team, after considering the options, I am directing you to action X, which appears to be the fairest." (Label your choice: *fairest, easiest, appropriate, strategic, graceful, swift* — with one word, identifying why you are choosing this option).

By labelling it, your team will see over time how you make decisions. You do not have to be liked, however, you do need to be respected — which is endorsed when you are seen as *fair* in your business practices. In my coaching work, by using powerful questions I draw out what needs to be focused on, then deepen the conversation to explore ways that my client might take action, to move forward towards the goal they have identified.

ACTION STEPS:

Carefully select when to use perhaps. In a fire drill, you are giving clear directions that need to be followed without any debate, which is a closed conversation. If you want to encourage debate or brainstorming, however, keep the conversation open. Open the conversation by suggesting that "perhaps there are other ways to achieve this . . ." To develop a shy staff member, try using perhaps when you are asking for a task to be completed, and see how others respond differently to you. Gather ideas in group meetings from everyone, as often the quietest person has the most well-thought-out ideas to share, yet may be shy to speak up. "Mary, perhaps you have something to add to this discussion?" This warm invitation without expectation draws Mary into the conversation without putting her on the spot. "Perhaps" is optional in this context, Mary does not have to give an idea — however is welcomed to. Next time you want to draw her into the conversation, you may opt to leave out the word perhaps. "Mary, what ideas can you add to this discussion?"

To build out your team of trusted staff, let them own their challenges and their solutions. Encourage them to think through a problem and always bring forth a few options rather than bringing you the issue without identifying any possible ways to solve it. Fostering independence and encouraging your team to think for themselves first (and only come to you when they have a bigger problem that they cannot solve or is outside their authority level) will prevent bottlenecks. This approach keeps you working on the strategic elements of your role, not solving a constant flow of low-level inquiries. The classic time-management square grid of tasks (urgent but not important, urgent and important, not urgent but important, not urgent and not important) shows how low-level urgent issues can take up so much of a leader's time, if staff are not encouraged to bring forth solutions, and work in an empowered way.

I have observed from managing staff, when they feel they are micromanaged, or you are not letting them be creative in how they do their work, they will lose their motivation. By trusting your team members are closest to the issue and know how it needs to be solved, you eliminate being a bottleneck and foster employee creativity. Freeing up your time enables you to work on strategic activities, your important-but-not-urgent work, which is less stressful overall and more effective.

2.3

Can't

Cannot is sometimes also spelled *can not*. The one-word spelling is by far the more common: Interest rates simply cannot continue at their present level. The contraction *can't* is most common in speech and informal writing.

Can't — the shorter version of "*I cannot*" is overused in today's world. What it really means is often that the person chooses not to do something, then looks for ways to justify why they do not want to do it. A much more powerful statement is: "I am choosing another alternative option, as that approach does not fit with my skills or values."

When you say, *I can't*, ask yourself why you are choosing to say that. Is it because you feel you do not have the knowledge to complete the task, nor the tools, do not have the finances or lack the support to achieve something, or just do not believe in the concept or likelihood of success? What is getting in your way of trying to achieve something? How often can you flip *I can't* to *I can do that, if I have access to X*? By saying *yes* more often, you move your energy into a positive vibration, and accelerate your growth by taking on something new or a stretch assignment and completing it.

If you are invited to an event, and you decide it is not a good fit for you (the people who will be there, the timing or topic of the event, your availability, or priorities) no explanation is needed or required. A simple "Thank you for the personal invitation, however, I already have plans that day/evening/lunchtime" is all you need to say. It is your time and you have control to select how you use it! Once it is gone, you will never get that time back, so treat this non-renewable resource as precious.

If you ask someone else to do something, and they say *I can't*, it is worth asking for clarification, to see if they are also lacking a resource, or perhaps not comfortable admitting this. If your son or daughter is saying that they *can't* do something, ask, "What would you need in order to complete this?" or "What would need to be in place for you to say yes to this request?" However, if you are asking one of your team to complete an assignment, remember a key component of your role as the leader is to remove all obstacles that are getting in the way of your staff being successful.

An alternate approach when delegating is to confirm what resources are available before you ask for their commitment. This could sound like, "I have talked with the engineering team leader about supporting your research project, and giving you access to the data you need to complete this assignment. How long do you feel it will take to prepare and present your findings?" You are not asking them a closed question: *"Will you do it or not?"* Instead, you are asking them when it *can* be completed, after sharing what potential roadblocks you have already cleared for them.

Generally, when asking a staff member to complete a task, make sure you have given them: authority, accountability, and responsibility — the core elements of delegation of authority. According to Henri Fayol's 14 Principles of management (Fayol was a French mining engineer, mining executive, author, and director of mines, who developed general theory of business administration and published his *Functions and Principles of Management* back in 1916) [40], delegation is different from abdication . . . As the leader, his theory suggests, your core functions are clear.[41] Based on watching powerful women leaders and research data, I suggest the following 5 consolidated practices with modifications (inside the brackets) to support feminine leadership:

1.   Planning (as a woman leader this skill is understanding the context)

    2.   Organizing (for woman leaders — prioritizing and delegating)

    3.   Commanding (for woman leaders — fostering accountability)

    4.   Coordinating (for woman leaders — managing towards the end goal)

    5.   Controlling (for woman leaders — collaboration and coaching)

However, Fayol also recognized that in a large organization, when you delegate responsibility for completing a task without first giving the employee the authority to complete it (and access the resources needed without further permission needed), you create a bottleneck. As a leader, setting your employee up for success will encourage them to say "yes — I can" more frequently, as they know and trust that you have created an environment for them to be successful already. While you hold the employee accountable for a completed task to a specified standard of excellence, you still hold responsibility for the work getting done, and retain the power to control or manage the outcome. (When you abdicate, you renounce authority — generally in a formal manner for a senior position or role in public office, or "relinquish a throne.")

Clear any roadblocks within the organization first, and clarify the scope of the project, clearly outline the budget available, and the measures of success. Confirm with your employee that they have all the tools, resources and connections needed to complete the assignment — then ask them when it can be completed. To ensure they are clear on how to begin, I also recommend asking, "What will be your first couple of steps to begin this project — what will you tackle first?" Their answer will give you confirmation they are heading down a path that will lead to success at the beginning of the work, or the opportunity for a course correction before they get too far off base.

Sometimes it is easier to see a solution and ask someone else to complete something than to see the answer for your own challenges (often referred to as a blind spot — something you cannot see). In a recent group learning session, my professional coach colleague Lynn Demers shared some excellent questions, and one in particular was intended to bring clarity regarding one of the biggest questions people struggle with — *What is my purpose in life?* One of the more challenging questions to answer after *Is this all there is?* This is a question which many people experience surfacing in their 30s.

Lynn asked a question that initially seemed a strange one, and as it did not flow easily, and yet it was so powerful I wanted to include it here: **"What is the one thing that you cannot *not* do?"** Go ahead and read that question again, as the answer you will form is significant and gives a powerful level of clarity to your activities and connects to your deeper purpose in life. Knowing what you are compelled to do, what you cannot help yourself refrain from doing, is significant. If you love to paint, and lose yourself for hours while painting, or just cannot leave the painting until it is completed and signed, this is an example. When you cannot *not* do something, it puts the spotlight on what you *must* do, you are compelled to do. What is that tractor beam calling you forth to do? For me, writing this book is something I cannot not do; it is constantly on my mind that I must finish it and get this work out into the world. So many of the examples in this book are from conversations held over and over again with my clients, that I know using powerful language and creating confident conversations makes a significant impact, hence I have to share ways I have learned to leverage this wisdom. I am compelled to share my insights.

In his book *The Law of Attraction*, Michael Losier states that often people "cannot" figure out what they want, but they know what they don't want. He describes this with his "Clarity Through Contrast" exercise. [42] True! I hear this in my coaching frequently when I ask for a solution to an issue and hear "I don't know . . ." He then shares a process of looking at opposites, to help define what the person wants instead. For example, "I don't like my boss micromanaging me and looking over my shoulder all the time." Agreed, not nice! So what <u>do you want</u> instead? The opposite of micromanaging behaviour is to allow independence and autonomy. So what you do want instead is to be able to work independently.

I have observed that people will often act only when the pain of change becomes greater than the fear of staying where they are. You might have a dream and yet remain reluctant to step towards it, because it will require change. Perhaps it is a change in mindset, in your job, home, location, the people you surround yourself with, leaving a strained relationship or an abusive spouse.

However, the pain of the situation eventually becomes a trigger for action. If you put your hand accidentally on a hot stove burner, you withdraw your hand quickly with the pain. Pain triggers action.

I loved Lynn's question, as it looked at what was missing, yet did so in a positive manner. It provoked me to consider what I was feeling compelled to do, to identify my calling, or purpose. What was it buried deep inside, that seed or idea, that if I did not act on it, I would be keeping my unique gifts from the world? What was it that I simply could not help myself but do, I <u>had</u> to do it, and it was easy for me and enjoyable, and purposeful? In this exercise, I realized that I loved to share information with others, to teach others, to give a nugget of information that could open their awareness to new possibilities. Writing, speaking, mentorship, and group coaching are ways that I could share information with a wider audience and impact more people. The seed of this book was sprouting . . . Once I realized this, speaking opportunities also magically showed up, endorsing that I had taken the right choice to step into action around my new awareness.

ACTION STEP:

What situations and invitations can you choose to say no to, without using I can't? What other words can you use instead of I can't? How can you convert that phrase to "I can do that, if you can provide me with X [state the resources you need in order to be able to say "Yes" with full commitment] then I can complete that task for you in a timely manner"?

Pay attention when others say I can't, and clarify what is preventing them from saying yes. How can you help others turn a low vibration phrase into a higher level positive one, moving from can't to can?

Use the following prompt in your journal: Recently I said I can't in the following situation . . . Instead, next time, I will say X.

2.4

Curious

In my professional work as a coach, I use the word *curious* frequently. I may start a question with a statement of my intention first, such as, "I am curious . . . What is the desired outcome for this project?" If I had launched straight into my question, "What is the desired outcome for this project?" the question may have been received quite differently, depending on my relationship depth with my conversation partner. If I am the designated leader for a project, I have the authority to ask for further details on the outcome of the project, and also the status of completion. By using *I'm curious* at the beginning of my question, the energy of positivity and possibility permeates the room. My question demonstrates caring not only about the outcome, but *how* the person is formulating their idea, and shows understanding for their measures of success or outcome/s for the project as well.

In order to build trust as a female leader, research shows we need to show three important characteristics: caring, consistency, and competence.[43] By stating your intention to come from a place of curiosity (using *I'm curious . . .* at the start of the sentence) you demonstrate caring. By listening to how the person is creating their project plan, how they are anticipating achieving project success, you show that you care about their success as well as the overall outcome. By repeating back what you heard them say (paraphrasing), you confirm that you are clear on their outcomes. Without saying so directly, paraphrasing implies that you approve their approach (or do not have any comments, guidance, or objections). By paraphrasing back to them, "What I think I heard you say is . . ." once again you demonstrate that you heard what they said and understand it. "Being heard" is another comment I hear frequently as an issue with my female clients. So be the leader who demonstrates hearing her staff.

In my twenty years of work in HR many of the conversations that went sideways involved the topic of performance. This is not simply because in larger organizations the task of performance management is generally administered by HR.

It is a frequent topic of frustration for new managers who are not skilled in delegation and managing task completion. Often the manager is busy and does not take the time to enquire about how the staff member is feeling about accomplishing their tasks, they focus solely on the outcome. A "get it done as quickly as possible" mindset. However, research shows us that people want to have the opportunity to not only complete a task, they want to understand the impact of their work. Staff need to see how their smaller piece of work may fit within a bigger project, and how this will ultimately benefit the organization or their customer overall (the purpose).[44]

In Pink's *DRIVE*, again his extensive research shows that people are motivated by autonomy, mastery, and purpose. They do not enjoy having their manager looking over their shoulder and watching them all the time, giving constant instructions and feedback ("micromanaging" them). People want to work with autonomy. By developing mastery and deepening knowledge on a specific topic, the work becomes more interesting and challenging, a key element Pink identifies, which contributes to engaging staff, helping with staff retention and reducing turnover costs.

Being a subject matter expert (SME) for an organization helps everyone know who the go-to person is for in-depth knowledge and for current trends in a specific area. An employee who is engaged with their organization is more likely to give discretionary effort — or to go above and beyond what is expected of them (Pink shares) and offer high quality work or service. "Engaged" employees are more likely to be innovative and bring their best ideas to their work, as well as more likely to have positive conversations with customers about their organization or add to the sales function.

What opportunities for innovation are currently being missed within your organization, because staff turnover is high (often highlighting a management or cultural fit issue) and engagement (demonstrated by staff working extra hours, or discretionary effort) is low? Where could you step into (or step up to) a leadership mindset, whether you are in a leadership role by title or not? What can you do to foster innovation in your organization, which will save the company money on expenses or supplies, to add new revenues with new product offerings or bundling services in a unique way and repricing, to retain customers, by demonstrating extra levels of care and attention?

What can you personally do to reduce staff turnover — you do not have to be in HR to impact this? Stay curious about opportunities to add value to your organization and offer teamwork alternatives.

By developing a volunteer team or committee to rally around a community cause that directly aligns with your company mission, you will be on the radar of the leadership team or executive, for your initiative and dedication. If you work for a pet food company, organizing volunteers for a "dog walking day" for seniors shows clear alignment, with pets being the common denominator. Community volunteer projects make great news stories, as TV and radio stations want to balance accidents, deaths, and horrific stories with heart-warming stories.

By staying curious about the current issues your organization faces and getting creative to find solutions to address these challenges, you showcase your personal leadership — and will be on the leadership radar the next time an opening develops. Being proactive in advocating in your career is one of my biggest coaching topics, as volunteer projects generally are more fun and less intensive than mandated projects deemed critical for success.

I worked in Calgary as an HR Consultant with the Wynford Group, a group of strategic compensation consultants, for several years, which offered an annual "Salary Survey and Recommended Best Practices Report," that included survey questions about what was important to their staff at work. For several years in a row, employees cited "having interesting and challenging work" in their top three answers as a key ingredient contributing to a great work environment.[45] The third research element identified by Pink is purpose — which showed employees desire making a meaningful contribution while at work. If their work ultimately makes a difference for their customer by improving the customer's life significantly (or helps the community or planet overall) it is seen as purposeful (and interesting). Coming to work each day and doing a task without knowing how it contributes to the customer experience often contributes to staff burnout, increases depression, and fuels low motivation. (Staff are also looking for quality feedback on their performance and seeking personal work-life balance.)

Overall, I believe we are currently experiencing a shift in the business world — a consciousness awakening — in which there is more awareness of the benefits of conscious commerce, and social enterprise is on the rise. It is becoming more frequent that organizational leaders are internally communicating the customer benefits with the impact of their products and services, and sharing these more readily throughout the organization. This is not solely with an external sales focus through marketing endeavours (for potential customers to understand); it helps if all employees understand the benefits their organization offers for customers. When employees are proud of the organization they work with (because it demonstrates being a great place to work), employees are more likely to invite others to engage with the organization (either as a customer or a potential employee referral).

Gone are the days where sales is the sole job of the sales team — sales can come from so many casual conversations at networking events, sports competitions, hair salon conversations — anywhere that people gather and connect. When you are proud of your work environment and the services or products your organization offers, you are proud when you are asked, "So, what do you do?" People want interesting, challenging and purposeful work — and of course, to be well paid for it!

Alison Donaghey, host of the radio show *Think Opposite*, as well as a speaker, author, and thought strategist, shared how she approaches business and staying curious.

> When I started one of my companies (a house painting company) I would look at the way the other guys were operating and ask how I could do it differently (as I did not want to do business in that way). I started with considering what would be opposite to their way? I would start at the opposite end and then move backwards gradually to something more conventional, until I found something that felt like a good fit for me. So my business encompasses my sense of self and service, not necessarily a typical business model.[46]

ACTION STEPS:

What can you become more curious about? How can you introduce I'm curious . . . into your conversations, today or this week? What else can you do to demonstrate that you care about the other person, with a question or personal inquiry? I encourage you to start thinking as a female leader, even if you are not currently in a role of formally managing staff, by being curious about where you can make an impact. What can you do differently or in an opposite manner to others, to embody your values in how you serve others?

For your own growth and expansion, consider volunteering as a way to gain experience or stepping up to a leadership role informally first. Volunteering has created some of the most amazing connections and opportunities for me personally, and the opportunity to develop skills in a supportive environment (without the pressure of a formal evaluation that generally comes with an employment situation). This chapter is about asking for what you want, and getting it, which means formulating intriguing questions. By staying curious and open in your questions and showing positive energy, you build trust and the likelihood of reciprocity.

A conversation is like a dance between two (or more) people, to understand each other and deepen appreciation for their perspective. A question can help move from uncertainty to clarity, so remaining open and holding an energy of positivity will ease the conversational flow. Note down in your journal what happens when you use the phrase I'm curious . . . and when you don't — and the difference in the outcome. (Please share your observations and results with me as I am curious to learn how the energy of the conversation shifts for you using this concept.)

2.5

Believe

This word is incredibly powerful! When you believe something with your whole self, mind, body, and spirit — it is a powerful force. If you lack belief in yourself, doubt will sabotage your efforts and easily derail you . . . It is a mindset shift that you can achieve. I am including this word in the section on asking for what you want because belief is a centre point for trusting that we *can* achieve something. My intention is to help you understand how to move from possibility to knowing — to fully believing you can have what you ask for from others — or for yourself.

A recent segment on one of OWN's online shows included a talk by Michael Bernard Beckwith[47], which put the concept of believing in a whole new light for me. Beckwith is an American New Thought Minister, author, and founder of the Agape International Spiritual Center in Culver City, California, (a New Thought church with a congregation estimated in excess of eight thousand members). In February 2012, he addressed the United Nations General Assembly as part of its World Interfaith Harmony Week. He is a global humanitarian, award-winning author and co-founder of the Association for Global New Thought (AGNT). As a minister, he has artfully blended Eastern and Western principles to share universal teachings to help us shift our beliefs and "participate in our own unfolding" like a beautiful rosebud which unfolds. Believing in ourselves is a key part of our personal growth. Beckwith recently shared his insights on believing, which really made me think differently:

When you believe more in what you can't see,

the things that you *do* see

are things that you won't see.

Yes, read that sentence again, to ensure it is clear for you. The things you can't see include love, harmony, peace, and joy. Whereas the things you can see are being demonstrated: violence, anger, fear, resentment, and prejudice, for example. When you believe more in harmony and peace, you won't see anger and fear any longer — because you begin to believe that you can change lower vibrational words and feelings for positive ones — like love and truth. The beautiful thing about a change in perspective is it costs nothing, is available to anyone, creates opportunities for something better to emerge, and when we believe, we can choose a new more positive path.

Beckwith also believes that we go through four stages of "unfolding to be our best self": being the Victim (a mindset of "someone is doing something to me" — rather than living with accountability for your own actions) being a Manifester (establish your intention and gain clarity — you create what you describe), and being an Instrument (there is a divine purpose or idea inside you that you choose to welcome in, and surrender to your potential). Lastly, stage four is Being (when you bring these elements together and authentically live into them — integration).

An interesting turn of events happened in summer of 2016 which cemented this concept for me. My husband John and my son Alex went shopping for Mother's Day. My son is very intuitive, and always seems to pick the most amazing presents, which turn out to be just what I need at exactly that time, interesting and meaningful gifts. One was a solar-powered butterfly, which when plugged into the earth circled the stake it was attached to, by flying around and around high in the air. I later came to realize at that time last summer I had been somewhat indecisive and was spinning in circles. While I was beginning to develop a new layer of clarity about my coaching work within my new brand, Flourish, I still was not quite able to connect the key elements of my work together in a way that made sense to me. When it made sense to me, I could then describe it with resonance to others, in words that flowed and embodied authenticity and truth. Clients who understand what you do (the transformation that you can help them to achieve) are attracted to work with you because of the energetic resonance they feel, and the belief that you can help them achieve their desired outcome. Clarity in your descriptor of the powerful transformation you help others make — while quickly describing who you are as a person — are keys to generating resonance.

At the time I received the butterfly, it seemed purely a pretty gift to put outside in the garden and watch how Shelby (our six-year old Sheltie) went crazy watching it circling around the stalk. The butterfly has long been an important symbol for me, a symbol of transition and freedom and the quiet time we must occasionally go through, cocooning the inner work needed to reflect upon before we struggle to break through and see a world of beauty on the other side — just like the butterfly breaking through the chrysalis. The butterfly breaking through is free, she has wings to fly, she can see the world from new heights, and soar wherever the breeze takes her. She softly drops down on each flower, and gently helps them to flourish, by carefully rubbing her legs on their stigma to release their pollen — their unique inner gifts. She flies and settles on each petal to populate and share wisdom with others by settling on each flower centre while on her journey.

The second gift was a beautiful pale turquoise spiral bound journal. The cover was matte and felt like suede, and softly called me in, to hold it and feel what needed to be written in it. Yet I was not ready initially to share heartfelt thoughts on the pages within (which ironically has flowers on the inside cover — that nicely connected to my company brand — Flourish! — my logo includes a light bulb with daisies inside it).

The new journal felt special — and the cover had an important message: "She believed she could, so she did," printed in beautiful filigree gold lettering. It felt so special that journaling, and the place I felt I was in my evolution, wasn't feeling quite special enough to begin opening such a beautiful journal. Symbolic perhaps of where I was in my journey, trying to articulate for the world how my services fit together.

By September that year, I felt the language emerging to describe the specific coaching I was providing. It was much clearer, and I boldly shared this clarity in a short video, what I was doing, and how I did it. "I am on a mission to uplift the spirit of humanity." I am doing this leveraging my passion — helping women have more joy in business. Helping women entrepreneurs' level the playing field of business, and professional women earn what we are worth. By helping women entrepreneurs have successful, flourishing businesses which expand and hire staff, perhaps more female staff — and women generally pay female staff fair wages, I help impact the inequality issue.

This is my contribution to leveraging my gifts of coaching and mentoring, to support women to have more confidence and set themselves up for success. The turquoise journal sat in my meditation room, unused until January 1, 2017 — when a perfect storm of sorts happened, and a new belief formed for me. The belief that it was now my time, time to step into a more powerful version of myself. From an astrological timing perspective, 2017 is the beginning of a nine-year period of renewal, and those who follow numerology and astrology were sharing what a great time it was for starting a new venture!

In January 2017, all these elements came together in harmony, and I finally *believed* I was ready to step into a bigger role, to see success in a new way, to own my identified purpose. The message on the turquoise journal cover now seemed to be calling me in . . . I now believed I could do it — so I stepped up and took action. I started saying *no* more often to activities that were not directly contributing to my four goals identified for the year, and I selected one word that captured the essence of what I wanted for the coming year — *adventure*. That single word emerged through a meditation and involved stepping out and living a new level of success, happiness, and confidence. As demonstrated by numerous speaker requests, when I started believing again, the universe began pouring opportunities to help me on my journey . . .

The late Dr. Wayne Dyer said: "When you change the way you look at things, the things you look at change . . ."[48] There is also another related expression: "If there is no change, there is no change" — supporting the fact that if we want our lives to be different, we have to be willing to make a small step toward making a change, in order to start the ball rolling.

Lisa Mundell-Lawrence, Woman of Inspiration 2017 Award Recipient (Mom-Preneur category), an executive Vice President of Western Canada of PMA-Brethour Realty Group, and one of the owners of the Cheap Smoke & Cigars Franchise shared that she believes her confidence comes from several experiences.

I was lucky, as I grew up with a single mum, her strength just stuck with me. When you are a single parent you have to show strength at all times. We have three girls and three boys and all of them are confident in their own way. We were taught that anything is possible — you just have to work hard to get there. I had cancer eighteen or so years ago, I was at the top of my field in sales working mostly with men, and when my power was taken from me, I found it puts things in perspective. I needed to balance my masculine and feminine energy, and learned during that life-changing time when I needed to show up as strong and powerful and when to be nurturing and loving. The Universe taught me that, so a favourite word is *unstoppable* and the phrase *I am possible* rather than impossible . . .

I also believe that all women have inspiration to share. Whether it be from sharing their stories of wisdom, from lessons they have learned or obstacles they have overcome, and women who have learned the art of checking their ego at the door especially, for the better good of all. Our franchisees are committed to starting a business, yet one with a little less risk. We do CPRs on an annual basis with each of them (defining context, purpose and results), by starting with their desired results, then backing into the purpose and then the context they need to create to achieve those results. This approach brings out their confidence when they write them out and clarify their action plan and see their business take off.[49]

While others can help to create a supportive environment for you, or remove obstacles to your success, it needs to be your inner motivation and belief that lights the spark. As a coach, I hold the space of possibility for my clients to believe a better way is possible, and support them as they take action and experience growth. I stand beside my clients, like a plant stake that you tie a seedling to as it grows strength in its stalk and deepens its roots, building strength to stand up in a windstorm. Seeing new possibilities is one of my gifts, and I use that to encourage women to explore options and choices, and take action on the one that best aligns with their purpose, and they believe aligns with their values.

Feeling you have possibilities, that you have a choice, gives a sense of inner freedom, a way to take control back in a situation that might have once felt like a tidal wave washing over you. When we **believe** we have choices, new energy of possibility flows in, and hope forms.

What you BELIEVE,

you can achieve!

— Mary Kay Ash, Founder — Mary Kay Cosmetics

ACTION STEPS:

Regardless of the time of year, ask yourself what you currently believe, and journal your replies:
1 — What do you believe could potentially be your next step in your life, or an area of growth for you?
2 — What is one action that if you truly believed you could take, would bring you deep satisfaction and joy?
3 — What is the one belief that is holding you back from taking a big step, one that pulls you backwards or causes you to doubt yourself?
4 — Would you be willing to consider it is time to let go of that belief?

*5 — If you took that doubt, reframed it, and created positive
energy in the opposite direction, what could that shift for you?*

Are you ready to take action,

to take a step forwards? When?

How about right now?

CHAPTER 3:

Elevating Positive Self-Talk and Confidence.

My mission in life is not merely to survive, but to thrive; and to do so with some passion, compassion, some humor, and some style.

— Maya Angelou

Certain words simply ooze positive energy! Words that are true, kind, and show generosity and respect for others, all resonate with a higher energy than negative or unkind words. Let's explore some of the most powerful words to add more frequently and focus on developing new habits — to elevate your confidence.

Abundant	**Accepting**	**Beautiful**	**Devoted**
Equal	**Excellent**	**Flexible**	**Forgiving**
Generous	**Harmonious**	**Honest**	**Humble**
	Inspired	**Liberating**	

3.1

Gratitude

Dr. Robert Emmons, Professor of Psychology at the University of California and author of the books *Thanks!* and *How the New Science of Gratitude Can Make You Happier* has been researching gratitude for over eight years. He is considered the foremost expert in this area, and writes: "Without gratitude, life can be lonely, depressing and impoverished. Gratitude enriches human life. It elevates, energizes, inspires and transforms, and those who practise it will experience significant improvements in several areas of life including relationships, academics, energy level and even dealing with tragedy and crisis."[50]

Much work has been done on this topic, with research by Emmons showing how to raise our energetic vibrational level with a daily gratitude practice. When I burned out, I stopped running in circles and took several months away from my client work, exploring self-awareness and my energy levels more deeply. When I started to focus more on myself and paying attention to what my body was experiencing, I realized that I was more tired than I had first thought (and having frequent bathroom visits). Armed with this information, I began paying more attention to my health, and was diagnosed with type-2 diabetes. Reading about the longer-term impact of this illness, possibly resulting in loss of sensation to your feet and legs, I had even more reasons to ensure that my livelihood aligned with my purpose, and to live each day without any regrets!

My coach, Jayne Warrilow, had shared in one of her sessions about her own recovery from a debilitating illness, and how she had found solace in a book called *You Can Heal Your Life*, by the late author Louise Hay. Hay believed that the body has wisdom to tell us, and there are just two mental patterns that contribute to disease — fear and anger. According to Hay, the real reason diabetes shows up is "longing for what might have been, a deep sorrow, no sweetness left, a great need to control." Hay recommended repeating a mantra to create new thought patterns as a way to heal yourself from a particular ailment or disease. To address diabetes, the mantra is: "This moment is filled with Joy. I now choose to experience the sweetness of today."[51] (I dug deeper into learning meditation practices that supported me staying present and increasing my awareness about joy-filled moments.)

Thinking about the probable cause of this disease, I believe that the emotional childhood trauma I experienced around my father's unkind words cut deeply, and that I was both angry (about his lack of support) and fearful (that his words may come true later in life). This anger and fear ultimately impacted why I strived for success for many years. I carried that negative energy with me for forty-five years, an energy of striving always pushing for results and advancement in my career.

With a renewed focus of bringing more joy into my life, I began looking for ways to add more activities that I enjoyed doing. As a child, what did I love to do? I developed a short list of the things that I found fun and brought me joy — one of which was creative projects: paintings, crafts, and stories — and how I used to love reading, and had written a few poems as a young girl. I loved painting, despite my father criticizing one of my art pieces (around age five), so I started doing more joyful activities, and even took my son to an art studio where we did some painting together on Mother's Day. He had a memorable time, and I really enjoyed reconnecting with my "inner artist." (He has since expanded his passion for art and is now selling his artwork to raise money for Operation Smile surgeries for children.)

In that phase of reflection and reinvention, I started looking for more joy. It was only after I stopped running around (in my post burnout phase) that I realized that I did not have to go hunting for it at all. Joy was all around me, I just had to be present, to stand still long enough to see it. (I wonder if you are nodding as you are reading this — does this sound like you?)

In my daily practice of journaling, I began tracking and noticing the things I experienced each day that gave me joy. I became more aware and started to see with fresh eyes many of the beautiful things around me that I had forgotten to appreciate while I was so career focused and striving for success. The beauty in receiving a bouquet of sweet-smelling flowers, seeing a glorious sunrise signalling a new day, appreciating a delicious meal triggering new taste sensations, and I rediscovered my love of ice cream! The silky, cool, smooth sensation lingering on my tongue — aaaahhhh . . . Being out in nature and appreciating the snowy mountains and the powerful ecosystem of animals and birds gathering around the pond by my house, drawing in a deep breath of fresh air while taking my dog for a walk. Accepting her sweet puppy kisses — all simple yet joyful moments I had been too busy to see before, were right under my nose. I focused daily on being grateful for what I had and stopped longing for what I didn't have.

Slowing down led to appreciation, for the small things that people do that show respect or love. It also led to a daily practice of gratitude, first thing in the morning before getting out of bed, and last thing at night before falling asleep. Being grateful for who showed up in my life that day, new contacts, friends and clients, seeing the small gestures from my son or husband showing love and respect. For having a safe home with a secure roof over my head, to be living in a peaceful country — with freedom of choice, to have a warm and comfortable bed to rest in, nourishing food on our table, resources available to me, money in the bank, and love in my heart. Regular appreciation of the simple yet meaningful things in life and showing gratitude to others is an important contribution I make in my community. My volunteer activities and being of service creates a calming effect on me.

Oxytocin, a hormone released by the pituitary gland, is sometimes called the "love hormone" because your body releases it at high concentrations during positive social interactions (such as falling in love) or when giving birth, and I experience it when co-creating possibilities or solutions with clients. Volunteering, or having a service orientation knitted together with a purposeful business for the common good (conscious commerce) fills up my soul.

Tracking these feelings in my journal and being grateful expanded my awareness of the joy all around me. In her article published in *Forbes* magazine — "7 Scientifically Proven Benefits Of Gratitude That Will Motivate You To Give Thanks Year-Round," author and psychotherapist Amy Morin found numerous research studies on the positive effects of gratitude.[52]

A 2014 study published in *Emotion* showed that "Gratitude opens the door to more relationships." [53] As I mentioned, Robert A. Emmons' research confirms that gratitude effectively increases happiness and reduces depression. [54] He showed that: "Gratitude improves psychological health and reduces a multitude of toxic emotions, ranging from envy and resentment to frustration and regret."[55] In an experiment by Dr. Emmons (at the University of California-Davis) people who kept a "gratitude journal," a weekly record of things they felt grateful for, enjoyed better physical health, were more optimistic, exercised more regularly, and described themselves as happier than a control group who didn't keep journals.[56] The Greater Good Science Center at the University of California, Berkeley — in collaboration with the University of California, Davis— launched the multi-year project "Expanding the Science and Practice of Gratitude." The general goals of this initiative are to expand the scientific database of gratitude, particularly in the key areas of human health, personal and relational well-being, and developmental science.

While I learned having a gratitude practice helped me to feel more grounded, more optimistic and appreciative personally, there is considerable research around the benefits of taking time to experience being grateful. Author Marci Shimoff, also shares more on gratitude in her book "Happy for No Reason: 7 Steps to Being Happy from the Inside Out" and a summary of my interview with her is in Chapter Five.

ACTION STEPS:

Start exploring what you are grateful for each day. Take regular breaks in your workday to step outside and simply take a deep breath, to fill your lungs with new oxygen and energy. Especially if you are stressed at work, after taking a break and a short walk outside, come back with a renewed attitude, ready to concentrate again and get that project done. (You may be thinking — I'm so busy I can't take five minutes to myself — and I am here to grant you permission to do just that!) When your prefrontal cortex is in stress mode, you cannot keep adding more to your brain — like a saturated sponge, the excess energy will overflow and not be absorbed. Take that short break!

Increasing your awareness of what brings you joy is one way to start seeing the small things around you that money cannot buy, those things that are so important to notice . . . The smile on a child's face, how your dog lovingly greets you at the end of the workday, when your spouse makes breakfast for you on the weekend without being asked, when you hear a joke that makes your stomach ache from laughter, the warm company of good friends, a sense of pride completing a big goal or project — it is the things that we cannot step into a store and buy, that we can be grateful for — the moments that really matter. Stop, breathe, and start noticing these moments of joy.

3.2

Appreciate

Close to gratitude is the word *appreciate*, and although we benefit by appreciating what we have and being grateful for the things in our life that bring us joy, there are other ways to use this word with positive results.

As mentioned in the section on gratitude, the more we are grateful for the things in life that we cannot purchase — things that are irreplaceable — the more we learn to appreciate others as well. When we show appreciation for someone, it can be with a small gesture, a smile or a nod, a simple touch on the shoulder for encouragement, or by giving an unexpected card or gift. Taking the time to honour the special people in our world makes life flow more easily. When we have built up our bank of favours, appreciation, or kindness — when we need to withdraw some (or need a favour from someone else) they know us to be kind and appreciative and are more likely to respond well. Those credit deposits have built up in your informal kindness bank over time and amassed significant yet immeasurable value.

If we appreciate something beautiful or valuable, such as a piece or original art, eventually it will also *appreciate* in monetary value. When speaking with others, one of the most important sentences to add is "I appreciate your perspective on this," which shows that you are interested and have heard what the other person is saying. Everyone wants to feel that they have been heard, that their opinion counts, that they are not being ignored or dismissed. This feeling of being ignored or not valued can lead you to stop believing in yourself . . . Appreciate others and watch what happens in return for you.

In a recent interview with Melinda Wittstock, Founder of the social media technology platform Verifeed, and the Wings of Inspired Business Podcast and Wings Business Summit, she shared how women especially benefit by supporting each other:

> What I have seen to be very effective in meetings is where women back each other up. Where a woman will say something, and then another woman will repeat it and say, "Yes, what she said was really awesome." Then a third woman also endorses, "Yes, what Yvonne said." When we work together, then we are heard (amplified) but when we are isolated it does not work as well. In advertising there is a study which shows that we are twelve times more likely to believe another person talking about someone than the person themselves. [57] Verifeed's "Return on Authenticity" algorithm measures this concept. [58]

By appreciating another person's opinion, you demonstrate that you value her viewpoint, confirm that her insights are valuable, (while you may not agree with her view of the situation and course of action). Appreciating and amplifying another woman in this way honours her contribution and showcases her ideas. When you share that you appreciate her perspective or opinion, even if you do not take her advice, or choose to act on what she has asked you to do, at least she sees you are being fair. Fairness contributes to building respect.

As a leader, people will not always like the decisions you make, especially when balancing the challenge of managing shareholder expectations as well as employee needs. However, when they appreciate that you are being fair, you can retain their respect. Another expression that works equally well, depending on the circumstances is: "Thank you for your opinion." You are not saying that you will change your mind now that you have heard their input, you are simply thanking them and acknowledging that you heard them.

As the mother of a special needs son, I have found it especially important for him to know that I hear what he says, and when he did not get that acknowledgment sometimes in the past, he would simply repeat the same sentence again and again, until I did provide an acknowledgement. He would simply add, "What I am saying is," in front of the sentence, to put additional emphasis on his next words. He is also very persistent (an excellent trait for a special-needs child to develop), which helps others understand what he needs. He is determined to get it, and even if he doesn't have the language skills (or sometimes the social manners) to ask for it with grace, he found workarounds to express himself and he gets what he wants . . . Except in some areas not open for debate, including safety matters (which require making decisions quickly in dangerous situations).

If you feel you are not being heard, feel your input is being ignored, try adding this sentence "Hmmm, what I am saying is X, which is important to me as it connects with my value of Y." When the other party understands why this topic is important to you, and a few of your personal values, they are often more inclined to acknowledge your viewpoint, and share their values and perspective on the situation. Stephen R. Covey, author of *The 7 Habits of Highly Effective People*, shared in his book, "Habit 5: Seek First to Understand, Then to Be Understood."[59] Use this approach to build your relationships, and increase the likelihood of an agreement — after hearing, really hearing — and understanding the other person's viewpoint.

My husband and I recently both read *The Five Love Languages: How to Express Heartfelt Commitment to Your Mate*, by Gary Chapman. *(Thank you to DreamBuilder coach Tracy Williams for that book recommendation.)* One of the five languages Gary identifies is appreciation. Through reading this book we both realized that if a spouse has a primary love language of appreciation, and you do not recognize this, and buy them a gift instead of giving words of appreciation, you will not be fully embracing the possible love moments in your relationships.[60]

In nature, to attract bees to a flower, the sweet nectar is buried in the centre. In life we allow our relationships to bloom and foster pollination when we give the sweet nectar of appreciation to others. Just as important of course, is to validate yourself. You deserve to be appreciated too, and your self-talk is even more important than what anyone else thinks of you anyway. Compliments will come and go, yet if you are honest with yourself and kind to yourself, you will be much more content in life — when living it on your own terms — validated against what you felt to be important and living in alignment with your values.

ACTION STEPS:

Pay attention this week especially to opportunities for amplifying the great ideas of another woman. In a business meeting, at an event when making an introduction, writing an introduction for another woman, a Facebook post or a referral connection — how can you amplify her? How can you "brag up another woman" and help showcase her capabilities? Women are often shy of talking about themselves, and yet we find it so easy to give a compliment to another person. Let's tap into this! Perhaps even pair up and plan this in advance.

Teresa de Grosbois (author of Mass Influence — which has been on the international bestseller list for the past two years) says "You can't make yourself famous, or influential. You can only give influence to other people, and they can give it back to you. Relationship Capital becomes an asset to your business."[61] Amplifying is an important way that you can help empower another woman, and when we reciprocate it has an incredible ripple effect.

3.3

Ask

While there are many definitions of this simple three-letter word, it is the overall concept of exploring with a question, or asking rather than telling, that is such a powerful one! When you stop telling others what to do, and start asking them how they will approach a problem or complete a task, it fosters empowerment and engagement. If you tell someone how to do something, it may seem quicker and simpler, however, it often stifles their creativity and disempowers them. Instead, encourage independence and problem solving.

As a coach, parent and leader, I have found that by asking instead, there are numerous benefits. I do not burden myself with all the decisions, have to know all the small steps involved, or keep current with the technical knowledge to complete the task myself. Most importantly, when I ask someone how they will complete a task, the other person usually gets much more excited about reaching the goal, because they can use their creativity to accomplish it. It is more fun for them — they feel empowered and excited and I do not have to follow up several times — because they are motivated to finish the job. Everyone wins!

As a director I learned to appreciate this concept when I had thirteen staff on my team. Each knew more about their detailed workflow and their technology system capabilities than I did. By letting each one know the required outcome, and clear timeline for completing a task, I let them determine how to actually get the work done. Then I asked, "Given the deadline and required outcome, what will be your first few steps to accomplish this task?" Their reply indicated how they would start and the opportunity to guide them if needed. It often indicated where to break the task into smaller pieces to meet the timeline. If their answer showed that they didn't fully understand the required task outcome, the start of the project was the best time to ensure clarity.

Notice here I did not say "desired outcome," as the choice to complete the task was not an option. I had a requirement, hence the phrase "required outcome." Be a firm yet compassionate leader, and gain respect from your staff as you empower them, letting them determine how the task is best completed. Earn their respect by being fair, encouraging them and giving space for each person to accomplish the directives. Ensure each member understands how their task fits with the overall department or organizational goal, and the impact of completing their smaller task well. ("Top-down objectives" is a common term to describe the ripple-down effect of having a corporate goal, broken down into more relevant and specific departmental goals, and then achieved by individual goals. Ensure each team member understands how their smaller part aligns to provide the overall customer experience — helping work feel purposeful.)

Telling someone what to do and how to do it disempowers them, and often creates unnecessary resistance, like pushing against a wall. When you are told what to do, do you like it? No, unless you expected this approach as you signed up for military service or a union role or a factory with mechanized or standardized practices. However, when you are asked or invited, and given a choice of how to complete the task, you can make it fun, use your creativity and own approach and resources to complete it.

Once again, when Daniel H. Pink conducted research for *DRIVE*, the evidence was clear. He identified three key factors: people wanted autonomy, mastery, and purpose.[62] When these three elements are evident in your work, you will thrive and be self-motivated. Neuroscience has proven creativity creates a release of endorphins — the chemical reaction that occurs when we exercise — we receive a hit of the feel-good chemical oxytocin. When we collaborate and share ideas or brainstorm work together, the endorphin release brings a feeling of happiness when making a contribution with meaningful work.

This good feeling is created when working together in search of a common good, the solution to a problem, to make a bigger idea work with the combined power of two or more creative brains. During my three years consulting with The Wynford Group, the data results reported that employees consistently identified wanting interesting and challenging work in the top two to three categories. Interesting and challenging work included purposeful work with the freedom to be creative and challenged, and to demonstrate solving a business problem or delivering a valued service. For example, working with a firm that conducts research and development and creates a better product or service, one that leads the field, or one that has a reputation for being innovative.

When passion, purpose, and freedom come together, a powerful chain reaction occurs. Mihaly Csikszentmihalyi (pronounced Chick Sent Me High), the Hungarian psychologist and distinguished professor of psychology and management at Claremont Graduate University, recognized this, identifying and naming the psychological concept of flow, a highly focused mental state. Over forty years ago, he began researching musicians to determine what makes a life worth living, after his own post war experience, in which much was stripped from him and his family. Noting that money cannot make us happy, he looks to those who find pleasure and lasting satisfaction in activities that bring about a state of flow.

When the work you do aligns with things you love to do and are good at, you can work on it for hours. You lose yourself completely, not being aware of the time slipping by, and have the glorious feeling of being in flow (described by Csikszentmihalyi in his research). Working creatively on something you love — something purposeful that has a heartwarming impact for others in your community — is deeply satisfying. His research showed that 30 percent of people (in the United States) since 1956 say that their lives were very happy, yet increases in material wealth did not increase their happiness level. He first started researching musicians and artists, those who were in the arts, creating beauty and something meaningful and worthwhile rather than working for material gain or fame and fortune. When a composer is creating a beautiful piece "spontaneous flow" emerges when they meld themselves with the music, and ecstasy results. Csikszentmihalyi describes this state of flow as experiencing "a feeling of serenity, spending time with a passion, when you forget yourself, and feel as though you are a part of something larger than yourself."[63] Fast forward to today and look at how many people sit watching television mindlessly, yet imagine they are in flow.

Your choice may be to ask for help from someone who has a skill they love to share, which brings them to a state of flow. When you are asking for help from others, bring in your curiosity, your softer feminine energy (rather than giving a directive that brings forceful male energy). Develop a balance of both feminine and masculine energies to live in energetic harmony, with yin and yang, positive and negative polarities.

When you are asking someone a question, you are drawing energy to you, rather than telling someone to do something, which is similar to hitting a ball, and pushing energy away from you. Asking shows respect that you want to know the other persons viewpoint and their ideas, that you value their time (key elements to building a relationship). In a sales situation, those sales staff who ask questions and listen keenly build rapport faster with a potential client than those who spew statistics, and quote "features and benefits" without listening first to the client's situation.

The salesperson who asks first has an opportunity to insert the benefits of their product into questions, remaining curious and not appearing pushy. If you have learned through an initial conversation that a potential client has doubled their sales in the past year, you can be sure something has changed. If the firm is now experiencing challenges delivering the volume of products in the same fast timeline their current clients have come to expect, you can connect that issue to your services. "Mary — I understand that your loyal customers have come to expect a high standard of service, and that excellent service is one of your company's values." (In your initial questions you have discovered what is currently working really well already for her business.) "I am curious, if I was able to introduce you to an employment agency who could shortlist candidates for an operations manager role, and provide you with excellent candidates who share your values, how could that help you continue your work of strategically expanding the organization?" You are now leveraging what you already learned from her and posing a solution or benefit back to her in the form of a question. In this manner you show that you care and are listening, and opening the conversation showing how you can provide a potential solution, using a question.

The conversation has been a dialogue — a verbal dance together back and forth, not a one-way monologue activity of "let me tell, tell, tell you" — and building the energy created in the co-creation conversation forms a more solid relationship. A customer who walks into a store at an airport may not receive quality service that will retain the customer, as there is a large volume of travellers who purchase just one item as they pass through the airport. Hence customer retention may not be a top priority. If you want to build a strong business with regular repeat customers buying a bigger service or product from you, building a dialogue through asking questions is critical. People will do business with people they like or respect, especially if there is a long-term service relationship needed, not a simple one-time transaction. Imagine working with a salesperson delivering multiple products or service over an extended period of time, with multiple points of interaction. You want to know that you can stand being in the same room as them! Getting clear on your own values first, then connecting with potential clients who hold some of the same values, is one way to build a strong client base and community, reducing your marketing costs overall through strong customer retention.

ACTION STEPS:

When you want to direct someone to do something, find a way to wrap a question around it, rather than giving a directive. If you want your teenage daughter to clean up her room for example, you may give an incentive, and ask "Do you want to go to the mall? As soon as you have your room cleaned up, we can leave. What time do you want to head out?" Or you could wait until your teenager asks you for a ride, then use the power of reciprocity to ask them to do something in exchange (Newton's law of cause and effect in action).

That conversation could be: "Mum, can I get a ride to the mall?" Response from you: "Sure, I can take you a little later this afternoon, if you can clean up your room before we go. How long will that take?" The likelihood of your teen saying no to your request, when you just agreed to do something for them, is very low. Give and take, positive and negative, yin and yang — Newton's third law in action.

3.4

Choice

One use of the word *choice* describes a luxury item. I believe that every single woman has the right to choose how we live our life, enjoy our time, and whom we surround ourselves with, just as we can choose our attitude, and choose items that exude quality and help us feel special. This book gives options to have more confident conversations with others, to ask for what you want, and receive it. An underlying gift though, as you probably are realizing, is to place focus on the words you use, and become more reflective about what you want to see shift by having those conversations.

If you were able to make one change, one choice that would help you to live a more joy-filled life, what could you change? What could be one small step you could take today, to begin moving towards that better choice, to having more joyful energy? Close your eyes, take several deep breaths, and clear your mind. Ask your heart for what you want, then decide what steps you are willing to take today to have what you chose. Breathe into the courage needed to take those first steps. Begin taking action towards your desires. When you express to others that you are not wanting to live in a particular way (or set of circumstances) any longer, and you are choosing to take a difference approach, you are taking a stand a different attitude from this day forwards.

When a coaching client makes the decision to move forwards, using their idea how to take action — their choice — it is much more likely to lead to a fruitful outcome. They are more committed to the change because they initiated it! They decided on their level of willingness to embrace a change, how quickly to move to a new behaviour or activity, and what success will look like in the future — success defined by their terms.

My professional coach colleague Tracy Williams shared recently with me that using the phrase "from this day forwards, I will be . . ." is like taking a "mental reset," telling our mind that we are not looking back any longer (at what has been) but moving forwards.[64] Are you ready to take a stand from this day forward for choosing to be more assertive in your life? Taking time to reflect what has been working really well in your life and choosing how it could be even better is stepping into new level of independence, choice, and confidence. You are no longer relying on others, you are taking a stand and taking steps towards new possibilities. By stating this is your intention, you are making a new choice.

Your mind is one of your most powerful resources, especially when combined with tuning into your heart and body awareness (through mediation and mindfulness practices) and making choices that feel good in your body. When you develop a new level of self-awareness you will begin to appreciate how your mindset and powerful words combine to create an unstoppable flowing river of passion and opportunity. You are likely already beginning to become more aware of how specific words feel in your body as you read this book. Does a particular word bring a knot in your stomach, or a lump in your throat? Does making one choice give you a prickly feeling under your skin or a feeling of anxiety rather than calm? Pay attention to what your emotions and your body are telling you about your decision to opt for one choice over another.

As I write about choice, I realize that you may be in a country where there is political oppression, or there are societal norms that appear to limit your freedom. Many cultures still have religious traditions that seem very rigid (and do not at first appear to offer you a choice). I encourage you to look for the possibilities, a situation or circumstance that has naturally occurred, and leverage this opportunity for a different conversation or perspective. Where has an event created controversy and commentary, where has a small crack of possibility already appeared in your society, town, or village? How can you leverage that small sign of positive hope starting to appear? When you have a small opening in closed curtains at your window, and bright sunlight shines in as the sun rises, it only takes the smallest amount of light to make a difference in what you can then see inside the room. Seeing new possibilities is the same. The small sliver of light shows us there are other ways. Look for role models from other regions, areas or countries for examples of alternate approaches.

The opportunity for a change could come from your son or daughter turning thirteen, turning eighteen or twenty-one — whatever age is a meaningful milestone in your particular culture — triggering a conversation about stepping into womanhood, manhood, or independence. Perhaps your child is moving into high school or senior high studies, graduating, or taking spring break, and you want him or her to keep family traditions and return home for the holidays. Perhaps to encourage him or her to take more ownership of their money (to prepare for university budgeting) rather than relying on you to do all the household finance management. Look for these types of external naturally occurring factors that can be a reason to introduce the conversation about making some positive changes, making some new choices.

It is easier to start a conversation with another person when there is an undeniable trigger causing a change to be required. When others realize that a change is going to happen anyway, it is easier to have a conversation about how they will adapt to it, and what choices this situation opens up. You may not be able to choose all that is happening around you, however, you can choose how you take action based on what is occurring.

In Craig Elias's book: *Shift!: Harness the Trigger Events That Turn Prospects Into Customers,* he expands on this concept while looking at sales scenarios. Elias shares how business owners and salespeople can tap into change to leverage conversations with those who "see it coming first, or know that a change is beginning". He also identifies several questions to ask to understand potential sales opportunities by creating a Window of Dissatisfaction by challenging their status quo.[65] A divorce lawyer is aware of a change in a client's personal living situation. If you are a real estate professional, having a relationship with a divorce lawyer makes sense. The lawyer knows who may be thinking about moving house as part of their transition to a new single life, and may be open to providing your contact information to their client as a trusted source who could assist them in finding a new home. Each situation is different and governed by professional ethics and confidentiality, of course.

Who do you know that already has connected or built a relationship with someone you want to meet? Who knows that an individual or an organization is more open to making a change, because an event is triggering change already? How can an event which is already occurring offer you an opportunity for a change of perspective, a timely introduction of a new and better way of looking at things? If you are working inside an organization that is rumoured to be making an acquisition or a merger, that could present an opportunity for you to request (yes, *ask*) for a meeting with your leader to review your current project successes. Book this meeting and prepare how to showcase your recent wins demonstrating you are ready for a more responsible role, or to step into a bigger leadership role (as you have already proven your capabilities, results and loyalty).

If your company's board of directors has just approved a new strategic direction, and geographic expansion is included, what choices does this open up for you? The expansion situation is already on their radar, something they decided upon, so exploring how that creates choices for you is much easier to have than trying to sell the executive on a plan to introduce remote teamwork, for example. When it is on their radar already, and it is *their* decision, it opens up choices that you can leverage in a much easier way. If you wanted to relocate or discuss remote working arrangements or telecommuting, what does the new situation naturally offer? When you feel that you have a choice, it fuels creativity. Feeling you have no choice in a situation can drag down your motivation, drain your energy levels and your sense of worth, until you give up.

In Africa, often families take advantage of this mindset. Families who have elephants helping them with large labour tasks will train the young elephants, to restrict their freedom. Having a wild animal charging around your property or farm can be very dangerous, so training from a young age often occurs. Newborn baby elephants weigh from two hundred to two hundred and fifty pounds, and full-grown elephants weigh twelve to fourteen thousand pounds. The young elephant is tied with a rope around its ankle to a central stake in the ground or to a tree. They pull and push, and twist and turn, and eventually figure out that they just aren't strong enough to break free of their rope shackles, so they stop resisting and just stay where they are. As the elephant grows, it becomes stronger; however, because it was regularly tethered from birth, its mind is trained to be given limits. It grows accustomed to being tied up, and even when it is much bigger and stronger, it will not try to break free of the rope. It has been tamed. In one story I read, an elephant at the circus was not even tied up, it was enough just to have the rope tied around the leg of the elephant, as it had been conditioned to think it was tethered, when it could feel the rope still on its leg.

Often the real difference between personal slavery and freedom is your mindset, and the world you accept for yourself, rather than recognizing when change occurs it triggers options to create a new reality. It is the awareness to recognize that it is yours to choose; that the chains with which you are held are mostly in your mind and not around your ankle.[66]

Where have you felt trapped, belittled, or put down in the past? In an article on "Shame" Jan Luckingham Fable points out, "Excessive shame is a prison. It keeps a person caged in feelings of worthlessness, self-hatred, and even despair."[67] Shame can be felt when you know that you could have done something better. This could be a more complete project, made a better choice for yourself, acted in alignment with your values, not reacted poorly to a situation, stopped at one drink rather than finished the whole bottle and regretted what happened next. It is more often tied to what others think of you, although people are often so busy with their own lives that they do not even notice . . .

We were given legs to run, jump, move, leap, and dance — giving us an opportunity to use them, to step into a new choice. It is more empowering and positive to be moving towards a better choice than running away from something out of fear. Taking accountability for a better choice and committing to yourself that you will take action, puts you back in the driver's seat. Waiting for other people to change is unpredictable and keeps you in a state of uncertainty. Don't like the unsettling feeling of uncertainty — take control of your situation. Step up and take action to remove yourself from it. Move to something better!

I understand about making new choices, and making difficult ones. When I left my first husband in spring of 2000, I had been unhappy in the marriage for two years, before finally deciding that it was time for me to break free from the relationship. I was not tethered like an elephant by a rope, nor in an abusive situation. However, I did not like who I was becoming in that relationship, or how it was impacting our special-needs son Alex (who was then six-years old), when he saw us in conflict. (Alex is very intuitive, an empath who picks up energy from those around him, and is easily impacted by the positive or negative moods of others.) For two long years, I tried to fix the relationship and agonized over the decision to stay or to leave. It was only when I was able to see a new possibility of what my future life could look like that I was able to finally make the decision to move on.

I had inherited some money after my father passed away and purchased a commercial revenue property, creating some passive rental income. After closing costs, I had around forty thousand dollars left, and was also looking to add another rental property to my real estate portfolio. I found a well-designed luxury condominium complex under construction, with an appealing California-style design of pretty coral-coloured stucco, and met the sales agent for a tour.

I remember standing in the bright and open two-storey living room looking up at the high window on the stairwell, and a random thought popped into my head: If I was ready to move out, I could see myself living here, this is really nice. As soon as the words bubbled up, from the place I now recognize to be my inner guidance system, it was like a bolt of lightning illuminating with clarity. What was really holding me back from leaving? It was late December, almost a new year, and time for a fresh start in January. It was only when I could visualize myself in a new home, a new cozy condo — with no outside maintenance to upkeep, where I could regroup from the emotional toll of my marriage — was I able to act and move out. I could see a better future, a better choice.

What big decision have you been putting off making?

(The one that your heart really knows that

you need to take action on . . .)

— Jo Simpson, Author 'The Restless Executive'

I believe we benefit from a powerful vision that acts as our inner guidance system, in order to overcome the biological protection system our brains have. According to neuroscientist David Rock, director of the Neuroscience Institute) "while our brains have evolved from cave-man times, we still have much of the physiology and chemical reaction to change occurring in our bodies. When you encounter something unexpected — a shadow seen from the corner of your eye or a new colleague moving into the office next door — the limbic system (a relatively primitive part of the brain, common in many animals) is aroused."[68]

Neuroscientist Evian Gordon refers to this as the "minimize danger, maximize reward" response; he calls it "the fundamental organizing principle of the brain."[69] Neurons are activated, and hormones are released, as you seek to learn whether this new entity represents a chance for reward or a potential danger. If the perception is danger, then the response becomes a pure threat response — also known as the fight or flight response, the avoid response — and, in its extreme form, the amygdala hijack, named for a part of the limbic system that can be aroused rapidly and in an emotionally overwhelming way.

Once we have mental clarity, we can channel our inner strength to take action. I had lost my belief for a while that I could have a different life, caught up in the dilemma of hurting another person during my divorce, while making the best choice for me. Like the elephant tethered by the small rope (who has been brainwashed to believe that he is confined) I was constrained in the relationship for months by my own mind, before realizing I could break the rope and begin a new life.

Only when I could see myself living in the new condo did the little voice inside my heart give me a clear insight flash — to remind me that I did have a choice — it was time to make a better decision. There are subsequent activities or consequences to manage when we take action, yet we always have a choice of how we respond to a situation.

ACTION STEPS:

Take time today to reflect. Look for external situations where a small crack of change has already appeared in the fabric of your society, town, or village, and a small chink of positive light is already starting to shine through. Where is there a naturally occurring event or trigger causing an opening for discussion about change? (Spring or summer, a business merger, a new supervisor, a graduation, a family death, or a new baby.) Then look at your own life . . . Where in your life have you become so ingrained in your habits you feel stuck, or feel restricted from the ability to act on something you feel passionately about? What (or who) is preventing you from choosing an alternative action, activity or mindset? Is it really them constraining you, or your own mindset? What is preventing you from exploring a new way, making a choice to think differently or act differently — to make a new choice that serves you better? Is there someone you need to ask for support from?

What belief may be holding you back, that may no longer serve you? Is it time to start taking your life back, rediscovering you, your true soul that is buried inside all the things you do for others? What is one choice, even a small choice that you can make today, that will begin to move you towards a stronger level of emotional independence? What are you willing to stop doing today? And what new action are you willing to start tomorrow?

Reflect, then commit to action. Try this prompt in your journal: "I am ready to make a new choice in this area of my life."

3.5

Intention

Setting intentions is incredibly powerful for our advancement and achievement, especially for building pride when we stretch ourselves and accomplish something we didn't think was even remotely possible. *Intention* is a slightly weaker word than *commitment*, as it sets the context that we will give our maximum effort, while we might not actually reach the goal.

Recognize that growth often comes by trying, whether we achieve the end state or not, as each experience teaches us something. It is the act of trying that is extremely valuable. Whether this is your future intention, or something else you are sharing with another person (your intention to meet them at six pm for dinner) it is important to distinguish between an intention and a commitment. The latter being a certainty, something you can rely upon to occur, when you make a firm commitment to another person.

When you say "my intention is . . ." you are sharing your preferred outcome, coming from a place of positive energy, with hope and strength of spirit, with a sense of opportunity (and often with multiple choices how you could achieve the outcome). When you refer instead to making a *commitment,* it is a promise, and reflects negatively on your credibility if not completed even once. If you commit to something and do not deliver it, others may begin to doubt your integrity or begin to lose trust in your capabilities, or possibly wonder if there is something dishonest occurring. One of the most important learnings about being heard is using powerful language; however, it needs to be combined with trust, and delivering on your commitments will avoid empty words and disappointment from others experiencing your broken promises.

Practise using the word intention rather than *commitment* and see how others respond to it. Most importantly, begin using the energy of intention in your own actions when you decide to act on something. Use the word *intention* where the outcome is somewhat uncertain (you are learning a new skill, or completing a new stretch assignment, or building a new relationship for the first time) and are less certain of achieving the goal. Use the term *commitment* when you are rock solid in your endeavour, and you will achieve it no matter what — you will find a way to overcome any obstacles on the way, because it is something that is absolutely critical to you and your reputation.

Making commitments to yourself is particularly important to build your self-worth and confidence. If you know you can rely on yourself to follow through on an idea, it creates an energy shift within you, one that supports manifestation. What you say you will achieve, you do, once you are committed to something, you make it happen. Mike Dooley, author, speaker, and entrepreneur in the philosophical New Thought movement, shares this concept in his book *Manifesting Change: It Couldn't Be Easier*: "All we have to do is define whatever it is we want, all the changes we wish to experience in terms of the end result. Define them 'as if you were already there' (which is what visualization is all about) and then begin moving in the general direction of your dreams, knocking on doors and turning over stones."[70] Take the first step towards what you want to achieve, and be willing to learn, stretch and grow during the journey.

Research by Astington and colleagues (1993) found that even three-year-olds are skilled at matching goals to outcomes to infer intention. If an individual's goals match an outcome, three-year-olds are able to conclude that the action was done on purpose. Although human behavior is extremely complex and still remains unpredictable, psychologists are trying to understand the influential factors in the process of forming intentions and performing behaviors.[71]

When you are unsure of another person's intentions, like the three-year old, I encourage you to trust your gut instinct first, and ask for clarity from the other person second. The expression of 'do what I say rather than do what I do' is often forgotten by parents, yet an important reminder that your intentions become clear through your actions. "Talk is cheap" is another widely used expression — and often people say one thing and yet do another opposite action, or act out of alignment with their stated intention. To advance in your career, trust is critical, as well as consistency and delivering on your promises. Endorse this concept by including in your conversations, "As promised, here is the report I committed to deliver today;" "As promised, I will pick you up at five pm." Help others trust your intentions by acting on them, reliably.

This book is intended to increase your awareness of how you use your words, how you can use them more effectively, and the importance of your behaviour authentically matching and aligning your actions with your words. You may think others may not notice, and yet, even a three-year old knows the difference. Setting an intention creates focus and is a first step to making a commitment and following through on an activity.

Monica Kretschmer, Founder of Canadian Business Chicks and Women of Inspiration shares "how important it is when talking on the phone or video to smile when you are speaking. The energy when you smile infuses your word to enhance the power of it, and then follow through with your intention." When your intention is to help someone else, or to listen carefully so that you can build a meaningful long-term relationship with them, you are happy thinking about this vision — and that aligns with a smile on your face! "Visualize that conversation playing out before you head into the meeting, and how you want to be perceived. It makes a difference. That intention is behind the words that you project," Kretschmer shared.[72] True! Your words must be in alignment with who you are as a person and your values. In my coaching sessions I can share specific language options, however, the words have to come from *your* heart and personality, and reflect your intention. In any conversation, it is important to consider "your ask," and your intention behind it (to share or collaborate, for instance.)

Stand up when making those important calls where you are requesting the other party takes action, which will share an intention, an energy of movement that is felt by the other person. In my level 2 reiki training, I learned how to share reiki energy over a long distance, to work with someone remotely in another location, city, province, or country — as energy is everywhere — like fresh air. You cannot see energy the same way you can see a physical object. Yet your phone is picking up a wireless signal, it is not plugged into the wall, however it allows the signal to send messages and calls to your phone.

Energy is everywhere . . .

What message is your energy sending?

ACTION STEPS:

This week, begin paying attention to when you use the words my intention is, or my intention was. When you are sure of something, exchange the word intention for commitment, and check in with yourself, noting how it feels different to take that extra step of a firm commitment to something, rather than the more flexible and looser intention to do something. Make journal notes on the different situations when this arises, and how your behaviour shifts with the use of the word intention rather than commitment.

Notice how others use the word intention rather than commitment, and the behavior that follows. Watch how others smile during conversation — does their smile appear sincere and match their words and their stated intention? What can you begin doing consistently to show up authentically, to be a woman whose actions match her intentions, and whose results match her commitments?

CHAPTER 4:

Awakening Key Words to Empower Your Success

Surround yourself with only people who

are going to lift you higher.

— Oprah Winfrey

4.1

Joy

Often, my coaching clients come to me for help making a difficult change, or for clarity because they are feeling uncertain about their path. To have a rational — yet unemotionally attached — wise person they can work with as a sounding board for their ideas is important. They have doubt and are not quite ready to make a major life-changing decision by themselves. A coach can act as a non-judgemental ear, or as a devil's advocate to help think options through before making the best choice.

I often ask my clients, "What brings you pure joy?" It is sad to learn that so many people rush through life, running to work, packing their day with busy stuff, and can't tell me where the joy is in their life. I understand this perspective well, because this used to be me too, and how I approached life before I burned out a few years ago. I was a driven woman, striving for what society deems as success (based on extrinsic objects). Busy! That was me, working in my corporate life in 2009, earning a decent living, yet not feeling particularly fulfilled, and feeling there was no room for my creativity to emerge. Even at the VP level, working within the corporate framework of traditions and rules, restricting my approach to problem solving and innovation. When I went ahead with something on my own, I would likely be criticized about the choice I made.

When we live in a busy world without taking time to be grateful for what brings us joy, life is dull. When we can step back and take time to look at what brings us joy, we are alive! This concept of stepping back is all about increased awareness, slowing down the pace of life to actually see what is going on around us, to see joy in the everyday. Joy is there, when you decide to see it, and celebrate it.

Each morning, take time to acknowledge what you are grateful for, and what brought you joy the day before. It might be as simple as watching a beautiful sunrise and seeing the sunlight reflected off the pond, or a glorious palette of oranges and pinks painted across the sky as the sun goes down. It may be hearing the laughter of a child, seeing an innocent shy smile as they get to know you better and draw you into their tiny world. A gift from another person, the gift of their time, deeply listening to your opinion, a feeling of being really heard. Someone in the local coffee shop drive-through line in front of you paying for your coffee in advance, and surprising you with their generosity. The gift of healing, when someone you love, or a family pet is showing they are feeling better after an illness. The freedom to choose who you love, to be free to pick your life partner. A warm and safe bed to rest in. A loving spouse who supports you to flourish in life. All these things and many more are examples of simple ways joy exists all around you. Stop, or slow down, and actually *see* it.

In 2014, my life was pretty busy. On top of a hectic work schedule (of my own creation in my coaching business), as I mentioned earlier, I was diagnosed with diabetes. As a fan of the author Louise Hay, I looked in her book *You can Heal your Life,* to explore her description of the cause of this disease, and discovered it was about "having a lack of joy in life." I was upset at my recent diagnosis and decided that I would start looking for more ways to bring joy into my life, shifting to a belief that I could eventually cure myself.

Do you remember in the movie *The Bucket List,* when the character played by Jack Nicholson writes down that he wants "to be kissed by the most beautiful girl in the world"? As an older man with a crusty demeanour, it is hard to imagine that happening, as many people think of a traditional version of a beautiful girl as a top model. And yet, at the end of the movie, he does get kissed by his definition of the most beautiful girl in the world, the granddaughter that he did not even know was born (the child of his estranged daughter who he had not spoken to in years, and finally reconnected with). In his eyes she was especially beautiful, as she was his adorable little five-year old granddaughter.[73] Having a focus on bringing joy into your life enables you to identify what you cherish and place value on, showcasing what lifts your spirits and makes your heart sing. By paying attention to what brings you joy right now, you can then look for other ways to have even more of it in your life.

According to Rhonda Byrne, author of *The Secret — The Power*, "everything has a frequency, and whatever you are feeling is bringing everything into your life that's on a similar frequency to you." (In other words, we will not attract into our lives the things we want until we are vibrating on the same vibrational frequency as the frequency those things have.) Like attracts like, just as a magnet attracts metal. It is science and universal law, and the gravitational pull of the universe. "Nature's great powers, like gravity and electromagnetism, are invisible to our senses, but their power is indisputable," — Byrne shares. "Likewise, the force of love is invisible to us, but its power is in fact far greater than any of nature's powers. The evidence of its power can be seen everywhere in the world: without love, there is no life."[74] As a mother, I know you simply have to gaze down at your sweet-smelling newborn child to confirm that love exists.

This wisdom is echoed further by Esther and Jerry Hicks. "You can't cease to vibrate, and Law of Attraction will not stop responding to the vibration that you are offering. Expansion is inevitable. You provide it, whether you know you do, or not."[75]

Take away love

and our earth is a tomb.

— Robert Browning, poet (1812-1889)

According to Evelyn Lim, author of *Abundance Alchemy,* and Jayne Warrilow, author of *The Secret Language of Resonance,* the Universe exists and operates by vibration.[76] Like everything else, you and I are also made up of vibrational energy. When your outer circumstances are less than what you desire them to be, there is something within you which is creating those undesirable circumstances, while at the same time keeping other, more desirable circumstances, at bay. You attract the circumstances based on the vibrational alignment of your thoughts and feelings.

Vibrational alignment, which can occur with objects and with people in the world around you, happens naturally, when you are "in tune" with them. When you make a point to focus on and enjoy a beautiful sunny day, for example, your brain begins to harmonize with the frequency of the earth, and the alpha state of relaxation and enjoyment generally occurs without effort. Your vibrational energy increases with the level of emotional energy. If you are hoping to attract more joyful outcomes, then you will need to be in a joyful state. Much like someone who wants to attract more interesting people into their life, *they* must become interesting to be around first — in order for others to be attracted to want to hang out with them. When the mind is focused on abundance, abundance is drawn to you. Guess what, as well when the mind is focused on lack, more lack is likely to result.

An essential element of Einstein's theory of relativity — the law of conservation of energy — states that "energy cannot be created or destroyed, it can only be converted from one form to another." We can see evidence of this when scientists measure electricity produced by the brain using electroencephalograph technology. Brainwaves occur at measurable frequencies. These frequencies directly affect your state of mind and your state of being. Vibrational alignment occurs when the frequencies produced by your brain are in perfect harmony with the objects and people around you.

My reiki master, Dixie Bennett, introduced me to a way to transmute energy from negative to positive white light, using the violet flame of transmutation, to convert negative thoughts and feeling into the white light of consciousness.[77] I have now included this practice in my daily success ritual and meditation time. Since beginning this daily regime, my ability to manifest specific things I request in my life has shifted significantly. Things now show up much more quickly after asking for them. Leveraging the healing energy of reiki is about tapping into universal chi energy, to direct or channel the energy for good. It can be used to heal, to break up energy blockages, to improve energy flow through the body, from your toes to your crown. As I added reiki healing to my toolbox and became a certified practitioner (level 2), I understand how to move energy flow through the body and remove energy blocks. I send positive reiki energy to others who require healing, or work with my clients to remove energy blockages that are preventing good flow.

Mark Waldman, author of *NeuroWisdom: The New Brain Science of Money, Happiness, and Success*, shared in a recent interview on the Wings Business Summit that:

> if you focus on being grateful in a mindful meditation, as part of your social brain (that gets turned on when we are around twenty-nine) and focus on gratitude for sixty seconds at the end of the day for seven days, it makes a big difference. Positive psychology research has shown that your self-esteem continues to grow for three months, stabilizes and the remains high for three months. [78]

WOW! Capturing JOY moments and being grateful significantly impacts having positive self-esteem.

ACTION STEPS:

Start to notice where you experience joy in your life. At the end of each day, note in your journal what brought you joy today. When you are aware, you can bring more joy into your activities. It may be painting, being with your grandchildren, singing, or simply being out in nature and feeling the breeze in your hair and the warmth of the sun on your face. Stop and notice, enjoy the moment. (To enjoy is: to receive pleasure from; take joy in, or to have as a condition; experience.) Be grateful for being in a state of pure pleasure and begin a daily gratitude habit taking note of what has brought you joy as an extension of this reflection time. By doing so you begin to raise your vibrational frequency and will find yourself attracting more of the things you identify that bring you joy, to enjoy.

4.2

Support

I find it intriguing that the word *support* can be used as a verb (used with an object), a noun (describing a state of being supported), and an adjective (used to describe how it supports). More importantly, when we see someone floundering, as women we often want to jump in and help them. Mothers are naturally wired for nurturing, especially when we see our children struggling with something. One common example is teenagers being tantalized by credit card companies (and keeping up with peers), and soon realizing they are in over their head with high interest payments accumulating, and not able to make their credit card payments based on their income.

While we as the parents can see how to resolve the issue, too many times in my conversations with other parents, I hear about women jumping in to save them and taking action to fix the problem for others. In transparency, as a young adult I also fell into this trap myself with accepting store credit cards quickly used to buy larger purchases (including furniture). My eventual solution was to admit I was overextended, had egg on my face, own it, step into action and apply for a consolidation loan. By creating one affordable monthly payment, I felt proud taking control back and cutting up those tempting plastic cards! Yes, been there, done that!

If you do not like the situation you are in, acknowledge it, own it (that you and you alone created the situation), step forward into it, and ask for support and help from a trained professional. (Silently drowning in debt is a sickening feeling.) Credit Counselling can offer options you may not be aware of, and help you dig yourself out of an uncomfortable place of scarcity.

Give a man a fish and you feed him for a day;

teach a man to fish and you feed him for a lifetime.

— Lao Tzu, the Chinese founder of Taoism

Although we love our children, if we solve *their* problems, we are not helping them in the long term to grow and become independent. We may have a quick fix, however, are not fostering independent thinking. You can invest in them today, or the problem may come back again and again if they do not learn their own lessons. Each time you solve it, they come back with a bigger mess to resolve, as they have not yet learned that lesson, so I encourage you to help them to explore their choices and actions when it is a manageable or smaller issue.

Do you recognize yourself doing this? If you do not support them, they can get angry as they flounder around trying to resolve it by themselves. That emotional tug is hard to manage and may appear as firm or cruel (in order to be kind). If you jump in too early in the problem-solving process with a solution, they can feel disempowered, feeling they have to accept the directive given.

If they start generating alternatives and you dismiss their idea without letting them explore and experience those choices themselves, they will not learn to problem solve effectively.

However, by standing beside them as they explore options, by staying with them and encouraging them to think through which choice makes the most sense, you teach your children a very important lesson. Firstly, to stay in conversation with things that are challenging and look at the possibilities long enough that the right choice will surface naturally. I believe our role as parents is to help explore which option has short term rather than long term implications, and which one resonates with them as *their* right choice. It is about holding two doors open and seeing which one they choose to walk through, not dragging them through one!

Next time they run into a challenge, they will be more likely to solve it themselves (or at least to come to you with some options already figured out, to perhaps gain your insight on the best one to act upon). If there is a really big life lesson to learn, perhaps as a parent you do not completely step back and let your child solve the problem independently on their own. Empower them (to give power or authority, or enable) and give them complete freedom to solve the issue their way. They may take longer than you would take, they may take a different route to get there, they may only fix half the issue initially, however — the act of struggling and achieving something that at one time they never dreamed even possible, is powerful fuel for the mind. If you achieve something that you doubted you could ever do, it boosts your confidence, and fosters a willingness to achieve something even greater.

I often look at lessons in nature. Take the emergence of the emperor moth, a majestic moth with its wide wingspan showing magnificently during flight. Before it can become a full-grown moth, it is a pupa in a cocoon, taking quiet time to rest in the dark before gathering enough strength from its transformation to emerge into the light. The restricting cocoon and the struggle required for the moth to wiggle through the tiny opening forces fluid from the body of the moth into its wings. However, without the struggle to escape through a tiny hole made in the cocoon, which causes the fluid to be squeezed out, the moth remains puffy and weak. If you encourage your children to take accountability for their actions, to struggle to figure out their own solutions (while knowing they are loved no matter what choice they make) this gift of independent problem solving is one of the most powerful gifts you can give them, the struggle to independence, leading to developing resilience and supporting their confidence to flourish. If you cut open a larger hole for the moth to emerge from, to make it easier for them to get out of the cocoon, they cannot fly, as they have not built up the strength during the struggle to do so.[79]

Abraham Harold Maslow, an American psychologist (1908-1970) was best known for creating Maslow's Hierarchy of Needs, a theory of psychological health predicated on fulfilling innate human needs in priority order, identifying levels of support that we all need. His triangular model outlining how our basic physiological needs must be our first priority, shows safety as the next most important priority, then leading to love and belonging (friendship and family). In Maslow's paper, "A Theory of Human Motivation — 1943," he argued that an individual was motivated to acquire self-confidence (one component of "esteem") only after he or she had achieved what he or she needed for physiological survival and safety, then love and belonging. At the base of the triangle are two levels including basic physiological needs (food, water, sex, breathing, and so on) and safety needs (personal security, shelter, our mind, family, and so on), and needs gradually rise to the top of the triangle, culminating in self-actualization.[80]

This theory is still taught in business and HR courses, as a way to understand that we cannot help others until we have helped ourselves secure our basic needs. Much like the airline safety demonstrations, you need to "put your own oxygen mask on first, before helping others." On that topic, women must be ready to ask for help — yes, *ask* for help and support. A picture of Superwoman comes to mind with her cape flowing and confident stance with feet wide apart and hands firmly planted on her hips. To maintain your confidence, and role model this for your children, know what your strengths are. What you are better at than anyone else? How can you share those strengths? Who needs your help right now? Swap your strengths with another lady who needs what you have to offer and let her help you as well.

Where do you need support and help yourself? Form a supportive circle, so that you know who has your back, because they have expertise or a strength in a specific area. Make sure you have their contact information handy (so you don't have to hunt for telephone numbers in an emergency situation). Practise asking for something small first, then lead up to something bigger, to build up your comfort in asking. Be ready with something that you can reciprocate with, which will make it easier for you to ask them. Reciprocity is powerful! Being willing to ask for support shows your awareness and is a sign of strength knowing that we all have skills and gifts in different areas. Know your skills and stay in flow vs. creating resistance by pushing uphill.

When you know you have a solid foundation and have the resources to draw upon to strengthen your resolve (including financial resources, reliable and generous friends, a safe home, and spiritual or energetic support), you can step more courageously into something new. Support cultivates confidence.

ACTION STEPS:

One of the things I had to learn in my coach training was to stop talking and let the other person figure out their solution to an issue. When I have asked a powerful question, I have become comfortable with the silence that follows while my client thinks or feels her way into her best choice or reflects on a situation. I hold my pen vertically in my hand and let it rest firmly on my top lip — my reminder to stay quiet. Who can you give the gift of empowerment to today, rather than jumping in too quickly to solve a problem for her or him?

Women often like to talk through different scenarios, to build support or collaboration for their next action. Men are generally more inclined to step in and solve the problem directly. I encourage you to have a confident conversation with your spouse (if you have children) and determine how you will handle challenging family situations before they occur. Agree on your ideal parenting style to empower your children, before the emotion of the moment distracts you. You may not be psychic, and not know all the crazy things that your children may tackle, yet it is easier to agree with your spouse while you are in a calm state discussing possibilities than to wait until you are in the middle of an emotional situation and cannot think straight. I know this, I previously had four young adults under age twenty living at home.

If you both agree that you want your children to grow up being as independent as possible, plan an overall approach that you can revert to the next time an emergency happens. Like practising a fire drill, it makes it easier to simply re-enact the drill more calmly in a real-life fire situation. By giving your children the gift of independence, you are stepping into a new role model of confidence yourself as a parent. Well done!

What about you? What are the resources that you need to shore up your foundation right now? Make a list of your strengths and make a list of what you can offer to others to support them. Where do you need help yourself? Note down what specific help you need right now, and who has the resources you seek. Commit to reaching out to them and asking for their assistance. "I'm curious… I have a challenge with XYZ (own your challenge). Can help me solve this, or do you know a trusted person who could help with this situation?"

For financial or legal matters, always seek out a qualified professional. When you own the problem and step into solving it, you diffuse any power of shame it may hold over you. Make sure you find a way to say thank you, or have something to gift back, to reciprocate. If you don't ask, no one will know that you need something, so ask! If you ask you have a 50 percent chance the person will say yes. If you don't ask, you have one hundred percent guarantee of life handing you a no. Generally, people are generous and do want to help, they need to know how you need help to support you in the best way possible.

4.3

Courage

Most people can look back at their lives and identify a few things they have done that are courageous or brave. Often they describe "having the courage to tackle something very difficult," which sounds as though courage lives outside them, as something that they can choose to put on when needed (like a coat) not something within. So, how do we actually find courage?

In several teachings, I heard a story of an eighty-year-old woman who lifted a car off her grandson, which sounds almost an impossible feat, until we learn more about the body's response to stress. In an article in *Psychology Today* author Jeff Wise shared: "Yes, You Really Can Lift a Car Off a Trapped Child." He shares, "The Science Behind Seemingly Impossible Feats of Strength Stealth Superpowers," and how the brain's automatic fear-response systems can unleash hidden mental and physical abilities. Wise shares a story of a man lifting a car (a Camaro) frame off the ground far enough for a trapped cyclist who had been dragged under the car to be pulled free. The world record for deadlifting a barbell is 1,003 pounds (he shared at the time of writing). A stock Camaro weighs three thousand pounds. He suggests that our fine motor skills tend to decline quickly when we're under pressure. But gross-motor skills peak much later — the closer a bear is to nipping your heels, the faster you'll run![81]

Penn State kinesiologist Vladimir Zatsiorsky shares that among the chemicals that the brain releases when under acute stress are two kinds, endocannabinoids and opioids, which are powerful analgesics (remedies that relieve pain). Their painkilling effects override the aching feeling we normally get when we try to lift heavy weights. Unfortunately, the effect is temporary. Fear circuitry can help us do things that would otherwise be impossible.[82]

Many years ago I attended a four-day experiential workshop (Warrior Camp with Harv Eker), where we were required to hike a mountain (Alberta's Yamnuska) with an elevation gain of nine hundred metres (2,952 feet) and given five hours to hike to the plateau peak and back down. At the time I was not very fit, so this seemed like an impossible task. The guides had marked success points at five levels, showing progress markers for each hiker, with the remaining distance to the summit. I was determined to experience all activities that weekend of personal growth offered me; however, standing at the base looking skyward I sincerely doubted I would be successful reaching the top.

The instructions given stated that all of our team members were to reach the top — including one member with his ankle in a cast who was walking using crutches — which added to my doubt of achieving this goal. While I was not being chased by a bear, committing to climb to the peak felt courageous, as I was not willing to let the team down. As I was concentrating on navigating the loose shingle, I wasn't looking up at the peak, and I was surprised to reach stage one easily. I kept going, and upon reaching level two, my legs were tingling and beginning to feel sore. I pushed on to level three, with my legs now beginning to feel numb. WOW, I made level three! By level four I could not feel my legs, yet it was replaced with a feeling of awe that my body was supporting me to achieve this climb despite the numbness.

Soon we reached the edge of level five, and the terrain changed from loose dirt to rocky, which required pulling ourselves up with our hands to continue the climb. Together, we helped our team-mate manoeuvre with his leg cast, and we all reached the flat summit plateau elated. I was stunned that I had made it! Even more inspiring was the image of our whole team lying on the flat rock looking over the edge at the sheer drop straight down nine hundred metres . . . What a magnificent view from the sunny mountain top!

I checked the time remaining for the exercise and realized I would have to run down quickly to get back to the base. My legs were still numb but beginning to tingle after the brief rest on the plateau, so I hoped I would have the continued strength to finish. Going downhill must be easier! One of my teammates and I paired up and started the fast descent back, running, yet intently avoiding loose shingle on the path. We had almost reached the bottom when one of our team mates, an older man, tripped and fell — banging his head. Now the race was really on, to urgently reach the base camp and get help, and my adrenaline really kicked in. It required courage to reach the top and focus on the loose shingle path to get down quickly and get help.

Unfortunately, he tragically died as a result of his injuries (which were combined with a previous health condition). I did not experience the planned fire walking event that evening as the agenda changed to a celebration of his life and a fundraising evening for our teammate. Together that evening, the group raised over $250,000 dollars for the shocked family to help offset the unexpected sad and tragic turn of events. This tragedy cemented two important lessons for me. First — Trust yourself to achieve despite adversity. Secondly — Take time to smell the roses of life as you run by, be grateful, as you never know how much time you have here. If the purpose is important enough to you, and significantly impacts others — not solely yourself — a surge of adrenaline is a powerful ally.

I learned how important it is to appreciate each day, as no one knows how long each of us will be on this earth for.

That incident seemed surreal, and highlighted how amazing our bodies are when we are required to focus our energy for short bursts of activity, especially when there is a life or death situation (whether being chased by a bear, lifting a car off a cyclist, or trying to get medical help for a teammate). Adrenaline kicks in! Adrenaline is produced in the medulla in the adrenal glands, as well as some of the central nervous system's neurons. Within a couple of minutes during a stressful situation, adrenaline is quickly released into the blood, sending impulses to organs to create a specific response.

Adrenaline triggers the body's fight-or-flight response. This reaction causes air passages to dilate to provide the muscles with the oxygen they need to either fight danger or flee. Adrenaline also triggers the blood vessels to contract to redirect blood toward major muscle groups, including the heart and lungs. The body's ability to feel pain also decreases as a result of adrenaline, which is why you can continue running from or fighting danger even when injured. Adrenaline causes a noticeable increase in strength and performance, as well as heightened awareness, in stressful times. After the stress has subsided, adrenaline's effect can last for up to an hour.

While adrenaline is an important part of your body's ability to survive, sometimes the body will release the hormone when it is under stress, but not facing actual physical danger. Stressful situations at work can cause this reaction too, when you feel under emotional stress. This can create feelings of dizziness and being lightheaded, and your vision changes. Adrenaline also causes a release of glucose, which a fight-or-flight response would use to spur on the body to defend yourself or run from danger. When no danger is present, that extra energy has no use, and this can leave you feeling restless and irritable. Excessively high levels of the hormone due to stress without real danger can cause heart damage, insomnia, and a jittery, nervous feeling.

If you can relate to these feelings happening to you at work, pay attention to what is happening immediately prior to adrenaline being triggered. Was it a critique shared by another person that triggered a stress signal? When your reputation is on the line, or your job is being jeopardized or challenged, this triggers stress, especially when it is important to keep your job and your salary (to support your family's survival). For women in particular, stress triggers an emotional release, often including tears (either accompanied by anger or feelings of not being good enough and disappointment for making silly mistakes that others have now seen). While crying for women may be a normal tension release mechanism, in the workplace it generally creates an awkward situation, as many male managers and leaders do not know how to handle this emotional reaction.

More women than men say they've cried at work (41 percent compared to 9 percent, according to Anne Kreamer's book *It's Always Personal: Navigating Emotion In The Workplace*). Their feelings about it afterward are particularly fraught. "In spite of the cathartic physiological benefits, women who cry at work feel rotten afterward, as if they've failed a feminism test," Kreamer writes. "Women feel worse after crying at work, while men feel better." [83]

In a *Huffington Post* article: "What 15 Female Leaders Really Think About Crying At Work," Mika Brzezinski, cohost of "Morning Joe" on MSNBC shared that "when you cry, you give away power. Being in control of your emotions gives you much more power at work . . . much more control over any situation . . . and much more dignity. I suggest never, ever, ever crying at work." [84]

The more senior your role, the bigger impact that showing tears at work can have on your reputation. In the same *Huffington Post* article, Sylvia Ann Hewlett, founder and CEO, *Center for Talent Innovation*, and author of *Executive Presence: The Missing Link Between Merit and Success* shared:

Executive presence is signaling to the world that you have what it takes — that you're leadership material. Senior leaders consistently report that crying detracts from one's executive presence, which rests on three pillars: gravitas (how you act) communication (how you speak) and appearance (how you look). Crying, I found in my research, is just one of a menu of communication blunders that, in a mere instant, can suck the executive presence right out of you.[85]

So how do you step into courage at work, when you feel the lump in your throat and the beginning of a well of heat erupting upwards, and the prickly feeling of tears forming? As soon as you feel the beginning of the emotion forming, stop and breathe — breathe deeply in through your nose and out through your mouth — to increase the flow of oxygen to your brain. Taking short staccato breaths will not fuel you to think your way out of the situation. Dr. Sneh Khemka, medical director at Bupa International, suggests to pinch yourself:

Crying is an emotional response that originates from certain parts of the brain — notably areas called the limbic system and the thalamus. You need to distract these areas into thinking your body is more active elsewhere. Pinching yourself in a not-too-sensitive area will be enough to convince your body it has better things to concentrate on, and suddenly those tears have gone.

Drink a cold beverage: Tears are stimulated by the facial nerve. So if you can get to an ice-cold glass of water in time, the cold sensation of the drink will stimulate other branches of the facial nerve, rather than the one that's about to start the tears rolling.

Think happy thoughts: It's always useful to have three or four 'happy thoughts' as a point of reference in any time of stress.[86]

I have found that using my forefinger (especially my nail) and pressing hard on my philtrum (the grooved part of your face between your nose and top lip) or pushing hard on my top lip with my nail will also be painful enough to stop tears.

If you just received a personal criticism, stop, take a deep breath, and ask yourself "Is that really true? What evidence exists that this is true?"

Perhaps you are put on the spot and asked something that you feel you ought to know, yet don't. No reply ready in the moment? Take a pause, or share a value of yours and make a request: "I value wisdom, and want to ensure you receive an accurate response. I'll research this further and get back to you." (If you share why you want a pause, or need extra time to prepare, mostly other people acknowledge and accept this willingly.) No one knows everything, there is simply too much new information forming constantly. Try not to say *because*, as this often sounds as though you are making an excuse. Stay firm in your conviction to seek out the answer. Acknowledge that no one knows everything, yet knowing who has the answer, or where to find it, is a key to retaining your personal credibility and self-confidence.

Perhaps you are giving a talk or presentation to a group making an important decision, to the executive team or a major client, and technology fails. Depending on the situation (and attendees) you need to decide if continuing makes the most sense, or as a last resort deferring and rebooking the meeting may be better. (I always have a printed copy of my slide presentation as a back-up, and have it on a USB stick to access it using in-house alternative equipment.) Consider though, by demonstrating that you can handle adversity and challenges with grace and resilience, it will help others see how you handle pressure situations with ease.

Rehearsing your presentation and knowing the time needed for effective delivery before your event makes the biggest difference. Recently, a technology glitch happened at a conference when I was speaking with an audience of five hundred women — my slides did not load for the projectionist (a bandwidth capacity glitch). As I had rehearsed several times, and my intuition guided me to take my paper printout to the podium with me, I easily stayed on track with my talk. I made a joke about the fact that the slides were not working, creating ease with the audience. In hindsight, I believe this issue showcased my presentation style in a much more authentic way, and the stories intertwined became more real for the audience. If you are nervous before sharing a group presentation, visualizing the audience with no clothes on can help. (Try imagining those around you naked, and see how quickly you smile!)

What if you reframed the concept of *courage* (from a frenzied energy with urgency) to *calmness* (with inner confidence and deliberate action)? Calmness is enabled by having at least three *pause phrases* prepared in advance for different situations that you have experienced in the past, to maintain your high confidence. When was the last time that you were on the spot, felt uncomfortable enough to be borderline fear, or were emotionally triggered? What was the situation, and what could you do differently if that were to happen again? Knowing how you reacted previously is a key to preparing yourself for a different outcome next time, a different *response*, and how to step into being more courageous. Preparation is a key to retaining confidence in the moment and being willing to act courageously with grace and ease.

Confidence is like a muscle,

it takes practice to build up your strength.

Momentum arising from being inspired has a very different energy than pushing or striving, which creates unnecessary resistance, rather than finding flow and the things that are working and doing more of those. In conversations, pushing is what causes resistance and objections from others. The energy of positive intention, collaboration and "serving rather than selling" is shared in your body language and energetic resonance, before your words erupt. Momentum created by inspiration supports stepping into a new level of courage!

How can you step into a more courageous version of yourself? When you know that the risk will be worth it! While you may not succeed the first time, your learnings are in themselves insightful. Each time your mind expands with possibilities, it rarely shrinks back. When you are clear on your value and contribution, possibilities are only limited by your mind and your beliefs. Recognize that beliefs and life experiences play an important role in being courageous. When the fear of staying in the same place is greater than the uncertainty of stepping into the unknown, you are ready to be courageous and take action.

For years, women have been held back in their career advancement by men requiring sexual favours and abusing their power. It's time for change! When you courageously speak up from the core of your being, your inner confidence and worthiness will support you. Describe your value from a business perspective in your career conversations. When you are clear on your value, you will feel the inner resolve to walk away from anyone who is abusing their power, especially at work. When you know you can find another job in a heartbeat, you know you have the resources in place that will support you, there is no need to put up with being manipulated or being bullied into something.

How can you quantify the work that you do by speaking to the results you achieve, in a clearly measurable way? Money speaks volumes! How does your role contribute to the organization generating more revenue, bringing in new clients or save them money by decreasing costs and expenses? When you can connect your role and results to clear metrics your value to the team becomes clear. (I referred three clients this month, which generated an additional fifty thousand dollars in revenue; by negotiating a better price with a supplier I saved over twenty thousand dollars in our purchase price, etc.) The more money (or value) you know you are contributing to your organization, the more courageous you will feel in speaking up when you experience being treated unfairly or abused. Take a few minutes right now to consider: How do you define your value in your current role or job? How could you add to that value, or measure it more effectively, showcasing an increase in percentages or dollars?

Courage comes in many forms. In my recent interview with Brigitte Lessard-Deyell, founder of Women Talk (rapidly expanding, with ten chapters across Canada at time of writing) she shared

> how crushing it used to be as a gay woman in society. Gradually society has started accepting it more. Now I am in a place where I am married to a beautiful woman, have two kids, and I can proudly stand and say I am an awesome person, and being gay is just a very small part of it, and it doesn't make it bad. I never really hid it; however, even two years ago it was not cool to go on stage or be interviewed and share that.

Brigitte — I believe that personal information share alone makes you worth celebrating, for being courageous and taking that story into the public eye! She also shared:

> I think a lot of it is a perspective, it doesn't matter what happens to you, because everyone has a story, but once you decide that I am who I am *because* of my story, you have a decision to make. Are you going to use this, or let it crush you? I love how Tony Robbins shares how he would not be the person he is today if he had the mother that he wanted (his mother abused and beat him). Once you decide to let yourself use it, it is a matter of being proud of who you are. We need every background, every perspective, to make this world a really great place, and whether you agree with it or not, we need to respect each person's truth. When women have a good support system around them, and listen to another person being brave and speaking their truth,

it inspires you to speak yours, to share it with the world.[87]

A word used in the right place, at the right time,

can be so powerful.

— Brigitte Lessard-Deyell

It is time to courageously take a stand, ladies! Let's take a stand as women deciding how you will, or will not, let another person treat you. You are the person who is in charge of your response to another person's words or actions. By doing nothing, you are also sending a clear message that the other person's behaviour is acceptable. If you are being mistreated, whether at work or otherwise, I encourage you to put yourself as a priority. Take the last fifteen minutes of your day to reflect on what you are grateful for, then ask yourself in important question: *How could my life be even better?* The positive energy generated while in a state of gratitude will provide the momentum and encouragement to fuel taking action.

It is easier to identify which one of those *better* ways that you are willing to act upon first. The most important element about this reflection is increasing your awareness. Using more powerful and confident language will be easier when you have a strong incentive and reason why action is important, and are fully committed to making a change. Change is difficult, as mentioned earlier, your amygdala will be sending chemical reactions to the rest of your body to resist change that may take you into uncertainty or danger. This is where the gems lie. Your biggest learnings are not in your comfort zone. Your biggest acceleration and development opportunities are when you are taking courageous action and seeing success. By stepping forward as I did, climbing a mountain one step at a time, I amazed myself by reaching the peak, and this spurred me on to greater achievements.

Are you ready for change? If so, it is yours to reach out and grab! Are you ready to courageously speak up for what you believe is acceptable or tolerable — or not yet? (If your answer is not yet, I encourage you, especially, to keep reading the remainder of this book.)

ACTION STEPS:

Own it! The value of making a change with the word courage is not within the use of the word, it is whether you claim it or not. Try saying "I am courageous" instead of "I seek the courage to," and really embrace and own your courage. Feel it in your body and be aware of the rush of adrenaline as you visualize achieving the outcome from taking courageous action. When you have courage and need extra strength, those endocannabinoids and opioids which are powerful analgesics will kick in, and so will their painkilling effects, giving you strength you did not even know you had. For mothers, giving birth naturally is an example of this, finding the strength to make that final push to bring your baby into the world.

If I can climb a nine hundred metre mountain, what can you do that you never thought possible? Start noticing more often how your body feels — check in when you feel a tightness or constriction, especially in your throat or your stomach. Journal your increased awareness and what is showing up in your body, check in with your energy periodically through the day, especially noticing when you feel stressed, and what were you doing, thinking or experiencing right before you felt that knot in your stomach forming, or sore shoulder aching. Start paying more attention to your words and pay attention to how you feel differently when using certain words. Stay curious about what your body is trying to tell you.

Develop three "pause phrases" for different situations that you have experienced in the past, to have ready for potentially stressful situations. (Such as, "Hmmmm, that is an interesting perspective. I will reflect on that and be back in touch with you.")

When you create your sentences, you will be more likely to remember and fully integrate them, when your words are in alignment with your personality. Write yours now, and practise saying these in front of a mirror. Watch your facial gestures, so you can see what others will see when you speak. Rehearse, rehearse, and rehearse — so that it becomes second nature to you. Just like a fire drill, practise what to do in an emotional emergency, be prepared with your pause phrases, and take a courageous stand for yourself! Remember too, take a glass of ice-cold water into a meeting, you never know when you may need it.

4.4

Trust

Trust — it is a soul investment in another person, a communication energy that cannot be bought, it has to be earned, and is typically expanded over time. Trust — can be difficult to earn, yet it is so easy to lose someone's trust. We don't instantly trust someone, even if a close friend introduces us. Although, in business, the concept of a warm introduction or a referral by a trusted colleague helps to pave the way to help a relationship develop. As long as expectations are met between both parties, trust evolves. When each person shares common values (excellence in customer service, high integrity, promptness, and so on) this helps interactions and conversations flow more easily. Yet trust is easily broken when commitments are not followed through. It is hard to extend trust to another if you do not trust yourself first. As motivational speaker Lisa Nicols shared in a stage talk around the time of her book launch *(Abundance Now: Amplify your Life and Achieve Prosperity)* trusting in yourself first is key, even if you feel that you have hit rock bottom. "From there the only way is up! Faith is believing in the unseen anyway. I had enough faith to say I know, like I know, like I KNOW – I don't necessarily need to see it yet. Abundance is available to everyone. I am not an exception, I am an average ordinary woman, who chose every day to make one more extraordinary decision." [88]

Trusting yourself includes understanding how you respond from a place of confidence and knowing your ability to choose when to be silent during times of deep emotion (anger, tears, disappointment, fear, and so on). If you are being chased down a dark alley then need to hide, the ability to keep quiet and not let a potential attacker hear you may save your life! Screaming at the top of your lungs may equally attract help and save your life. In everyday situations, your ability to resist blurting out an angry response may keep a relationship intact. Can you trust your emotions, using your voice in strength and trust the signals your body is expressing, and interpret them wisely? Can you recognize the rush of energy and heat in your body, feel where it appears first (stomach, throat, head buzzing, and so on)? Feeling heat can indicate stuck energy. In my reiki studies, I learned how to recognize and interpret when energy builds up in various parts of the body. Feeling a lump in the throat often indicates you are angry about not speaking up, or a lump of stuck energy in your stomach may indicate disgust mixed with anger.

When you speak up, you trust that your opinion will be accepted rather than rejected, or at least be heard and validated. Recognize that you have your opinion (something you value and want to take a stand for), and others may not agree or have the same insight or perspective as you do. When you trust that you have been heard, you will be more willing to agree to disagree if your conversation partner has an opposing viewpoint.

Confident conversations evolve by building positive energy and synergy, by stepping forward in a collaborative dance of discussion. Build a relationship first by looking for common ground items or viewpoints before moving to more contentious issues whenever possible. Moving too soon to put the spotlight on something that is not working, or about an injustice or unfair practice when trust has not yet been earned, is like (pardon the analogy) "jumping into bed on the first date," as my colleague Teresa de Grosbois, author of the bestselling book *Mass Influence*, says.

Build the relationship first. Get to know the other person and their perspective and understand what is important to them in the discussion. Why does this matter to them? As mentioned in Chapter One's section on the word *why*, use an open question initially, such as, "What is important to you around this topic?" or "What would a successful conclusion look like to you?" or "What would the fairest alternatives include?" Most people want to feel a negotiation is concluding in a "fair" way. Before sharing your opinion, gather your facts, the indisputable statistics or outcome examples, and bring an open mind combined with a few possible solutions, ready to co-create through collaboration. Remember the expression "there is no "I" in the word "team," and watch a better outcome emerge through discussion, brainstorming, and co-creation — and *trusting* that the process will conclude positively. Pay attention to the body language of the other person and watch to see if they are leaning into the conversation with interest or sitting back in their chair (with a reserved pose of observation).

Set your intention for the conversation before you begin, to guide your conversation flow. In business meetings, agree first on the outcome of the meeting (when it is arranged) to ensure that you are fully prepared with ideas and data, and that the right people are involved in the meeting. When you reach the predetermined outcome, you can often conclude before the scheduled finish time. Have you ever attended a meeting that was not fruitful, and you felt it was a waste of your time? Having a clear outcome identified and preparing your questions in advance will show you how you could benefit from attending.

Jot a few critical bullet points down on the back of your business card before joining the meeting, to keep your intention clear. Writing notes generally aids in remembering important details as well as the action items you committed to completing, as you demonstrate competence and reliability. When you make a firm commitment to show up as the best version of yourself, and are prepared in advance, you can foster trust from others more readily.

The poem "Make a Promise to Yourself" puts it so well. This poem, first published in 1912, is a reminder to each of us to trust in our own capacity to stay grounded in service, to ourselves and others. In 1922, it was adopted as the "Optimist Creed" by Optimist International, a global service club which raises its own funds and chooses its own service projects, to improve the lives of children.

Make a Promise to Yourself

To be so strong that nothing can disturb your peace of mind.

To talk health, happiness and prosperity to every person you meet.

To make all your friends feel that there is something in them.

To look at the sunny side of everything and make your optimism come true.

To think only the best, to work only for the best, and to expect only the best.

To be just as enthusiastic about the success of others as you are about your own.

To forget the mistakes of the past and press on to the greater achievements of the future.

To wear a cheerful expression at all times and give every living creature you meet a smile.

To give so much time to the improvement of yourself that you have no time to criticize others.

To be too large for worry, too noble for anger, too strong for fear, and too happy to permit the presence of trouble.

To think well of yourself and to proclaim this fact to the world, not in loud words but great deeds.

To live in faith that the whole world is on your side so long as you are true to the best that is in you. [89]

Advancing into leadership requires trusting your ability to clearly communicate expectations and timelines, while expecting a positive outcome. It is a key time for observing how trusting you are with others, and for learning how each of your team members works most effectively. When you move from being an individual contributor to achieving goals by leading others to complete their work, it can be challenging. By leading fairly, handling staff matters consistently, maintaining confidentiality, as well as being reliable and competent, your team will learn to trust and respect you.

Find ways to showcase your values through your authentic leadership style. For example, if detail-oriented, you can showcase this in your first impression, reflecting a neat wardrobe style and thoughtful coordinating accessories, showing attention to the finer details through concepts like top-stitching, colour-coordinated buttons or well-fitting tailoring. This value is echoed in your timeliness, how you lead your team, manage project timelines and meeting discussion points effectively, paying attention to the details of each team member's contribution to the overall project success. Demonstrating the company values aligned with your own leadership values fosters authenticity and builds trust from others.

In a recent Underground seminar, Kimbel Musk (brother of Elon Musk — investor and founder of Tesla) shared that "Trust is the new currency." [90] Trust is so important to building authentic relationships it is almost more valuable than gold. Building trust is like building credits in a bank, you can take a few credits out if you mess something up, and still have a solid balance — when you pay attention to nurturing relationships.

ACTION STEPS:

Decide today that you can trust yourself first — go ahead — put your feet firmly on the ground, sit still and close your eyes, take several deep cleansing breaths. Breathe in the words "I trust myself," and on your outbreath say "completely!" Repeat that mantra breathing in — "I trust myself," outbreath say "completely!" by repeating it several times. I recommend you incorporate this mantra daily for the next twenty-one days. Research has shown that twenty-one days is the length of time it takes to embed a new habit — so make it a habit to believe and trust in yourself — to believe that life (I call it "the Universe") has your back and supports you in all you do. When you begin trusting yourself fully and believe that there are no mistakes in life — simply learning opportunities, you can more easily shift your energy to a place of expanded possibilities.

Reframe the word mistake and open your opportunities to learn, grow and develop — experiencing less stress and less worry. When you trust yourself, the opinions of others are not judgemental criticisms, they are simply their opinions — not your truth. Build a stronger level of trust with yourself by writing down three things each day that you will complete, and making a commitment to yourself, and follow through.

If this is new for you, start with three smaller goals that you know you can commit to completing easily. Complete them and celebrate that you honoured yourself enough to trust that you could make a self-promise and follow through in it. Embed this habit daily for twenty-one days. Gradually build up to bigger daily goals and celebrate each evening that you have completed your stated goal. Journal how it felt to achieve your goal. What was the outcome of achieving it, and who else did this also impact? (Helping others as well adds a "bonus feel-good moment".)

This continued activity of "committing and following through" builds self-trust, and self-respect — when you know that when you give your word you commit, it is truth — you will get it done! Each day as you build up your "trust muscle," it will become stronger and support you more fully in exchange. What we focus on, we get more of — so trust and commitment go together to build up your self-respect, and others will increase their respect for you as they see your declarations become reality. While building your own trust level, your bonus reward is having others trusting you more readily, just by role modelling it yourself! The conversations you have with your soul are just as important as those you have with others.

4.5

Freedom

What does it mean to *be free* or to *have freedom*, and how does this connect to building your confidence, depending on your location, circumstances, and lifestyle? For those living in war-torn countries, it may mean safety — not living in constant fear of aggression or losing your life. For the average North American, who lives in comparative luxury (compared to those claiming refugee status or living in many war-torn countries under siege), freedom is more often thought of as financial freedom. In my experience, money does not buy happiness; however, it does create more choices, which creates a short-term extrinsic reward and *sense of freedom.*

Freedom for many is choosing to take a day off work without the worry of missing a paycheque, or to choose to operate your own business rather than working for someone else. Freedom to run your own business if not set up purposefully can simply be buying yourself a job.[91]

As this chapter is about *awakening key words that empower you to success* — determine where you experience freedom today. Confident women *trust* that they have the resources at their disposal to remain independent instead of living in fear when they are feeling constricted by something or someone. By having a sustainable income, you create more *choices* for yourself. As mentioned earlier, according to Maslow's Hierarchy of Needs, safety and shelter are basic needs that must be met first. It is hard to step into having confident conversations when you lack resources, it feels like wearing handcuffs, restricting freedom. When your income flow is restricted, your behaviour changes as you operate from a scarcity mindset, and you tightly clutch the resources you do have. Your energy is restricted and feels small and withdrawn, and others around you feel that scarcity energy.

If you are an hourly paid professional, your income will become capped, as eventually you will run out of hours that you are able to work (and be paid or invoice for). How can you create more value so you can continue to increase your hourly rates, or if you are employed, negotiate a salary or rate increase? If you enjoy writing, could you write a blog to attract or nurture your organization's clients, fostering retention? Can you find ways to save costs with an innovative idea? Can you volunteer for a special project and build relationships with other departmental team leaders to showcase your value, leading to an internal transfer and salary or rate increase?

If have your own business, with any rate changes, your clients need to clearly see the value of the expanded services, and how these warrant your described fee increase. Being free of the hourly grind, even if you love the work that you do, requires some creativity. By designing your service in packages or bundles, you can choose to pull together service offerings and value-add items for your clients' needs and determine a bigger fee for your bundle of options instead. What can you develop once, and sell multiple times, thereby leveraging your time? What can you repurpose and evolve into a new client offering with minimal work, or align with a new customer group at your expanded rates?

If you are intrigued by entrepreneurship and passionate about a hobby, consider creating a side business from that interest, and gradually expand. Move gradually from your hourly work to your passion when you know it can financially sustain you. As a coach, I have encouraged many corporate professionals to make a transition to their passion project as it develops consistent, sustainable income. By evolving on a part-time basis, you minimize the risk and gradually replace your original income — yet have more passion, purpose and fun! Creating your own income rather than relying on a job to support yourself elevates your confidence. You are then solely relying on yourself (and happy clients are recurring clients, who are often willing to pay a little more for reliable and higher quality services). Financial independence is another way to feel more confident, knowing you have a sustainable income!

When charging for a result or specific project outcome rather than hourly pay, you may opt to hire staff on your team to complete the work, while you develop the systems to ensure the quality of their results and invest time to oversee and supervise your team. You can then scale up your business and take a periodic vacation (once they are trained). If you enjoy having confident conversations with potential clients, as the founder of your organization, you are the best person to be speaking passionately about your product or service. As you generate additional revenue, your value to the organization is much higher than if you are completing less complex or administrative tasks that a more junior person can take on for you.

Hiring an assistant (or VA — virtual assistant) frees up your time for more client meetings and generating new business, with more mental bandwidth for strategy and innovation, as well as keeping your awareness of synchronicities occurring signalling growth opportunities. If you are technically inclined, there are numerous technology and automation options to systemize repetitive tasks. Adding systems to your business or work regime fosters consistency and reliability and ways to easily train others for solid orientation to your organization and their specific role.

Freedom is valuable, so confident women do not waste their time, they honour it! Learn to be even more efficient with your time. Once time is gone, you can never get it back. When you love the work you do, your passion and confidence shines through, and your conversations with clients, colleagues and staff will flow more easily. Passion is contagious!

Freedom may mean negotiating your working hours. If you are bundling your services, agree to complete the work by a predetermined timeline, giving you the freedom to work on it when it fits in your calendar and around your family. *Freedom* may be taking four-day weekends or working specific chosen days of the week. Bundle your services, and be paid for your intellect, not your hours worked. If you have earned a post-graduate level degree, have ten years of working experience, are required to maintain a professional accreditation — all this experiential and professional value is worth adding up and reflecting in your fees. It is your problem-solving capacity that your client benefits from, and your professional guidance and advice (depending on your job and role). When you pay a dentist, you pay for the outcome (a completed, and hopefully pain free, root canal, or a tooth crown); you don't pay by the hour, you pay for their years of experience (including years of education, accreditation, dental association fees, receptionist, office rental, anaesthetic and sterile tools, and so on). You want a trained professional who can treat your teeth, with minimal pain, and are paying for that result. Accordingly, you and your services are valuable too, so charge what you are worth!

If you are in a corporate role, how can you approach your leader to have a salary increase conversation? First, plan out the conversation, connecting the current business objectives to your specific role. If you have a formal performance review, examine how your work success is measured. What are the specific metrics that your leader will be evaluating your performance against? What matters most? (Accuracy, current industry knowledge, meeting numerical or sales targets, profitability ratios, customer relations or retention, professionalism, presentation skills, attitude, leadership, delegation, teamwork, and so on.) Is there a portion of the work which you could complete faster or more accurately if you were away from the office environment without distractions, triggering a telecommuting discussion and a benefit for you also? (If you are in a customer service role currently in a call centre, it may be harder to negotiate to work from home.)

Look at your work and get creative about how you could to it differently, to enable you to have the freedom you desire. What would be the benefit for your leader or your team/organization by suggesting alternatives and making a change? With technology advances, many organizations offer flexibility to staff who complete work online or remotely, giving freedom to complete projects from home if desired. Working remotely from home one to two days a week can reduce research time or improve task completion if you are focussed and not distracted by co-worker interruptions or by ringing phones. If you can negotiate more freedom in your role, such as a day a week working from home, how can you use your previous travel time to re-invest in yourself instead? (Reading an e-book, completing an online course, or additional reflection and journaling time?)

Research shows that the average office worker is interrupted seventy-three times every day. The average manager is interrupted every eight minutes (telephone calls, incoming email messages, interruptions by colleagues, and crises). Statistics tell us that it takes twenty minutes following an interruption to get back to the level of concentration that we were at prior to the disruption. These statistics alone offer substantial reasons for initiating a conversation with your leader about working remotely.[92]

Additionally, researchers at the University of California (Irvine) found after careful observation that the typical office worker is interrupted or switches tasks, on average, every three minutes and five seconds. (Their research showed it can take twenty-three minutes and fifteen seconds just to get back to where they left off.) Jonathan Spira, author of *Overload! How Too Much Information Is Hazardous To Your Organization* estimates that interruptions and information overload eat up twenty-eight billion wasted hours a year, at a loss of almost one trillion dollars (to the U.S. economy).[93]

Fending off interruptions is an art, one of the Modern Arts of Confident Conversations. Try these activities to confidently take control of your work day and minimize interruptions:

- *Arrive early, before others are in the office.* You may be surprised how much you can get done before others have the opportunity to interrupt. Closing your office door, and putting your telephone on Do Not Disturb, are simple yet effective ways of keeping your focus as others arrive and distracting chatter in the hallways begins. Managing your available conversation time is just as important as the conversations are…

- *Don't invite additional work* by saying "how can I help you?" unless you are in a direct customer-service role. Your conversation partner will find something and you have now added to your workload — so do not offer this "help you" invitation until your own work is completed first. If you have spare time, invest it strategically!

- *Limit casual visitors.* Have a stack of files or binders piled up on your spare chair, so that visitors who stop by and ask "if you have a minute?" receive just what they asked for — a minute of your time (assuming your door is open). Most guests will not take the liberty of moving things off the chair and making themselves comfortable and cozy, they will stand and take one minute of your time.

- *Manage your availability.* When someone comes into your office casually, stand up and walk towards them, which gives the impression you were leaving so you only have a moment or two, with no words required. You can also confidently suggest that they are "making an interesting point, and perhaps booking time to discuss it more fully could be worthwhile" so you can give them your full attention, then reach for your calendar and book the new time so you can quickly return to the task you were working on.

- *Set your work area up for success.* If possible, position your work area so it is not directly facing your door, where you will see everyone walking past in the corridor, creating a visual distraction. Ensure your back is not facing the door though where visitors can come up behind you — creating poor Feng Shui energy. A sideways position works well if your office or cubicle furniture options can be set up in this way.

- *Meet your conversation partner in their office* or workspace, or a neutral meeting room or coffee area that offers freedom, so you can choose when you are ready to leave. (Having a chatty person in your office may require you once again to stand up, signalling when the conversation has concluded.)

Feeling confident in your office environment can be thoughtfully created, while being highly productive without distractions will help you have more confident performance reviews, based on your excellent results and your achievements, created through your laser like focus.

Financial resilience is easier with a regular income, yet financial "freedom" can be achieved through a passive income stream. (Passive income flows in each week or month, regardless if you are working or not in the business generating the income.) Receiving interest from an investment, a dividend, royalty payment or rental income are examples of creating sustainability. In rental properties, your tenants, once in place, continue to pay rent each month, even when you are on vacation (screen them carefully during an interview, and complete a credit check validating their history of paying their bills regularly). Many of the world's millionaires made their fortunes with investment property. An empty property without tenants does not generate cash by itself, unless it is an estate home used for other rental purposes (such as movie filming or retreat rentals). Hence, the tenants are the "investment" since they generate your income, so screen them well with powerful questions and pay attention to your gut feelings regarding their fit for your property, and the likelihood of them carefully maintaining it as a home. (If you have a full-time job, consider hiring a property management company if you have good rental income, to leverage your time effectively.)

If you design a product that can be sold multiple times, after the initial development time invested, especially if it is an information product (an e-learning course for example) revenues flow easily when you have automated sales and delivery systems set up. If you have money flowing in whether you are working 9am to 5pm or not, for many women that is the ultimate freedom, creating more time with your family or children. Being in a family relationship where both parties fully respect the other, creating an open and honest, loving relationship may also be considered freedom. The freedom to choose who to love or marry is an important freedom cherished by many women.

ACTION STEPS:

In your journal, consider: What can you do to enhance your freedom this week? It may start with inner reflection and defining what freedom means to you, and determining tangible goals to work towards that will expand feeling confident.

If you are feeling oppressed, how can you do to take back your freedom or independence in one to three areas of your life, to boost your pride and increase your confidence? In your journal, list three actions you commit to act upon, beginning today.

Who do you need to open a confident conversation with to remove a restriction in your life impacting your current freedom level? Draft that conversation and commit to a date when you will communicate your needs clearly, with commitment.

List a few "passive income" opportunities to explore and test out, and your first action steps to begin moving towards a more purposeful job or financial freedom.

4.6

Receive — Verb (used with object)

Based on thousands of interviews and hundreds of conversations with coaching clients, I know that most women give more than they receive. With the smaller percentage of executive and board positions held by women (according to Catalyst research), many of the lower-level roles which heavily emphasize serving rather than strategy, are held by women. When giving to others, serving others at work, attending to children, and taking care of the household or elderly parents, often the equation of giving rather than receiving becomes out of balance.

Many religions share that it is better to give than to receive, or groups encourage service before self, although when women continue trying to give from an empty fuel tank, this giving imbalance doesn't work. Have you offered to help another person, then realized that in doing so, you now have very little time for yourself, for your exercise and fitness, reading, quiet reflection and journaling, studies and continued growth, or rejuvenation — including sleep? Women have been socially trained that giving is one way to show love for others, and others will like us if we are nice and generous. Additionally, when we are giving, kindness triggers one of the happy hormones that feels good: oxytocin, so we are hardwired to give, and further encouraged by socially accepted norms.

Oxytocin is a hormone and a neurotransmitter that is involved in childbirth and breastfeeding. It is also associated with empathy, trust, sexual activity, and relationship-building. It is sometimes referred to as the "love hormone," because levels of oxytocin increase during hugging and orgasm. (It may also have benefits as a treatment for a number of conditions, including depression, anxiety and intestinal problems.) Oxytocin is produced in the brain's hypothalamus. Females usually have higher levels than males.[94] When a hormone is released that feels good, it is not surprising that we continue looking for ways to repeat receiving a hit of positivity.

Philanthropic giving, as many successful entrepreneurs, business owners and wealthy people have discovered, also triggers oxytocin. Hoarding large amounts of money or being devoid of having a purpose greater than yourself, eventually feels hollow. Using wealth to make a social impact for others nourishes the soul. Giving is a way to balance the energy expended following business success, hence the rise of more conscious entrepreneurs, social enterprises, and mission-inspired business ventures today. (Millennials especially love this trend.) Use your time in ways that nourish your soul and connect to your purpose.

One of the things frequently crowded out of a busy entrepreneur calendar is transition time. The opportunity to catch your breath between appointments or activities, to quiet the mind for a few minutes, switch gears between activities and calm the mind chatter, to give yourself time to prepare for the next activity — purposeful, meaningful activity. ***Time to put yourself first!***

Mark Waldman, author of *NeuroWisdom*, knows this. As mentioned earlier, in his recent book, *NeuroTips for Money, Happiness & Success: 21 Productivity Tips for your Brain,* Waldman (who also wrote *The New Brain Science of Money*) shares how important it is "to take three ten-second relaxation breaks each hour. Compassion increases, self-love soars, and a new voice can be heard, one that will guide you toward greater awareness and serenity. Repeating a positive value word (like peace, love, integrity, confidence, etc.) for five to ten minutes will turn on as many as 1,200 stress-reducing genes."[95]

Waldman also recommends (as I do) "keeping a Daily List of Your Accomplishments, knowing that the brain registers small goals the same as large ones." By tracking a list of your accomplishments, having a conversation with your leader to showcase your results on a regular basis is much easier. Many organizations have an annual review process, yet it is easy to forget specific results and learnings gained over a whole year. Maintaining your own career plan and measuring your evolution is one of your best tools for increasing confidence and receiving recognition. Track your own successes. As you record your accomplishments, detail when challenges arose and how you handled these, to demonstrate your growth and showcase your learnings from that experience.

Becoming aware of what you find easy and brings you joy, enables you to add more of these joyful moments into your day, and swap out the negative or energy draining activities. An excellent book on the topics of receiving and staying positive is *Happy for No Reason: 7 Steps to Being Happy from the Inside Out*, by Marci Shimoff, who has also coauthored books in the "Chicken Soup for the Soul" series with global trainer and author Jack Canfield.

In a recent interview I hosted with Shimoff, she shared her own personal turning point story. She shared,

> I had just finished delivering a speech to eight thousand women [in June 1998], had three books on the bestseller list, and I was achieving my goals. I had previously set five specific goals: to have a great and successful career helping people, a wonderful husband or life partner, fabulous friends, a comfortable home, and the equivalent of Halle Berry's body, and had worked hard to have these things line up in my life. After autographing 5,432 books, I returned to my hotel room and walked over to the big window overlooking the beautiful Lake Michigan view, and burst into tears. I could not fool myself anymore into thinking that "next thing" would bring that juice inside.

She started researching happy people and practising what she learned: "We think that these successes are going to make us happy, it is the other way around — the happier we are, the greater success we have. To be more confident, work on raising one scientifically determined and proven thing — your happiness 'set-point,' and shifting into a soul-based life rather than an ego-driven life." [96]

Marci also encourages you to ask... What is your soul calling forth from you? If you are not sure, pay attention to how different thoughts feel in your body. Being willing and opening up to being able to receive is key to any success and to feeling worthy. In our interview, she recommended asking yourself these five questions:

> 1 — Do you push away or have a hard time accepting compliments? ("What a great job — oh that was nothing . . .") Instead, say "Thank you, I appreciate you noticed this, I worked really hard on it and am happy with how it turned out."
> 2 — Do you feel guilty when people offer to help you with things, or open up and receive help?
> 3 — Do you have a hard time accepting help, or asking for help? ("That's okay, I can do it.") Instead, gracefully accept their support with a simple "Thank you for caring to offer your help."
> 4 — Do you have a hard time accepting gifts (or letting in things in any way)?
> 5 — Do you downplay your successes around others, so that they do not feel bad about not having similar kinds of things? (Or let others say "you are just lucky" . . . No — you worked hard, so acknowledge that effort!)

As Marci shares, "If we push away the small good things, then we are pushing away the good that the Universe wants to bring to us . . ."

ACTION STEPS:

Focus on your conversations this time with yourself. Start noticing how you are receiving help or pushing away offers of help, or resisting. Notice it, and ask, "What can I do to be open to receiving more now?" Practise the concept of receiving, and include this habit in your daily reflections or journal.

Although women often find sharing their success with others a challenge, highlighting your results is simply keeping your leader current on your contribution to the team objectives or departmental goals. That is pure fact, not bragging!

If this "highlighting" initially feels uncomfortable for you, it gets easier with practice — as you build your "confidence muscle." I recommend using the format of WHAT you did, WHY it was important, HOW you used your particular skills or talent uniquely to complete the task, WHO was impacted (and how) and WHEN you completed it. Show you were on-time and budget — or even delivered your project before the required timeline. Journal this week: WHERE you saw success using the format above to document results, and prepare to share this with your leader. Take charge and book a meeting or find a way to introduce this result into conversation. Increase your comfort level talking about your wins! Practise in the mirror if needed.

WHAT you did.

WHY it was important.

HOW you used your particular skills or talent uniquely to complete the task.

WHO was impacted (and how).

WHEN you completed it.

4.7

Perspective

One of the patterns that drains women's confidence is worrying about things that we cannot control. While we certainly are multi-talented, we often try to do too much for others, and often end up taking on other people's problems and trying to solve them. In the same manner that we say "sorry" too often, excessive worry drains energy, and impacts sleep patterns. Adopting the perspective of "if it is not life or death — it is just stuff!" is a fresh way to look at life in a calm and stress-free way.[97]

Women are often the most stressed when something is happening with our children. My son Alex turned one year old and was showing flu-like symptoms. While his skin was quite pale, he was running a high temperature. My mother's instinct told me he needed to see a doctor, and as the closest clinic had closed, we went directly to the local hospital. After being in the triage area with a six-hour wait, he was sent home with a flu diagnosis. As he was looking pale and his breathing was shallow, I decided to stay up with him, which was when he had his first grand mal seizure right in my arms. It was a scary experience watching my young son convulsing and shaking slowly from his left hand, up his arm and rippling down the left side of his body. Back to the hospital! My lesson in perspective came while in the emergency room, watching the ER physician poking him in the neck to infuse medicine directly into his jugular vein to stop the seizure fast.

A mother's pain when her child is sick is almost unbearable! The smaller our baby, the more we feel their pain. In that moment it truly felt as though he might have died right in front of me, as it took what seemed like a lifetime to gain control of the seizure activity and see his tiny body gradually stop twitching. After having several more seizures that year, he did have an MRI, which identified the root cause. My son was born with special needs, and epilepsy was one outcome of his complex medical issues. I spent hundreds of hours in doctor's offices and hospital rooms over the first five years of his life. I learned the message loud and clear: "If it is not life or death — it is just stuff!"

When women worry, often our sleep is impacted. Experiencing restful sleep is important, especially for women with young children to look after. According to Dr. Steven Shea of the division of sleep medicine at Harvard Medical School, our breathing patterns change during sleep.[98] When we are awake, breathing is usually quite irregular, since it is affected by speech, emotions, exercise, posture, and other factors. As we progress from wakefulness through the stages of non-REM sleep, our breathing rate slightly decreases and becomes very regular. (During REM sleep, the pattern becomes much more variable again, with an overall increase in breathing rate.) One of the greatest changes induced by sleep is an increase in the release of growth hormone, influencing the metabolism of proteins, carbohydrates, and lipids. Certain physiological activities associated with digestion, cell repair, and growth are often greatest during sleep, suggesting that cell repair and growth may be an important function of sleep.

When women lose perspective and are not confident they have the resources to manage challenging situations (including conversations) I have often observed that they *bury their head in the sand* or run away from the situation. It is an instinctive reaction to recognize when to run from a perceived danger, known as the "flight or fight" response, secreted into your blood system by your adrenal glands. The fight-or-flight response (also called hyperarousal, or the acute stress response) is a physiological reaction that occurs in response to a perceived harmful event, attack, or threat to survival. (It was first described by Walter Bradford Cannon, American neurologist and physiologist, who was the first to use X-rays in physiological studies.) Major events in the fight-or-flight response include the secretion of cortisol, adrenaline, and or adrenaline from the adrenal gland.[99]

This secretion reaction is instinctive, just as babies are born knowing how to feed from their mothers, while mothers also know when there is something amiss with their offspring. It is the proverbial "sixth sense" we have shadowed behind the five testable ones: see, taste, touch, smell, and hear. Listen to your sixth sense, your intuition, and keep things in perspective: "If it is not life or death — it is just stuff!"

To produce the fight-or-flight response the hypothalamus activates two systems: the sympathetic nervous system and the adrenal-cortical system. The combined effects of these two systems are the fight-or-flight response. When the hypothalamus tells the sympathetic nervous system to kick into gear, the overall effect is that the body speeds up, tenses up and becomes generally very alert. If there's a burglar at the door, you're going to have to take action — and fast! The sympathetic nervous system sends out impulses to glands and smooth muscles, and tells the adrenal medulla to release epinephrine (adrenaline) and norepinephrine (noradrenaline) into the bloodstream. These "stress hormones" cause several changes in the body, including an increase in heart rate and blood pressure.[100] By maintaining perspective, living your values authentically and working in an environment that acknowledges your contribution, you can live with much less stress in your life, while having more restful and rejuvenating sleep.

Practicing mindfulness can also reduce stress. Mindfulness is the art of paying attention to the present moment[101]. Done so in a particular way, that is on purpose, without judgment, this attention to being in the moment can open up a world of possibilities around you that previously would have been ignored, or unnoticed.

This particular way of being present in the moment has been a practice of various backgrounds dating back more than 2500 years. Often associated with Buddhist philosophy, the basic mindfulness attitude can actually be found in a variety of secular and philosophical traditions, across the world.[101] The practice of mindfulness is long standing and crosses many cultures. It is a way of paying attention to the present moment, moment by moment. When done so in a particular way, it can help enrich lives and manage difficulty.[102]

- Mindfulness is a practicable skill.
- Practice has been linked to enhanced happiness.
- Mindfulness can be used to manage depression and anxiety.
- Mindfulness can be used to manage chronic pain.
- Mindfulness can be used in the management of stress and stress related disorders.

Evidence is growing showing the usefulness of mindfulness-based strategies in the management of depression, anxiety, chronic pain, stress as well as related disorders, and others.[103]

ACTION STEPS:

What "issue" have you taken on that is someone else's problem to solve? How can you reduce stressors in your life right now, and ensure you are sleeping well at night?

Knowing you have resources to draw upon (friends and family members, financial resources, transportation options, and trained professionals) keeps stress in perspective. Have your "emergency contacts" list available in an easily accessible place for all of your family members (such as a printed copy on the side of your fridge that can be grabbed as you leave in a hurry). Convenient access matters. Having the information in your cell phone can be cumbersome when driving or juggling a sick child.

Being resourceful and prepared, as well as committing to a daily mediation practice helps to calm and ground your energy for the day.

Note in your journal:

1 — What can you take off your activity list to reduce your stress?
2 — How can you move from chaotic energy to calm energy?

Explore the work of expert Jon Kabat-Zinn on mindfulness (https://www.mindfulnesscds.com/).

CHAPTER 5:

Eliminate Negative-Nelly and Low-Vibration Words

Do one thing every day that scares you.

— Eleanor Roosevelt

Well-known author of *Happy for No Reason* Marci Shimoff, mentioned in the previous chapter, shares that, according to scientists we have about sixty thousand thoughts a day, and our mind is always on. That's one thought per second during every waking hour, and "of those sixty thousand thoughts, 95 percent are the same thoughts you had yesterday, and the day before, and the day before that. Talk about being stuck in a rut! For the average person, 80 percent of those habitual thoughts are negative. That means that every day most people have more than 45,000 negative thoughts." [104]

  Here are a few words to pay attention to, and remove from your vocabulary, to make room for higher vibration words.

5.1

Should

How often does someone else tell you that you *should* be doing something, approaching it differently, which often makes you feel wrong or inadequate? First of all, unless you are a student and your teacher is telling you the steps to a scientific or chemical experiment that needs to be done with specific repeatable steps, in order to achieve a consistent outcome — I believe that almost everything else is negotiable. When baking a cake, you have the basic recipe; however, if you decide to add lemon or cherries to the batter, it simply enhances it. When you say to another person "you should have done it this way, or you should take this action" — you are asserting your will on them, and often giving unwanted advice. How often do you think that you know better, because you are their parent, their best friend, their mentor, or their conscience?

To have confident conversations, first ask if the other person is open to another opinion or new idea. "Hmmm, that is an interesting approach, and I wonder how it will turn out. What will be the expected result doing it that way?" Notice that I did not use the word *you* in the sentence, I kept the focus on the approach or the action, and desired outcome.

Often in my coaching conversations I listen to a woman sharing a current issue. I'm an excellent problem solver, and often can intuitively see how they may take a shorter path to reach their chosen outcome. Have you ever had someone telling you what to do? How often do you take their advice, rather than acting on your own idea? When you think it through an issue (prompted by insightful coaching questions) and determine your own action plan, you are much more committed to it.

On occasion, a client is simply stuck, and so stressed that no blood is pumping to her frontal cortex and she cannot see or verbalize a solution. If she's completely stuck, one of my favourite questions is, "Hmmmm, I am curious . . . Is XYZ a feasible option?" No amount of verbal stick-poking, "you should do this" or "you should do that" is likely to encourage her to take action. *Should* has an energy of obligation to it, of rebuke — as though you made a mistake and now awkwardly have to fix it. (Often a more gentle nudge to consider a possible option is enough to open an idea that piggy-backs on my XYZ comment, yet appears as a aha moment, and is easily committed to.)

As your confidence level matures, and you begin to trust yourself more, you will stop listening to what other people tell you that you *should* do. After all, it is their opinion, not your truth. Even when something happens in our lives which seems to be disastrous, there is always a valuable learning from it. Our greatest learnings come through dealing with those challenges, not the easy moments in life. What you *should do* according to someone else's opinion, and what you *could* do, are two very different things.

I recently watched Amelia Purdy in her POPTECH 2012 YouTube video [105] Amelia "Amy" Purdy (born November 7, 1979) is an American actress, model, world-class snowboarder, and 2014 Paralympic bronze medalist. In her video she shares her story. At nineteen, Amy thought she had caught the flu, but actually had bacterial meningitis, and ended up in hospital in a coma for three weeks. During this time her kidneys shut down, her spleen burst, she lost the hearing in her left ear, and she lost both feeling in her legs below the knees when her body went into toxic shock. (When in toxic shock the body will draw blood from your extremities — arms and legs — to sustain blood to your heart, lungs, and other major organs.)

This toxicity resulted in her having her feet and calves amputated on both legs. The doctors did not give her much hope to walk again without a cane, let alone snowboard again. She actually did achieve this seven months later — she loved snowboarding so much that she refused to believe it was not possible that she could ever do it again. If she had listened to what others were telling her she *should* learn to live with, the world would have missed out on such a great role model of women's resilience. She now describes herself as a "fembot," taking advantage of her bionic legs, and co-founded Adaptive Action Sports with her husband leading a non-profit for youth, people with disabilities, and wounded veterans, to help them get involved with active sports.

Before contracting meningitis, she shared that she had a strange premonition after hearing about one of her friends' neighbour's son (also nineteen) who had contracted a strange disease that had caused him to lose both of his legs. "If I ever suddenly lost my legs, take me to a bridge, and I would be going over" is what she shared she thought at the time. Her twenty-first birthday gift from her Dad was a kidney, to help her live without medical mechanics supporting her life. "I slowly started to embrace what could be, and the unlimited possibilities with my new legs. When I embraced the things that made me unique, I realized that an entire universe of possibility opened up to me."

Sometimes *should* mind-chatter doesn't even come from the outside, it is your own self-talk! How often do you say *I should* . . . to yourself? Often this ends up becoming a berating moment, where you tell yourself you *should* have taken a different action, and you would have ended up with a different outcome. Of course you would! Be aware that you made the best decision for yourself at that moment, with the advice and experience you had. You made your best choice under the circumstances, hence *should*ing yourself is not useful, and second guessing yourself feels crappy. When you think you *have* to do something, rather than when you choose to do something, it feels quite different in your body. By making a new choice your action has fresh energy, an invigorating *intention*, not oppressive or feeling like a burden or obligation.

In an interview between embodiment coach Christina Marlett and John Gray (author of *Men are from Mars and Women are from Venus,* and relationship counselor) Gray gave an example of how it feels when your language is burdensome: "I have to pick up my kids from school," and feeling a tension of obligation. Marlett shared in my interview with her:

> If instead I choose "I get to pick up my kids," and look at WHY I "GET TO" or "WANT TO," and explore that, I realize instead I WANT to pick them up because I love them! I don't want them standing on the curb wondering how they are getting home, because I love them. The inner talk then becomes "I am going to pick up my kids because I love them and want to spend time with them" which has such a different more positive energy to it. [106]

Should is a word carrying negative weight with it, a feeling of judgement and condescending in most circumstances. When you share with someone that you feel they *should* do something this way, it is telling them your opinion, your judgement, based on your values and experiences and your version of the "right thing" to do, or the "right way" to do it. One of the best ways to push others away is to provide your unsolicited opinion. Ask first if you can share something with them, and after their *yes*, give your ideas, ideally in the form of a question. "Have you considered any other options, such as XYZ?" Help your children grow into contributing members of society by letting them decide how they will accomplish something. Not by *your* rules, but by helping them to think about *their* options and choices, use *their* imaginations, and pick one approach to move into action.

Ladies, let's decide right now to stop giving advice to others unless they ask for it!

Let's help our friends and colleagues flourish by making their own best choices, help them grow strong and for children especially, to cultivate their independence. Even if they do ask your opinion, take a stand for helping others to figure out their own problems, and explore their options first, before jumping in and trying to solve the problem for them. Ask them to share more: "How do you plan to accomplish that?", or to share their first steps towards this action or goal. It is more empowering than telling them and confining their actions to your ideas — let them explore and grow! Let's take Lao Tao's advice — "Give a man a fish he feeds for a day — teach him to fish and he feeds for life."

ACTION STEPS:

Exchange the word should for could — to move the energy of the intention from judgement to "possibility," from telling to asking — it is a powerful shift . . . If you could do something, it invites a choice rather than identifying an obligation. If you choose to complete a project, to take a gift to someone in hospital instead of having to do this, this shift in your language and attitude subsequently creates a sense of freedom. (When you make a choice, it carries a lighter more positive energy of movement.)

Should carries a static "must do this" energy. However, choice equals freedom. When you are free, you can be yourself — a more confident and decisive self. Giving other people advice often creates tension, especially as you will often feel ignored if they do not take action on your advice. Instead, don't offer unrequested advice in the first place, releasing you also from the circle of tension which follows if you have given advice, and the possibility of becoming "attached" to their outcome.

Instead of jumping to offer guidance, ASK them a few questions first to see if you can help them solve their own problem. They will feel more committed to act upon what THEY decide is their best solution, because it was THEIR idea and they know how willing and how quickly they are to act. If you are the recipient of unrequested advice — simply smile and say, "Thank you, I'll consider what you have shared." (You aren't saying you will or will not act upon it, you're simply acknowledging you heard them.)

Note down when you used the word should recently, and how it made you feel.

Did others give you unsolicited advice today? How did that feel, and how did you reply?

5.2

Fine

I was surprised at how many dictionary definitions and ways there are to use this word, from "fine art" to being "punished with a monetary fine," to something "pure and unblemished," to a "fine day with nice weather." While these are all clear descriptors, I want to focus on the frequent usage of this word in everyday conversation.

How often do we ask, "How are you today?" and the answer frequently comes back: "I'm fine," or "Fine, thank you," often followed by "How are you?" — A customary North American greeting. What do we really mean? That we are "pure and unblemished", or that we are "feeling like a sunny day," or "asking for someone to punish us by issuing a ticket for payment"? How did we move away from the origins of this word ("the highest degree of honour") to have common usage as an introductory statement, providing a lacklustre description of how we are really feeling? *Fine* sounds like a measure of mediocrity — the comfortable companion of satisfaction — this is not really living! This boring description is not a confident reply!

Ask yourself each morning, "How am I really feeling today?", then pick a more descriptive word, one that truly expresses how you are feeling. Being authentic in how you are feeling, and not covering up your true emotions with a blanket word like *fine* — which is meaningless to really describe how you are feeling — you step out courageously! If you are saying you are *happy*, yet actually feeling *depressed*, your body will display signals showing how you really feel (your energy will appear low, possibly your eyes will be downcast), and others around you will intuitively know that you are *not happy*. I am a fan of owning that you are *in the process of . . .*, not *fake it until you make it* — which is inauthentic, and others will feel this.

Confidence comes from the inside, being true to yourself, owning that we are each on a journey and life gives us experiences of both joyful times and sorrow. On heart monitors in hospitals, you see the lines moving up and down, they are not showing a flat line until someone passes away ("flat-lining"). A life without the peak to extreme joy would be sad, and a life without challenges and learning lessons would be boring. Having appreciation for a dipped line into sadness periodically enables a fresh perspective when you come out the other side. I recommend acknowledging the gifts that come your way, happy and sad, then choose to live your life authentically, in full glorious technicolour.

In my recent interview with Christina Marlett (founder of the Courageous Self-Care Movement, a global embodiment coach for speakers, and author of *How Ugly, Awkward Dancing Changes Everything*), she shared how important it is for women, especially, to "get out of their head and into their body." She explained how we learn best through movement (just as kids learn through movement and activity experiences).

> Every word has energy, has its own vibrational level, so it is important to carefully choose which words we are thinking and saying. This is important because those words become our reality, our signature vibration going out into the world. One word I hear when I ask people, "How are you," often their reply is . . . *busy*. Busy is not a state! Neither is fine . . .
>
> What you are really saying with the word *busy* is that you are stressed out, depleted, and running on empty. The origin of that word is actually anxious, so what we are really saying is, "I am anxious" — probably not the confident greeting you want to share with others . . . I found myself saying this word, and decided to go on an epic search, a quest to find a new word that better explained and matched the new vibrational energy I wanted to be. For a while I would say, "My life is really full," which felt that I had no room for anything else — however, after a month-long search, I now use the word *exciting* when others ask *how are you*. I have now eliminated *busy* from my vocabulary. When I take my kids to martial arts I am *excited* to do that, and excited to see they are learning and growing. *Bad* is another word that has low vibrational energy and is weak not descriptive . . . [107]

By being authentic in your reply, you may be offered help to get out of feeling *depressed*. You may uplift someone else with your answer of *joyful*. (In nature, one rotten apple can spoil the whole basket, and attitudes are contagious too.) Be prepared for others to act surprised at first when you respond (as the typical response is *fine*). It will help them wake up and take notice, because you are not doing what everyone else is. My husband likes to see the faces of store clerks in response to their cash-desk moronic question, *"How are you today?"* when he gaily responds, "I'm fantastic, how about you?" The look on their face is priceless if they are paying attention, then quickly moving to curious — as his reply is not what they typically hear. It is a great way to start a conversation!

Fine is overused and misused in everyday language as a cover-up, a non-descript word to say that you are simply doing "okay." Many women are using this response because they are in pain and don't want to explore digging into what is causing it, or are burying dealing with the underlying issue causing the emotion. If you don't like how you feel, acknowledge that, and ask your inner wisdom to guide you to take one small step forward to a better choice . . .

When my previous mother-in-law Mary (my ex-husband's mum) passed away, it hit home for me how we over-use the word "fine". Mary was very active in our lives, and even though she had six children, she would call each one every evening to find out how their day had been. She would visit regularly and was one of the small circle of trusted babysitters we could leave our special-needs son with when we had an invitation to an event. Grandma Mary was one of the kindest people I ever met, with a beautiful generous heart, and always giving to others, who was missed terribly when she passed away. The entire family was devastated by this loss.

After the funeral I went back to work the next week, although I quickly realized I was not emotionally "ready" to be there. I was still in shock and grief and barely coping, sleepless nights were my new normal, and I was unable to think straight or make any large decisions. It struck me then how casually staff members gathered at the workplace coffee machine and asked, "How are you today?" without pausing to really hear the answer. I suppose *fine* has become customary as a vague reply, more out of a duty to respond and be polite.

Each time I was asked the question, tears bubbled up. "Actually, pretty crappy — my mother-in-law just passed away, and I miss her so much!" was the real answer. However, this honest response stopped team members in their tracks and frequently halted the conversation, and they did not know what to say next. What is the best response to someone who lays their heart out in the open, and tells you sadly how they are really doing that day? I could feel many people shrink back and not know what to say next. So mostly they simply said, "Sorry to hear that, I hope you feel better soon." *Feel better soon*? This was not a cold I was getting over, this was dealing with a gaping hole in my heart!

Inside, I was in so much pain, that one question almost seemed like a stab to my heart — and at the time I didn't have the words to be sorting through my emotions and didn't want to be poked every five minutes by others asking me about how I felt. I could have answered *fine*; however, that was not how I was really feeling. I have learned that when someone asks me about my feelings that my honest answer is what comes forth, no cover-ups, no lies, I am compelled to share my raw authentic truth. Not everyone is ready for that truth.

Subsequently, I learned to greet others in a different way. To pay close attention to their body language, and then ask, "How are things going?" This question, which seemed more generic, gave them an out to not have to share how they were really feeling — unless they wanted to. To ask about their overall circumstances, rather than their feelings. The other alternative I ask is, "What's new in your world?", which feels more positive, as this could equally be something great that was happening and told me much more about how they were really feeling, by their positive or negative answer. Body language gives so many clues . . . In general terms though, some signals are: if someone is carrying their head high — confidence. If looking down more at the ground — trying not to be see or catch anyone else's eye — uncomfortable. Chin up — defiance or a feeling of I'm better than you are, or I know more than you do. Arms crossed over the front of the body — closed to new ideas and information. Sociologist Amy Cuddy has researched this topic extensively, and I highly recommend watching her TED talk "Your Body Language Shapes Who You Are." [108]

ACTION STEPS:

Pay attention when you greet people to the words you use. Try asking: "What's new in your world right now?" If you ask: "How are you today?" listen, really listen to the answer, pay attention to the person's tone, their eye contact, how their shoulders go back (taking a proud stance) or curve inward and forward (pulling in and being more closed about their response). Watch how many people move through life with a bland answer of fine.

Ask yourself, do I really want to know how this person is actually doing, and am I prepared to support them with kind words during the bad times, and celebrate with them during the good times? Only ask: "How are you feeling?" when you are prepared to listen and help the other person if they need your support. My husband raises an eyebrow when he hears others say they are fine, as he learned that this word is an acronym for fearful, insecure, neurotic, and empty. Let's stop being casual with our greetings, be more mindful, and find a way to meet others where they are, in a way that helps them be authentic and whole. Greet them in a caring manner that you would like to be greeted.

Become more conscious of the words you use every day. Try to use fine to describe something of "high quality, for the discerning taste" — a fine wine or jewelry piece. Replace fine with a clear descriptor of your actual mood or energy level at the time, being creative yet honest and authentic about how you are feeling. If the temptation is to say fine, perhaps it is time to question how you can bring more joy into your life, so that you can respond, when asked, with "I'm fantastic," or "I'm joyful today." Try infusing your conversations with new descriptors and encourage others to do so as well. When they say, "I'm fine," I say, "Really — fine, hmmm, how are you <u>really</u> feeling today?" This approach encourages people to wake-up to their real energy state and consider how they are really feeling in that moment. Using some colourful language (a Tony Robbins technique used to shock people into waking up) will get their attention too. "I'm f*cking awesome" will create a jarring effect and totally surprise the other person — so be choosy regarding who you use that response with. Perhaps not the first impression you want to make with your new father-in-law or your boss . . .

What other descriptive words can you use to replace fine or busy? Which words could elevate your energy and vibrational level by just saying them? Select a few descriptors can you use instead of fine, good or bad. List ten descriptive words now in your journal, words that you can integrate into your greetings and conversations, and note how you feel inside when you say your new descriptive word choice. Does your energy expand or contract when you say "I am . . ." (A sample list is available at: <u>https://www.cnvc.org/sites/default/files/feelings_inventory_0.pdf</u>

Note by the language you use if the descriptor falls into the category of "feeling satisfied" or "unsatisfied" with having your needs met.) If you are more frequently using "unsatisfied" descriptors, what needs to change in your life overall, so you can step into a happier and more confident version of yourself? Where are your needs not being met? What is one small step you can take today towards removing any obstacle to your overall satisfaction and happiness with your life?

5.3

Wrong

I often hear clients and colleagues talking about something *going wrong,* someone *being wrong,* or *it's wrong.* Are they referring to breaking the law or an accepted moral code, or is this statement their opinion when someone does something in a different manner than they personally would? When did we become a society that thinks that so much is *wrong*? I believe that there are no mistakes in life, there are simply lessons — ways to put the spotlight on an event — a thought, a pattern, a circumstance — and then pose the question: "what needs to be different for a more positive outcome or experience?"

I spent much of my childhood according to my father, being *wrong.* When I was growing up in England, as a fun-loving creative and adventurous child, I loved to explore. My elder sister (by three years) had a much quieter personality, more introverted and studious, getting her homework done first — then playing later. I preferred to be in the park climbing trees or on the playground swings than doing my homework. I valued practical learning experiences rather than the theory taught in school, cultivating common sense and exploring with my "trial and error" experimentation approach. I wanted to squeeze every drop out of life, and the stuffy school environment and aggressive home atmosphere I lived in didn't support massive growth and expansion. My Father wanted me to conform.

My parents experienced scarcity living on government rations during the Second World War, saving everything that couldn't be readily purchased at the store. I watched my mum hoarding things and repurposing almost everything. She would save the wrappers that butter pats came in, to wipe inside her baking pans for Friday's baking ritual. She would rinse off aluminum foil and reuse it several times over and over, until the crinkles in the foil became holes from being folded over so many times. My Mum learned to be thrifty through the war.

Aluminum foil is great for keeping food hot, however, you cannot see what is inside, so covering leftovers with see-through cling wrap is easy and timesaving, and became a popular choice in our house. Why do I share this journey down scientific memory lane? I see being *wrong* akin to aluminum foil. Those who think you are wrong have created a solid idea of how things *should be*, which may or may not fit with your values and actions. What if instead, we saw life through the lens of cling wrap, seeing through the veil of transparency, looking at what is possible instead of the static wall of aluminum foil — the closed mind of a solid cover? If you choose to look at life through the lens of clarity (clear plastic wrap that keeps things fresh and lasting longer) you can more clearly see how mistakes in life are actually lessons. Lessons are opportunities, they are generally not right or wrong.

The Post-It note is a popular office helper. According to *Wikipedia,* this product resulted from an experiment that technically was a mistake — was the wrong formula for the desired outcome. In 1968, a scientist at 3M in the United States, Dr. Spencer Silver (no relation to me!) was attempting to develop a super-strong adhesive. Instead he accidentally created a low-tack, reusable, pressure-sensitive adhesive. Eventually 3M launched the product as Post-Its in 1979, and it continues to gain popularity today, with all shapes and sizes now available, based on the original yellow pads.[109] On a scientific level (a repetitive process that does not produce the desired outcome consistently) when things *go wrong* being open to possibility is about reframing the outcome and how it can be leveraged, even if it was an unplanned result.

ACTION STEPS:

What if you eliminated the word wrong from your conversations? How could your life be much more open to possibility, to staying curious and looking at "what is and what could be" rather than closing the door on options and choices? Criticizing others does not build collaborative relationships, as no one wants someone else telling them they are wrong. Find ways to celebrate what is working well right now, and then explore "how could it be even better?" The sage advice of "attracting more bees with honey than with vinegar" is still true. Positivity is like magnetism, it draws things and people to you. Who wants to be around a miserable pessimistic person who frequently thinks things are wrong?

Numerous sages and successful people have shared that "we end up at the same level as those we surround ourselves with". Therefore, if you want to elevate your perspective, find groups of people who share the viewpoint you aspire to — who leverage lessons rather than cursing over mistakes — and create opportunities out of adversity. Connect with a new group who already demonstrates the characteristics you respect, and those that you aspire to develop. A rising tide lifts all boats . . . Look at your current close circle of relationships. Who do you have in your life who has negative perspectives, engulfs you in their negative energy, or doesn't show support for attaining your hopes and dreams? It may be time for a relationship cleanse . . .

Just like the example of emptying your closet in the section on space, who do you want to surround yourself with, to help you stay as positive as possible? In order to bring more positive people into your life, make space by reducing the time spent (and it is "spent" rather than invested) with those who are dragging you down, "toxic people".

Start today by identifying those people who you no longer wish to spend time with. List the first five people that come to mind. Beside each name write down one action item or strategy to stop letting that person drain your time, your confidence or your positive spirit. (If it is your mother-in-law for example, you cannot completely cut off relations with her without upsetting your husband, however, you could change from frequently meeting her in person to having a short periodic phone call, or share an update text message instead. (Begin limiting your time being around negative energy.) How can you take control of the time you spend with those who drain you, and increase your conversations with those who are more confident and positive? Write down each person's name, followed by your "toxic reduction" strategy or action required.

    Periodically, on a quarterly basis, review who you spend the most time with and who you have "outgrown" that may be dragging you down or holding you back with their lack of ambition or floundering self-growth. Take action — time for a toxic cleanse! You are responsible for your own calendar, so include those people who make you smile and uplift you, who fill your cup, not empty it. As you create space in your life, consider who could help you grow, provide a supportive environment and exudes positive energy instead.

    Identify 5 people to start who you find elevating to be around. How can you more deeply connect with them, to build a network of friends and colleagues who will help inspire you, enabling you to expand and grow, while cheering you on? Write down your strategy or action to develop a connection with each of them. (Approach each one with a specific opening topic or knowledge area that you are curious about and ask if they are willing to share their perspective or experience with you. Most people want to help others, and successful people are generally happy to share and to help others grow.)

5.4

Fear

A powerful word that can be used to stir people into action or paralyze them, it may be considered the opposite of confidence. Dread or terror of taking action may create such anxiety that you become frozen and take no action at all, as your head conjures up unpleasant possible future outcomes that may not actually occur.

    I have experienced fear many times, yet while it has not prevented me from taking action, it has taught me a few things. While taking an experiential learning weekend course, I realized that fear is a "future state." During one of the exercises in an outdoor adventure program, I was required to climb up and then stand on top of a telephone pole (thirty feet up in the air on a pole that was approximately ten inches wide) — yes, really! On my way up to the top, climbing up the pole, I was present, concentrating on taking one step after another. When I got to the top of the climbing handles and had to balance myself on the tiny flat top of the pole, even though I was wearing a safety harness, I started imagining… *What if I fall? Will I be able to keep my balance? Will the harness hold me up if I do fall? How am I going to get down again safely?* Once my nerves took over, future possibilities of various dangers took over stirring up the mind-chatter in my head. Once the possible outcomes for failure popped in, it was harder to stay focused. However, if I stayed present, breathed deeply and told my mind to *stay present, right here — right now,* I was able to prevent myself from letting my imagination run riot. (I navigated the course and a safe descent, and now use that approach of deep breathing and self-talk whenever I am in a fearful situation.)

Joseph LeDoux, professor of neuroscience and psychology the Center for the Neuroscience of Fear and Anxiety based at New York University says: "Fear is the response to the immediate stimuli. The empty feeling in your gut, the racing of your heart, palms sweating, the nervousness—that's your brain responding in a pre-programmed way to a very specific threat. We come into the world knowing how to be afraid, because our brains have evolved to deal with nature." [110] We have come a long way from our cave-woman days and the danger of sabre-tooth tigers.

Joy Hirsch, professor of functional neuroradiology, neuroscience and psychology, and director of the program for imaging and cognitive sciences at Columbia University, shares, "If you were in a dark alley and something scary jumped out at you, it would be the amygdala that would contribute to your decision to run." [111] The amygdala is one of two almond-shaped groups of nuclei located deep within the temporal lobes of the brain. Shown in research to perform a primary role in the processing of memory, decision-making, and emotional responses, the amygdalae are considered part of the limbic system. [112]

Fear, alarm, and *dread* all imply a painful future emotion anticipated when confronted by threatening danger or evil. Alarm implies an agitation of the feelings caused by awakening to imminent danger; it names a feeling of fright or panic: "He started up in alarm." *Fear* and *dread* usually refer more to a condition or state than to an event. *Fear* is often applied to an attitude toward something, which, when experienced, will cause the sensation of fright: *fear* of falling. Being pro-active and facing your fears is the best way to overcome them. By dreaming up possible negative experiences that may not come to pass, you stay in fear. Instead of letting fear have "power" over you, <u>take action</u>! By taking one small step *towards* the fear, you begin to shift your mindset to step out of fear and into possibility.

On the theme of money again (since this is often a source of lack and fear impacting confidence levels) if you fear that you may not be able to pay your electric bill, you can wait and take zero action, wondering what will happen and creating all kinds of possible fears in your head. Or you can take back your power by picking up the phone and calling their billing (or collections) department and negotiating a payment plan. Vendors usually want to retain you as a customer, and understand that sometimes circumstances beyond your control may impact the capability of a client to pay their bill on time.

It's not the fact that you found yourself in a pickle, it is what you decide to do next that will keep your friends or relationships intact. It is HOW you choose to handle it — try to bury the issue or lie, or face it head on — own it and deal with it. Your confidence will rise with positive self-talk, brainstorming different possible solutions, and then moving forwards into action.

By choosing to take responsibility for your actions, your energy will shift, and you will show up differently to the world, more authentically. Friends and colleagues can feel your energy shrinking when you are in lack, or when you are embarrassed about something and not returning telephone calls. Your body language changes too (often with your head lowered, not willing to make eye contact, and with shoulders often curling inwards and forwards — unconsciously trying to make yourself seem smaller so no one will notice you) and while you hide from the uncomfortable action needed to take to feel better, others will *feel* something is amiss. Your energy will feel dissonant and disjointed. Remember the last time you struggled with making a decision, and then the lightness of hope that you felt when you finally made the decision? Indecision drags your energy down, decision-making lifts it!

If a fear seems overwhelming, imagine standing on top of a telephone pole! Take a few deep breaths, and move back to the PRESENT moment, as there is no fear right now (fear occurs when you project forward into worrying what MIGHT happen). Consider one SMALL step you would be willing to make to begin moving out of fear, shame or embarrassment into integrity. What CAN you do, who can you ask for help (in the case of the example money issue, there are many free money counselling and debt control consultants giving advice on how to resolve the issue).

Take action! The longer you put off dealing with the issue, the longer your confidence will be deflated, and you will be blocking space in your mind with the uncertainty. Hanging onto unfinished business saps your energy. It is like waiting for an axe to fall on you — instead, stand up and face the axe, as it will not have as much distance to fall if you are standing rather than sitting, and will not hurt as much. Make a choice today that no matter what your circumstances are, that you refuse to live in fear. When you picked up this book you CHOSE to own your freedom, to take back your personal feminine power, and to take action! Even if it is a small step, GET MOVING towards something that feels more expansive and more in alignment with who you are.

In her article "5 Ways to Stop Sabotaging Yourself," posted in *Psychology Today,* Andrea Bonior, Ph.D. shares that there are

> several behaviors that often keep people from taking action. These methods of self-sabotage can prevent them from getting where they want to be, fixing what they need to fix, and becoming the person they would <u>love</u> to be. Dwelling on "If only

. . ." keeps you stuck. Repeatedly revisiting "if only" fantasies when they involve things we can't do anything about, keeps us idling in neutral. Burying your feelings doesn't work. Try not to think of a rhinoceros in a bikini, and bam—there she is, and she's wearing quite a hot number! Feelings, when hidden, grow bigger and bigger, letting inertia harm you. Build the right day-to-day structure in order for new habits to take hold.[113]

ACTION STEPS:

There are numerous things that could stop you from achieving your career goals, or your life, if you let them including: perfectionism, fear of failure, or procrastination. Choose to put the spotlight on a few areas of your life that you know you have been hiding from — yes, do that right now and own it, then take action! If you want to step in to a more confident energy, it is time for a frank and intimate conversation with yourself. Knowing yourself from the inside out significantly contributes to shining brightly in a clear, honest energy of truth. No cobwebs, no muck to be stuck in, moving freely and with integrity, being proud of yourself for taking action to move away from fear!

What are some of those messy things you need to dig into and clear up, starting today — that are awkward, embarrassing or things you want to hide from others? Write down a list of "messy things I choose to clean up," and for each, list the "action I am taking to move forwards".

5.5

Strive

Often our measure of success is determined by the size of our home, type of car we drive, bank account or investment portfolio. Only measuring success in extrinsic or monetary ways will often keep us striving *(to struggle vigorously, as in opposition or resistance).*[114] Why live in fear when you can live confidently, trusting that life is working *with you* rather than against you?

Strive is an old word which became popular as we as a civilization began to commercialize our world. Originally, people bartered or traded items of value for what they wanted, a spear for some food, or shells collected for early jewelry. [115]About 2,700 years ago, the first coins appeared in ancient Turkey in Lydia, a kingdom on the Aegean Sea. The amount each coin was "worth" was stamped right onto round, flat coins made of gold and silver. Coins were small and easy to carry, which made trade simple, especially with visiting merchants who came by sea. The concept of metal coinage spread rapidly, and by 2,500 years ago each Greek city-state had developed its own coinage.

Coins made it easier to count who had more and who had less, shifting the way society now often evaluates people, by the size of their bank account rather than their contribution.[116] Your bank account size is just one reflection of the value you contribute to others. Author Lisa Nicols, author of *Abundance Now: Amplify Your Life & Achieve Prosperity Today,* shares that "abundance is available to everyone.

> It is a myth that abundance is singularly based on possessions and money – it's all about what you drive, what house you live in, how much money you make – when in fact that could not be further from the truth. Wealth is about possessions and money. Abundance is a 360 experience. True abundance is your health and the quality of your relationships you have. At the end of your life you will literally measure the quality of your life by the quality of your relationships you have, all the other stuff will fall away in the area of importance. The relationships you have with your children, how they relate to you, how your siblings relate to you, do you have love in your life. You will start

looking at relationships at a higher level, as you get older." [117]

Your contribution and giving are real measures of how others will respect you. Confident women know they have the resources they need, as well as to look after their family. When your contribution to others comes from your heart, you will never be short of resources. Generosity is generally reciprocated.

It is interesting to note that in old French "strive" means *to quarrel or compete.*[118] Although when we push too hard to create something, when we struggle vigorously, we often create resistance, making it harder for us to achieve our goal. When you push against a brick wall, it is hard and resists your energy. When you try to push another person to do something, you often create unnecessary resistance from them, creating tension in the relationship. I encourage a "pull energy" rather than a "push energy" — creating an invitation that attracts rather than pushing and creating resistance. When you embrace the concept of asking curious questions, it is easier to understand and appreciate what your conversation partner values.

Around 2014, I realized that this push energy was driving my work life, and in conflict with my values. I had been offering HR consulting services (as well as executive coaching) after working in senior HR roles for over fifteen years. One particular experience confirmed when the goal is solely focused on earning money, it is often hollow in its reward.

At that time, I was asked to complete a delicate harassment investigation (often conducted internally through an HR department). In 2013 and 2014 I was very focused on reaching my financial goals, so when a new client with a five-figure project was referred, it was appealing. The organization (I'll call them ABC Company for confidentiality) was facing an impending revolt in one field site location, with employees reacting angrily to the culture clash of comments made by a senior leader. A harassment complaint had been reported to the organization's senior leadership, and my contracted role was to investigate, present my findings, and make a subsequent recommendation. I fulfilled that obligation to investigate with the local staff and delivered my "Executive Summary and Recommendations;" however, an interesting lesson followed.

After weeks of interviewing staff members, documenting my findings, and as a certified HR professional sharing my professional recommendations for change — the senior leadership team reviewed and then ignored my feedback. Yes, I was paid well for the hours put into the task, and yet I felt treated like a street vendor — I felt used and underappreciated, hollow inside. This feeling of *not being heard*, nor having my opinion valued, was endorsed by behavioural observations. The client only returned my calls when he had an urgent question, while many days would go by before my questions were answered. I felt that my professional opinion was not appreciated or valued after ABC's leaders decided to ignore my guidance and chose a different direction.

Occasionally, I am asked to coach an individual who has no desire or the willingness to make a change, which I refer to as *un-coachable*. Coaching is a powerful self-development method that leading organizations use for development of valued staff. Investing in those who have already proven alignment of personal and organizational values, and are committed to high-quality delivery for clients, makes good business sense. The leader under investigation displayed few of these qualities, and I believed was not a smart coaching investment. This experience created a hollow feeling and space for a flash of insight which followed, triggering a major turning point in my life. Following reflection, I made an important decision to create better measures for my personal success, and chose to redesign and rebrand my business model, and changed the name accordingly.

For those readers who have never experienced professional coaching, it is a goal-oriented process that addresses the gap between where you are now and where you want to be in the future. It is a collaborative partnership that facilitates excellence by supporting you in discovering and optimizing your personal and professional potential. In each meeting, you choose the focus of the conversation in alignment with your articulated coaching goals. My role as coach is to listen, observe, and ask thought-provoking questions which will expand your thoughts and energetic alignment, to enable you to self-discover powerful insights, (or provide "blind spot" feedback) leading to new choices and actions.

As coaching leads to creating action, the recipient of coaching needs to be ready and willing to "act." I may suggest "practices and exercises" to complete between coaching sessions that will be closely related to expanding on coaching goals. This interaction provides an opportunity for increased clarity, which triggers action toward the realization of your values, vision(s) goals, and aspirations. Coaching requires willing participation.

In this case, ABC ignored my recommendations, and I heard later they were legally requested to attend a human rights tribunal — which could have been so easily avoided had they followed my professional advice. Although I was fairly paid for completing this project, it left a hollow feeling inside me about the type of work I was doing, the type of client that I had accepted working with because of the contract value. When living in fear of not knowing when my next billable project would show up, I strived, and projected an energy of scarcity.

My business earnings were leaving me hollow, yet in my volunteer activities I felt how working on heart-centred projects with impactful success was genuinely invigorating. When I was making a difference and feeling enriched about how I was being treated (where my professional opinion was heard and valued), my heart sang and work felt "in flow".

I was subsequently asked to coach the site leader who I felt was "un-coachable," however, what needed to change was based on his personal values. His values were in conflict with my values, fuelling an energy of resistance. It was then I realized when I was *striving* — simply for the money — I did not feel intrinsic motivation from within (*intrinsic — native, innate, natural, true, real).* [119] Money provides an external (extrinsic) short-term incentive, as I know from building HR compensation strategies (including short and long-term rewards programs, to help motivate and retain staff.). However, intrinsic motivation lasts much longer.

Money can motivate in the short term, however,

in the long-term having an impact

greater than ourselves

is a key to feeling accomplished and purposeful.

In my striving to "make a buck," accepting the contract based primarily on the monetary value, I realized I had lost a part of myself, and felt my soul was being sucked out of me like preparing a hollow egg for painting at spring (or Easter) celebration time. No amount of money could offset my need to be heard, to have my opinion validated, to have my values of responsiveness and quality customer service, not respected by my clients.

I realized I had fallen into a common trap where a consultant is brought in to complete a work project, simply to pay "lip-service" later on when questioned by either staff, senior executives or the provincial authorities. "We did not ignore the problem, we brought in a consultant and did an investigation . . ." — yes, but then you chose not to listen to my recommendations and created a bigger issue! In my striving I compromised my personal values. It was a critical turning point for me.

When external events trigger an emotional upset, it is so useful to reflect on what happened and what learnings you can take away from a painful situation. This project with ABC showed up in my life for a purpose. It helped me to make better choices, to choose to stop — take a step back, to clarify my values, to complete another layer of inner reflection and emotional healing. I re-evaluated how I would select my future clients to avoid this situation occurring again. My reflection showed I had been striving so hard, I had already started heading towards burnout. A key lesson was also to know my values and only work with those who share common values. (If you have not yet taken the VIA free values assessment mentioned on page 36 – I encourage you to take it now and begin paying attention to how you are living into your top ten values every day. Ask potential clients, employers and friends to help you get to know "what they value the most in your relationship, by sharing a few of their most important values, and help you work more effectively together".

In 2014 I was invited to be an expert panelist on a six-day global tele-summit with Tenacious Living Radio, with expert speakers sharing expertise on the topic of "emotional overwhelm." My segment was scheduled for day five, speaking on "Moving from Career Stress to Career Joy." The session was pre-recorded a few weeks prior to the tele-summit. Upon kickoff, I listened to the first few days of each speaker defining *emotional overwhelm* and how it shows up in our behaviour. Listening to the experts' descriptions, and what happens within the body, I quickly realized that I was already in overwhelm personally. I had already started sliding down the slippery slope myself — without even realizing it! It is so easy and unconscious, like a slow pain that gradually dulls the senses and becomes a new norm.

I was glad that I had already prepared for the event in advance. With my strategies to help with shifting this for others to share in my tele-summit segment, I now had action steps to help me move out of it personally. I used my own system (originally intended to help others) for myself — and it worked amazingly well. I stepped into a new level of self-awareness and learned how to live with a new level of confidence, in alignment with my values, and to honour myself with an expanded level of assertiveness.

If you don't honour your values, you'll miss the feeling of being fully grounded and the sense of wholeness that comes from deep inside. It is a solid feeling of deep clarity when you know who you are and what you are willing to take a stand for in the world. Acknowledging and accepting who you are and why you are here (your purpose) gives a feeling of standing on concrete rather than quicksand. With that innate confidence you will feel strong enough to stand solidly in the windstorms that life brings, without getting blown over by a strong breeze (not swayed in your values by another person) — creating a feeling of rock-solid integrity and resonant energy.

When attending an event or gathering, there is typically at least one person "resonating," that you feel energized by, just by being close to. You can sense their strong vibration as they exude an energy of resonance, of solid truth — you can feel this. "You will see heads turn when a person with strong resonance comes into the room," as my coach, Jayne Warrilow shares. They are powerful because their energy is vibrating at a higher frequency, and you know this person has much wisdom to share. They are attracting people to them like bees to a honey pot.

After a few months of deep reflection and resurfacing after my burnout, I felt rock solid. It was time to rebrand my existing business (previously named "The Shattered Ceiling") to a new brand, one that acknowledged the fresh energy of integrity and growth I was feeling. I equated my new fresh energy to the lively spring burst which occurs in nature —sprouting up a new shoot straight for the sky, with a vibrant green freshness. When you initially plant a small seedling into a flower bed, it has a weak stalk, and is likely to get washed away from its earthy bed if a heavy rainstorm occurs. In a blustery windstorm, a new baby plant will often have an under-developed stalk and snap off.   In rebranding my new company name: "Flourish — with Yvonne Silver," I saw my role as a coach similar to the role of a plant stake, supporting my clients' evolution. Gardeners place a plant stake beside a new plant, to provide strength during growth, while it develops a strong root structure and thicker stalk. My coaching role echoed the strength of a plant stake, by providing value, support and strength to my clients, as they deepened their self-awareness (akin to their roots) growing stronger in their capabilities and resilience (their stalk or trunk).

If you look at the logo in the About the Author section at the back of this book, you will see that I chose the light bulb to represent my creativity and problem-solving gifts, helping others gain clarity. The centre filled with Gerber daisies is reflecting my work with growth-oriented and vibrant female clients. I am passionate about supporting women in their evolution and growth, represented by the flowers. Each one is different (reflected with varied coloured flowers, and even one with a bent stalk, as we are all different in our abilities and physical attributes). Coaching is not about fixing something that is broken, it is about exploring possibilities to step into your greatest potential.

Coaching is about creating more, bringing out the best of your natural talents and leveraging those unique gifts and insights.

The new energy of growth with "Flourish" felt so different than that of "The Shattered Ceiling". I moved from a scattered energy made up of broken shards of glass, to flourishing in a new clear and solid awareness, sharing my creative mindset, with a focus of making an *impact* rather than chasing monetary goals.

Shortly after this insightful event, in 2016 I learned about a book called *Evolved Enterprise* by thought leader Yanik Silver. He explores how to "re-think, re-imagine and re-invent business to deliver meaningful impact and even greater profits." His collection of social enterprise examples making an impact (while having significant growth) included many well-known public examples. He explores iconic brands including TOMS Shoes and Warby Parker (glasses manufacturer) who have exploded through their connection of a social impact and common good, with a profitable and scalable business. Using the B1G1 impact model ("Buy one and give one" for every pair purchased) TOMS Shoes expanded rapidly as their customers became their raging fans, who loved the concept that every pair of shoes they purchased also provided a pair to a shoeless child in a poor country. Warby Parker expanded using the same B1G1 model (one pair of glasses donated to someone in need for each pair sold) and advanced quickly. TOMS donated over 1M shoes in under four years of conception, which shows significant growth and is such a heartwarming story.[120]

Social enterprise models offer an opportunity to operate a "for-profit" business, making a "social good" impact. Silver's book showcases eleven various examples of "impact business models," all tapping into a socially good cause, and being profitable. "Business with heart" — now that resonated with me! The energy of striving no longer appealed. By moving towards a business model with an "impact measure" of success, I am now committed to donating one copy of this book to a women's shelter, not-for-profit or foundation, for each one purchased (B1G1). This initiative helps more women become aware of their words and elevate their confidence, appeals to my compassionate and creative personality, and fuels my desire to make a positive difference.

This book content emerged during 2017 and 2018, as I realized so many of the concepts I was sharing with hundreds of my clients, had helped them significantly evolve. Many concepts included reusable approaches worth sharing. I watched the results from some of the simple language and word concepts that increased confidence, lifted energy, and created more aligned and purposeful career choices. My clients developed new levels of awareness, and became more articulate about their goals, and what they wanted to take a stand for. Many became stronger and more confident leaders, more assertive wives and mothers, and each one gained clarity around their priorities and a developed a clear vision.

When you know who you are, leverage your values, appreciate what is important to you, and measure your success in collaborative and impactful ways, you attract others to you that will support you — as they are on the same vibrational frequency as you. With my BIGI donation focus, I can give hope to women who may not be able to afford to purchase their own copy, so please do recommend it to your friends or women's resource centre at work, or recommend it for a book club or reading group. If you purchased your copy and have a particular request for your second donated copy be shared with a specific woman's charity you support, please let me know, so that we can honour this by emailing: Admin@WordsWomenAndWisdom.com. This book becomes a central element of my new business model, teaching women to Flourish in business by helping you to elevate your confidence, and ask for what you really want, and receive it! Let's help more women to do that too.

ACTION STEPS:

Stop striving and start living in alignment with your values! Think back to the last time that you felt out of alignment. This could show up as anxiety (your head feels so full of thoughts that it is spinning, you can feel the blood pumping through your veins, or you get a massive head ache in your front temple). Recall, what was the situation right before you felt like that? What was happening that may have contributed to you feeling deep anxiety or a strong sense of unease? What opportunities exist for aligning your values and tapping into your talents and gifts, to bring these into closer correlation with each other?

Pay attention to events that you attend and see if you can pick out a few of the people who are emanating high energy and personal power, those who you feel have integrity, are solid and trustworthy. How do you feel when you're around these people? Start taking back your own power by saying no more often, not spending time with people who you don't resonate with. Notice when you feel your values are being compromised. Your confidence will grow by understanding your character strengths and values, using the free (professionally developed) VIA assessment which I encourage you to take online at: https://www.viacharacter.org/www/Character-Strengths-Survey

Live your values every day. Find an organization where your values align closely with those of the organizational culture, the team goals and align with your potential leader, where your gifts can be fully expressed. Working in alignment with your environment and your values can be a beautiful and soulful fit.

If you are an entrepreneur woman reading this, take the VIA as well, and see how you can bring more of your personal values into your leadership style. If you don't have a social enterprise element already in your business, find a way to incorporate one, to prevent you from working hard and burning out without living purposefully. (If you need support with this, reach out to me through the Contact page at: WordsWomenAndWisdom.com to brainstorm ideas for your business.) When your business venture has an impactful "mission-inspired" soul, this emanates generosity when you are creating an impact for many others. Showing up as who you were meant to be in this world, by being aware and awake and living purposefully, is simply a more joyful way to live.

*Take the free VIA assessment, created by Martin Seligman with The Happiness Institute[121] (link above) which takes ten to fifteen minutes to complete online. Note down in your journal your top ten values shown on the screen (or chose to purchase a more detailed report) and visualize how you can live more closely in alignment with those values, noting these ideas down. For instance: "Value = **Creativity** — I find three ways each day to use my creativity (at work & at home) and these are A, B, and C."*

CHAPTER 6:

Sharing Harmonious Words for a Happy Home

6.1

Enough

"Am I enough?" I have heard that this question comes up for many women, especially as we gradually deepen our awareness. When we wake-up from the corporate mindset of living paycheque to paycheque and being led by success measured primarily by our bank balance, a whole new world of awareness awaits. When you value yourself based on intrinsic motivators (doing something for pleasure) rather than extrinsic measures (receiving an external reward or outcome, or to avoid punishment) your perspective on your own self-worth shifts.

Is it time for you to stop doubting yourself? To step up and step out with more confidence? If so, you will benefit from committing to daily powerful inner reflection, exploring the things about yourself that you love, and perhaps those behaviours that you are not proud of (your shadow side) . . . What have you learned about yourself so far, and where are you feeling there is untapped capacity? Where do you have even more potential to live into and experience a joy-filled and purposeful life?

If you feel a ripple of emotion in your body as your stomach flutters, your heart pounds, or a lump in your throat emerges — take these feelings as signs of your potential readiness to expand. A lump in your throat may indicate blocked energy, a desire to speak up about something buried deep inside. It may signal a desire to advocate passionately for a cause that energizes you, or take a clear stand for an injustice you see occurring in the world. Take time to reflect and sit with these feelings, allowing time each day to deepen your awareness, and ask your soul what it wants to show you right now, through your emotions.

Often, our emotions are triggered by other people. When you notice a specific behaviour in someone else that you don't like, often you see that behaviour it them for a purpose. When it triggers an emotional response in you, your soul knows deep inside that you also express that behaviour at times. If you don't like seeing it expressed by others, you likely know that you need to work on changing this behaviour yourself.

In his book *The Presence Process,* author Michael Brown outlines a method to deepen awareness and enhance the ability to observe events as they occur, using deep breathing exercises and mediation. He teaches how to step back from an emotionally charged situation which triggered a reaction in you, and how to slow down your thinking enough to see what is happening and observe where there are learning opportunities.[122]

We are all made up of energy, and energy cannot be removed from the universe, however, it can be transmuted from negative energy to positive energy. Brown believes that when something is causing pain, a leading cause is having "un-integrated emotional energy around this situation, and until the energy is integrated the same situation will keep occurring over and over again." I have personally experienced this when "the universe keeps on tapping me on the head until I finally get the lesson." Can you think of an example when you have also been in a recurring and challenging situation before?

Often these unintegrated energetic occurrences seem to happen or reoccur in seven-year cycles Brown shares. His book explores how we develop in three phases. The first seven years of our lives ("emotional development") the second phase, age seven to fourteen (the "mental development" phase) and finally from fourteen to twenty-one (the relationship development phase). By reflecting on painful situations arising in your current life, you may also see how these seven-year cycles show a recurring issue that is ripe for "energetic integration."

If you want a situation to change, *you* have to change it, by changing your own behaviour first, then speaking up to confirm your chosen course. You can choose not to be in that situation (the place, the scenario, in relationship with another person) by taking charge of whom you invest your time with, by how you invite their opinion or not, or by how you let them treat you.

You could begin managing your boundaries more effectively. I prefer showing up whole in my authentic true power and using my words wisely to manage my own self-talk. Then I show others how I want to be treated rather than hiding behind a boundary. Putting up boundaries may keep others out, however, like the emotional shield I used to protect me in the past, boundaries also keep you contained — and keep you operating in a much smaller way than your true potential.

In nature, when you see a beaver dam in the river, it has created a jam — a boundary that blocks the flow. The resulting stagnant pool does not create new life, and it gradually grows cloudy and smells bad. No flow, no life — it is the same effect with a blockage of the Chi energy running through our bodies, as with a beaver dam blocking a flowing river. No flow, no life.

Try switching out the word *boundary* for *tolerate*. Darren Hardy, founder of *Success Magazine* suggests deciding what each of us will *tolerate*. I like this word much better, because it is a firm way to show your truth, what you want to take a stand for, to serve your needs. When you refuse to tolerate how someone else treats you, or tolerate being over your chosen weight, or to tolerate holding an unsatisfying job or being in an abusive relationship any longer — it is easier to be fired up to take action!

When you move from acceptance to "taking a stand," you show to others that *you* are the one choosing how you live your life. Your value does not depend on how others may judge you, it comes from how *you value yourself*. I have worked with many resilient women who have come through tremendous challenges and emerged like a butterfly from a cocoon, to express their true beauty. You are already enough — strong enough, smart enough, aware enough, open enough, loved enough. By being willing to take action on the exercises in this book, you will deepen your awareness further, evolving into feeling more grounded and more confident in your ability to express yourself.

You teach people how to treat you,

by your silence and acceptance, or by your actions.

— Dr. Phil McGraw

ACTION STEPS:

Are you enough? If your mirror reflection comes back saying no, you have an opportunity for growth. Find a quiet place (out in nature always feels good for me), sit quietly, breathing deeply, and if safe to do so, close your eyes. Ask yourself "If I were enough, what would that look like for me? What would I be feeling or doing that I am not doing today?" Listen deeply for your inner guidance to emerge and feel what bubbles up. What is your soul calling forth from you? What can you take action on? How will you show up differently when you "are enough"?

If you want a situation to change, YOU have to change first. If you want to have a more interesting job, look for ways that you can bring new life to HOW you do your work. Can you use new technology, approach work with a new cheerful attitude, engage others in new ways to add new energy to an existing project, opt to volunteer for a not-for-profit group (outside your current job) and feel a warm rewarding glow as you are appreciated, and make an impact for those less fortunate. You may not have to change companies, perhaps a lateral move to another team will increase the acknowledgments for your efforts from a new leader seeing your accomplishments with fresh appreciation. (If your values clash with those demonstrated by the organization, I highly recommend exploring work with other companies whose values more closely match your own.)

If you want to step into a healthier lifestyle that enables you to feel slimmer and fitter, identify one small step that you can take today towards this. Can you start taking the stairs rather than the elevator, or park at the far end of the parking lot giving yourself extra exercise? Cycle to work? Jog with your stroller while giving your baby some fresh air, or pick up your walking speed to a brisk pace? Bring an eight-glass canister to work filled with your daily quota of water, and sip it throughout the day, reducing your reliability on caffeine. Take the initiative, and make a change yourself — if you don't put yourself first, no one else will.

Are you serving others enough? Volunteering can be extremely rewarding and can often be woven into a family activity or a corporate event for your team. Before you take on a new volunteer role, make sure you have the capacity to give from a full heart, as often women over-give. It is hard to give from an empty fuel tank. I have had numerous experiences where volunteering has led to building amazing and impactful relationships and valuable projects.

Define your "non-negotiables" — those values you hold dear and will not waiver on, the things you are willing to take a public stand for. Are you willing to "call out" a teenage boy for not offering his seat on the train to enable an elderly man or pregnant woman to sit down? Are you ready to attend a public women's march to show solidarity for equal pay legislation and awareness?

If you want someone else to change, it could be a long wait. Teach others how to treat you according to your values. Take a stand for yourself and what you will or will not tolerate any longer. What beliefs and values do you hold that are misaligned with how you are letting others treat you? What actions will you now confidently take instead of acceptance in silence of a situation that does not honour you?

You are enough, you are worth it! *(Review the section on value if you need to further explore why you are valuable and enough exactly as you are.) What beliefs has this chapter stirred up in you? Examine your values (from the VIA assessment mentioned previously) and decide where you need to take action to live more closely in alignment with your personal values. When you do, you will feel more grounded, more resonant energy, and know that "you are enough." Try this journal prompt: My* *value/belief is X. To live in closer alignment, my new action that supports me better is Y.*

If you are in a leadership role at work, remember that you are being observed by your staff every time you make a decision. They look at your behaviour expecting a role model for the company values. Even leaders sometimes act out of alignment with corporate values when under stress. What is one thing that you have acted upon recently that you were not especially proud of, and yet, you learned an important lesson? Write it down: My Lesson was X. My alternative action or behaviour next time will be Y.

In case no one told you recently, you are enough already! You can always enhance that, much like a talented violinist can keep practising to hone their skill and deepen their ability. Being enough is like a rose, a tight bud is enough, and yet you deepen your beauty and inner confidence each time you blossom further (like the rose petals which slowly open to reveal the sweet nectar buried deep inside) showing who you really are.

In your daily reflection, include reciting this mantra out loud (in front of a mirror, every day, is even better): "I am willing to take a stand for myself, and I am enough." Own that!

6.2

Self-talk

There is power in what others say to us; however, remember that what is shared is only *their* opinion, it is simply their perspective. Unless they are sharing the evidence of an experiment (repeatedly conducted using a controlled environment) their perspective is not science nor truth — although it may be said with such strong opinion that it feels like the truth. However, it is *their* truth, not yours.

If a friend said that your hair was green, you may double-check by briefly looking in the mirror, only to find that in fact it wasn't green. You would be confident and know that was not *your* truth. However, if your friend told you that she thought your husband was having an affair, and you also had some doubts about him coming home late recently from several times, your imagination might begin conjuring up possibilities, and you may believe her.

When you doubt that you have the knowledge, the words, the insight or the clarity to take action on something, your doubt will show up as hesitation, a crack in your confidence, which often stops forward movement. In a recent interview with a colleague, she spoke on the importance of self-talk. The concept equally applies to reaching goals you have for your personal development and growth (or goals at work). Your personal growth and success ultimately impacts your family and home life too.

Dr. Dahlia Mostafa, professional certified life coach, counsellor, leadership consultant with the Canadian Life Transformational Academy, believes that

> confidence stems from being clear on your self-worth and your identity (how you see yourself, your best qualities, how you speak out in public, your storyline), which you have the power to change as you grow and expand, describing your true essence. Confidence comes from valuing your unique combination of characteristics rather than letting the layers of negative experiences hide your true self. Fear experiences as a young child (fear of judgement, fear of failure or often fear of success) all contribute to shake your confidence. Using "I AM" statements (I am able, capable, skillful) are extremely powerful to reinforce your capabilities when you frame these ideas in the brain and then anchor these traits with knowledge and practice.

If you decide you want to go back to school and take evening classes, have an open and honest conversation with your spouse or children about why this is important to you. When they understand how it will benefit them as well (the WIIFM — What's In It For Me concept) you will have more support. When they understand the ultimate overall gain, when you are studying in the evening (and not as available for their needs) they will be more accepting if they can appreciate the potential long-term family benefits. (Sharing a vision of taking a tropical vacation together or a family camping trip, or tour of Disneyland often helps!)

Dedication then reward, dedication then reward — you are also role modeling an important lesson for your children — showcasing the practice of focus and achievement. (If you don't engage them at the beginning of the process, often children — or sometimes husbands too — will act up when they are not receiving enough of your attention, unless they know *why* you are investing significant time into your studies.) Is there anyone in your life that you need to have a conversation with, to clarify your goals and your actions to achieve them, and why this is important to you? I encourage you to make time for that conversation in the next few days, to clear the air and create space for your dreams to emerge, with the support of your family.

As a regional vice president for RBC, Tasha Giroux has been with the Royal Bank of Canada for twenty-five years, receiving numerous regular promotions. Tasha is an active participant in the RBC Diversity and Inclusion Initiatives, and an advocate for changing how women are evaluated for promotions and included in succession planning discussions. She regularly speaks on topics relating to women, diversity, and personal growth issues, especially for those women who work in a predominantly male work environment. In a recent interview with Tasha, after she was promoted to a regional vice president of commercial banking role (for Alberta and the Prairies) she shared how she reassured herself every day with motivating self-talk for six months after earning that promotion. "I had to keep telling myself every day, that I *could* do this, and perhaps even more importantly, that I wanted to do this."

Many years ago Giroux developed her own career development plan, and using this document as her compass, reviewed it regularly for action items then discussed this regularly with her leader. Her career advancement shows this focus, proactive dedication and demonstrated results have earned her a senior position, with significant responsibility. She now role models senior female leadership within RBC and her advocacy contribution advances the development of diversity initiatives that support a better working environment for women.

Whether you are at the VP level in your career, or just starting out, self-talk is incredibly powerful! When you feel a pain in your body, it may be indicating that energy is stuck somewhere.

Pay attention to these feelings. A hollow feeling may indicate that something is missing in your life right now. Is there something that you are not being recognized for? Where do you want to place focus to build up a new skill or expand your knowledge, and how will you do this? Giroux shared how important it was to ask yourself, "Am I doing my best? I also ask my children when they are going into an exam, have you done your best, have you studied as much as you can, and feel as prepared as you could be? Then you have done your best." She also shared a key element for success in her career advancement.

> "I have always had my own development plan in an organization. With a quarterly review every year, my development time goes into my manager (including training budget approval). My plan was holding me accountable for the things that I thought were important for my own personal and professional growth. I think from a woman's perspective, you never get what you don't ask for, and my plan guided asking.
>
> Don't be afraid to state your intentions, to ask for help, don't be afraid to ask for what you want. The worst thing that can happen is someone says *no* to you, and that's not that painful once you get used to it. Hearing *no* can create some of the very best opportunities for stepping outside your comfort zone, beyond what you thought were your pre-established limits. Challenging yourself not only opens so many doors, but boy it makes life fun! Because you're able to continuously learn and grow and develop."[123]

Many of us have "mind chatter" or your "inner critic" periodically appearing, that inner voice which tries to guide your decisions and tells you when you are heading off your path. Listen to your mind chatter if it is supporting you, and remember that the voice within is often your amygdala chattering away to keep you safe. Your amygdala is the part of your inner brain that keeps shouting, "danger, danger," when you tackle something new or scary, which may create physical or emotional danger — when you step out onto the ledge of life, onto the slim end of the branch. Yes, that little voice is "mind chatter."

Standing on the ledge of life anticipating an exhilarating jump can be the best feeling in the world — pure anticipation, followed by a rush of excitement! The end of the branch is where the newest, sweetest shoots are, where the most delicate flowers bloom. It is where the sweet nectar of life exists, ready to be harvested and pollinate other flowers, continuing life's existence through the power of bees.

The amygdala is the almond-shaped structure in the brain; its name comes from the Greek word for almond. As with most other brain structures, you actually have two amygdalae (shown in the centre in the drawing below). Each amygdala is located close to the hippocampus, in the frontal portion of the temporal lobe.

Limbic System

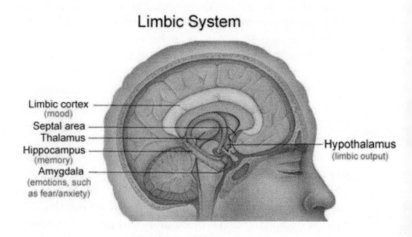

Ref: Conway.psychology.webs.com

Your amygdalae are essential to feel certain emotions and to perceive them in other people. This includes feeling fear and the many changes that it causes in the body. If you are being followed at night in a parking lot by a suspect-looking individual and your heart is pounding, chances are that your amygdalae are very active.

According to Bruno Dubuc, Douglas Hospital Research Centre funded by Canadian Institutes of Health Research: Institute of Neurosciences, Mental Health and Addiction, the amygdala enables one of the forms of implicit memory: emotional memories associated with fear. Various aspects of an especially emotional situation such as a car accident, will be processed both by the hippocampus (memory) and by the amygdala, working in parallel. Thanks to the hippocampus, you will remember whom you were with, what you did, and that it was a particularly painful situation. Because of the amygdala, when you remember the event, your palms will sweat, your heart will race, and your muscles will tense. Although you can remember the *emotional* pain of an illness, your body cells do not retain memory of the *physical* pain.

Mind-chatter is often created by fear coming from our subconscious, creating potential scenarios that may not even come true. One of the best ways to manage mind-chatter is to stay present and centred on what is happening right now (as with my telephone pole example). Overcoming fear or self-doubt starts with awareness, followed by honestly assessing your abilities and acknowledging any shortcomings (and determining your development opportunities). Each one of us has strengths that when overused in excess, can become a weakness or area for development. If you are outgoing and friendly, when taking this to the extreme with excessive talking, you may end up ignoring others' opinions, and appearing to hog the conversation. Everyone likes to talk about themselves, so an overly "talkative Tina" is not always very popular, when no-one else can take a turn in the conversation.

Any strength when overused can become a weakness, so pay attention to what you do extremely well or quite naturally, and how others around you are responding to your actions. Are they engaged with you and leaning into the conversation, or pulling back and showing signs of being bored (eyes wandering around the room, fidgeting, scratching their head, etc.)? Here are a few approaches to manage mind-chatter:

Do not try to push these thoughts down, as it is like saying "don't think about yellow elephants" — the mind goes right to elephants! Sit still with your feet firmly on the floor. Breathe slowly in and out. If the occasional thought slips in, let it simply waft in and away without placing your focus on it.

Practise becoming more aware of your actions and be willing to learn by becoming the "observer or neutral witness" of your thoughts. This takes practice in examining the last time something happened, what triggered the event (what circumstances happened immediately prior to the event under examination — your pre-trigger)? Reflecting on a few occasions of a recurring issue will typically highlight a pattern forming. With this increased awareness, the next time the pre-trigger situation happens, you will be more likely to see it coming, and be ready to observe yourself in the midst of the situation.

Notice a sensation of first feeling uncomfortable, or the impulse to want to *do something* in response to events. Simply observe yourself. Be kind to yourself and acknowledge your awareness of the pre-trigger (*here we go again, it's that thing again*) when you tune in to what is happening around you. Often your responses will seem to happen in slow motion. As you notice your behaviour, stay present and feel into the energy of the situation. Stay in that energy until you feel it subside. After the event, plan out how you will respond differently next time, only after letting the emotional charge of the situation integrate in your body (your emotions, thoughts and feelings).

Take a stretch break. (as recommended by *Mark Waldman* earlier[124]) slow your breathing or find a focus point and stare at that single object for a minute or two with no thought.

Create a blank space. Visualize an Etch-A-Sketch [125] screen where you can shake the tablet to erase the current words or picture creating a fresh blank screen. When negative mind chatter creeps in, stop — take four deep breaths — and shake your head (left to right) like the tablet, to create a new "blank screen" in your mind.

Practise increasing your focus. Increase your attention on each part of your body, as you might do in a yoga nidra class, beginning at the tip of your pinkie (smallest) finger on your right hand. Slowly breathe in and out while concentrating on each part of your body for five seconds, focus on each finger first, and then on your wrist, forearm, elbow, and so on. Travel up your arm and down the right side of the front of your body to your toes (concentrate on each body part or toe individually for a few moments), then travel up to the heel, up the back of your legs to your crown (going down and up your arm to each body part), then bring your focus back down the left side of your back body, then down to your toes and up the front side, and travel up again and back down your arm to your left pinkie finger.

ACTION STEPS:

As you become more in tune and aware of your language, and which words are triggering specific emotions for you, journal these observations. What is causing your mind-chatter? When you feel your inner critic rising up tell that inner voice of doubt to look for clear facts and observable signs that show the truth (like not seeing real green hair in the mirror). What actually occurred? What is your truth, not another's opinion? Journal your success signs. When you did clearly ask for what you wanted — what happened?

Write down actual events and what you noticed about yourself (and how others responded). If you didn't like the outcome, then changing your self-talk and exchanging low vibrational words for positive ones will likely have a different outcome next time. As you build your confidence, be prepared to look at all situations with a "glass half-full" mindset and use each circumstance with an unexpected ending to explore what could have been an "even better" outcome.

Ask yourself, "What could I do differently next time?" Life is an adventure, a constant petri dish of learning opportunities — stay observant and open to evolving. Switching your language, as mentioned in previous chapters, makes a huge difference to your internal chatter. By changing should to could, moving from self-talk of obligation to possibility over HOW you take action, you create your CHOICES.

Have you set clear intentions for how you want to live your life, and what you want to achieve (as Giroux did) over the next three or six months? If not, do so now. When you have a clear and meaningful goal, your focus will increase and mind-chatter decreases. Your mind will become excited and full with the new project rewards, filling open space so that no doubt and mind-chatter can creep in. (If you do not have a measurable "end-goal" in mind, determine one. Otherwise how will you know when you reach your destination with no predetermined success measures?)

In accordance with the Law of Attraction (Michael Losier and Rhonda Byrne concepts) your reticular activating system will help filter valuable information that your brain needs to notice. When your goals are clear, your attention will be guided to useful and relevant information you need related to achieving that goal.

(When you are pregnant you will suddenly notice pregnant women everywhere — right? Or you decide to buy a white Buick Encore, and everywhere you drive you keep seeing white Buick Encore SUVs — you notice relevant information that is important to you based on your goals.)

Is there anyone that you need to have a conversation with, to clarify the support you need to achieve your plans or desired goals? Who else needs to understand the actions needed to reach those goals, and why this is extremely important to you? In order to grow you need space in your life to do so, and asking for help from others (especially family members) will often create the space you need. When others ease your load, you free up your mental capacity for learning, while achieving your goals. Reflect in your journal the actions you will take next, based on the guidance above.

6.3

Doubt

Passion in your DNA is one of the determining things for entrepreneurial success.

— Kym Gold, co-creator of True Religion Brand Jeans; author of the business book, *Gold Standard: How to Rock the World and Run an Empire*

Self-doubt is an uncomfortable feeling. Yet uncertainty, one of the causes of doubt is something that almost all of us have experienced. As young children or students adapting to a new school or learning a new skill, in an interview or the first day of a new job, there are many circumstances which may create doubt. When you feel unsettled in your stomach, or mind-chatter is trying to creep in, it is sometimes much harder to step back into feeling confident . . .

In her book *Lean In: Women, Work, and the Will to Lead,* author Sheryl Sandberg (CEO of Facebook) discusses an interesting topic: *Imposter syndrome* (also explored in a Harvard Business Review article by Gill Corkindale). Women are especially prone to this issue. Imposter syndrome can be defined as: a collection of feelings of inadequacy that persist despite evident success. "Imposters suffer from chronic self-doubt and a sense of intellectual fraudulence that override any feelings of success or external proof of their competence."[126] Imposters seem unable to internalize their accomplishments, however successful they are in their field. High achieving, highly successful people often suffer, so imposter syndrome doesn't equate with low self-esteem or a lack of self-confidence. In fact, some researchers have linked it with perfectionism, especially in women and among academics. "Success is no big deal" is often the inner dialogue, and yet for women it actually *is* a big deal.

Why? Women are more often judged on their past performance when being considered for a promotion — so feeling successful and talking confidently about how you achieved those results does matter. You are the best advocate to showcase your own success! The tendency is to attribute success to "luck," with a belief of not deserving success, or to worry that success brings the added pressure of responsibility and visibility.

Professor Carol Dweck at Stanford University suggests embracing self-doubt by acknowledging "I'm not there yet. But I can get there." Dweck's research has found that

> self-doubt is often fed by a fixed mindset that invests in the belief that we're born either smart or dumb, talented or ordinary. Over the past decade, neuroscience research has confounded these beliefs with the discovery that with effort and practice we all have the potential to improve our abilities. LET ME REPEAT THAT — *with effort and practice we all have the potential to improve our abilities.* If life

were one long grade school, women would be the undisputed rulers of the world.[127]

I know that many times in my life I have set a goal to "go on a diet." Some of the popular guidance suggests creating affirmations with "I am" statements, and yet saying "I am one hundred and twenty pounds" to myself over and over in front of the mirror just felt wrong. I am not one hundred and twenty pounds, and with a diabetes diagnosis impacting my insulin production, I may never again achieve that weight, so as soon as I state this, my mind knows it is untrue, and starts "doubting mind-chatter." However, if instead my daily affirmation is, "I am in the process of developing healthy eating habits leading to a weight of one hundred and twenty pounds", my mind can agree this is true — "I am not there yet," however I *am* "in the process of . . ." Be kind to yourself as you are embracing new activities, learning new techniques and becoming the best version of yourself.

A toddler did not walk overnight, they tried and wobbled, fell down, got up, wobbled and tried again, tripped — sound familiar? For parents with children who are now walking, sometimes there is even a longing for those previous days when your children were not so active and easier to keep an eye on. I remember around age seven sitting with a friend in her summer flower garden looking down and realizing it was the first time I did not have an ugly scrape or a fabric bandage on either of my knees.

It is about doing your own personal best, and reaching *your* maximum potential, whatever that may look like. Your success level is not fairly compared with someone else's, as they may have taken the same course as you, yet may have more concentrated study habits, a higher IQ level, have volunteer experience in this topic or have a friend tutor them. Comparison creates doubt, so please stop comparing yourself to other women. You are unique! With my special-needs son, comparing his ability to walk with that of other children, would have been disheartening. Alex was diagnosed as developmentally delayed at one-year old and would likely never walk, according to one doctor. As a determined mother who was ready to go to bat for my child, I refused to believe this to be true, and helped him gain strength in his legs, then gradually learn to walk (albeit a very clumsy gait initially) at around age two and a half. While he was not able to ride a bicycle without stabilizers as his balance was impacted by his physical challenges, he was incredibly popular with young female store clerks, and learned excellent negotiating skills at an early age. He eventually learned to compensate with what he *could* do, not worrying about what he *couldn't* do. What do others tell you are some of your natural abilities and talents?

If you ever doubt the power of the human spirit or the power of the heart to persevere, there are many incredible TEDTalks and YouTube videos of people who have attained incredible success in life despite significant challenges. Four highly motivational examples[128] are:

> *Sean Stephenson, Top 10 Rules for Success —*
> *https://www.youtube.com/watch?v=50vKBG4NTE8*
> *Amy Purdy — https://ed.ted.com/on/EEqOvVLr*
> *Nicholas James Vujicic, No arms no legs, no worries—*
> *https://youtu.be/8jhcxOhIMAQ*
> *Conjoined Twins Abby And Brittany —*
> *https://www.youtube.com/watch?v=VMzK6iz6uVs*

Do you have children? What have you already learned about giving them feedback, so that you encourage their desire for learning and do not create doubts or crush their fragile confidence? You may not be one hundred percent sure that one of your children will be able to learn or complete something, or know that one of your team members or a friend will succeed in achieving a goal. Be kind and supportive (rather than judgemental) or don't say anything at all. What can you share with them that will help? Can you give them *constructive* feedback that they can choose whether to take action on?

For many years after I left home and moved away from my mean father, whenever I was being given "feedback" it still sounded like "criticism." In my early childhood I had experienced years of being constantly told to "be quiet like your sister," or "be home from playing in the park for supper at five pm — don't be late!" It seemed I rarely did something good that was worth celebrating in his eyes. It took many years to realize that there was a subtle difference between those two words *feedback* and *criticism*. I believe it begins with the energy behind the intention (criticism being judgemental and feedback being encouraging). What is your *intention* when you speak — is it to inform, to inspire, to encourage, to guide, or to stop or scare the other person by creating doubt in their mind?

When you have an urge to give another person feedback, consider first what value does sharing your insights offer the other person? If there is a clear and important advantage (it will keep them safe from a fire, their action will severely hurt another person or possibly gamble away the family fortune) ask for their permission before you share your thoughts. "May I make an observation?" is a respectful way to begin the conversation, and confirm they are open to feedback. After they confirm they are open to hear more, then share your insight kindly and constructively. While speaking to an adult, co-worker or subordinate in the same baby tones as you would with your young children is not going to win you any prizes, be compassionate with your words when giving feedback to others.

You can awaken them to a blind spot by using an open-ended question which invites action rather than a closed statement. This could sound like: "Mary, I see that you completed that project to the best of your abilities, and I am curious about your process. How did using that approach help to successfully achieve your goal?" or "What did you learn from this activity?" Or, "What worked really well, and how could it be even better?" Use open questions, which invite reflection. By focussing on the positive elements of the project or task, and helping Mary self-discover what she could do differently next time, this constructive approach helps engage staff to explore their own learning opportunities.

At work, where there is a clash of organizational values and the person's behaviour is clearly misaligned with the values of the organization, more direct feedback may then be needed. Each person has his or her own unique set of values, which are intertwined with his or her life experiences — which form his or her beliefs. If your values are opposite to another person's, you can spend many hours in discussion or defending a point judiciously and still not reach agreement. (If, based on my values, I think something is black and, based on your values, you feel it is white, we are likely never going to agree on middle ground — seeing it as grey.)

Your values are your inner compass, your truth, so when another person disagrees with your values, it rarely results in agreement no matter how long you talk about it. Better to "agree that you disagree" and look for things that you can find in common in the situation or focus on future action items.

How can you rein in doubts? Get comfortable with uncertainty yourself. Begin with "What if" I did know, how could the situation or outcome be different, and how might I feel differently about myself? Then, take something small that you are flexible about, asking yourself, "What if I didn't know the answer?" and move from doing this with smaller and then gradually bigger decisions.

Stay flexible and stop trying to control things that are not yours to control. Trying to control someone else's behaviour will often set you up for frustration, as their values and beliefs guiding their actions will be different than yours. You do have control over how you *choose* to respond (note I did not say *react*). By staying flexible and open to options and possibilities, I am frequently amazed at who (or what resources) magically show up to help a situation become a valuable learning opportunity for growth.

Sometimes situations present an opportunity to reframe in order to put something into a more positive statement, which is especially useful in job interviews and performance review meetings. In a recent conversation with Catherine Brownlee with CBI (a global talent management search firm) she shared that when interviewing candidates who have been employed for a long time (who are often not very comfortable in an interview situation) that she often helps them "reframe their accomplishments."

She does this by "drawing out who was responsible for which specific tasks. The team did a really great job, we outperformed other teams by . . ." She will ask, "Did you lead the team, which part were you responsible for? There may be an opportunity to share that you led, were responsible for, which part was the most successful part?" She shared that "All people have a difficult time promoting oneself in interviews, so it is also up to the interviewer to help them with that. It is up to our recruiter to make sure we ask great questions to find out what role was played, what were the measured results, and really pull out some of that (valuable) information."

Catherine shared:

> I will help them reframe their answer for the next time (when interviewing with a prospective employer) to practise promoting themselves. For

example, a candidate may say "The team did a really great job and outperformed all the previous teams by X percent. Then I start asking probing questions such as: did they lead the team, were they instrumental in being part of that success, and what did that actually mean?" Then I will suggest "you know there might be an opportunity for you to say, I led a team of six that did not have previous experience, or I was responsible for, I was accountable for" and we can reframe and showcase their abilities.[129]

Catherine also suggests staying away from *but*, and *however*, or blaming anyone else (such as a previous employer) and always try to represent yourself in a positive way. No matter what the negative situation may have been, there is always going to be a positive aspect. Rehearse, rehearse, rehearse before meeting with an interviewer, it could be life changing to secure that new position!

Set your intention and preferred outcome, and consider different possibilities that could happen in the meeting and practise "reframing." As an expert interviewer, Catherine shared how she "typically asks an open-ended question to let a candidate be very broad in their story, and (listens carefully for) anything that I feel could be perceived negatively." At the end of the story she inquires "this is what I heard, is this what you meant?" Often it is not what they meant, they were in the mode of storytelling rather than in the frame of mind to really listen to the words that they were choosing before their answer. One way is to paraphrase, to confirm: "what I heard you say was . . . and what I think you meant was . . ." which clarifies we are not jumping to an incorrect conclusion, and still honouring what the person is trying to say (while it may not have sounded the way they intended it to the first time). "I hear you, I understand you, and now I am choosing to respond."

Knowing how your success will be measured if you accepted the role is a critical piece of information, that will enable you to leverage your skills and set yourself up for maximum success, if offered a job. When you can talk comfortably about your measurable successes, you stop doubting yourself, and show up in a grounded and confident way. At the end of the interview remember to ask, "What does success look like over the next three months in this role? What will be some of the expectations to get there, to reach that success level"? If you take an inventory of your skills before an interview and find ways to showcase your clear results with measurable statistics, you will often have a choice of several job offers from numerous employers. Consider your skills, interests, passions and unique abilities, and how they could contribute to the success factors identified in the new role. Know yourself and your proven capabilities and reduce doubts.

ACTION STEPS:

Acknowledge your progress when you're "not there yet." Journal the small steps too, all movement is good (remember the tortoise and the hare race?) even if slow and steady. Be kind to yourself — using language such as "I am in the process of X."

At work, ask a colleague who has seen your results to share what skills they observed that uniquely helped you be successful — accept all comments as "feedback" and simply an opinion. Remember, everything has a learning opportunity, and there are no mistakes in life, simply lessons . . . When you remove the word failure from your vocabulary, life feels lighter and brings forth optimistic energy!

Do not compare your results against those of others, as each person has skills and abilities at different levels, and both can reach an outcome, possibly taking very different routes. Instead, at the end of each day, take a few minutes to reflect on "what is working really well, and how could it be even better"? Go ahead, begin a new daily habit today in your journal and list five positive things that you may be learning, however have absolutely NO doubts about accomplishing!

6.4

Value

One of the most important takeaways of this book is to know your personal character strengths and values (through taking the VIA). Your values underpin your personality, guide your decisions and help you choose what you will take a stand for. They are an integral part of who you are, and how you show up in the world. It is easy to tell when you are acting in alignment with your values, you feel happy and open with expansive energy. In reverse, misalignment shows up as a feeling of nausea or stress when you're in any environment that conflicts with your personal values. If you are feeling unsettled, yet had not been able to "think" through why this was, this could be a nudge from your values and intuition asking to be recognized by how you "feel" instead. Pay close attention to what your body is showing you, where you feel nausea, pain, a dull ache, or anxiety . . .

When you understand your values (and character strengths) you can look for ways to align these with your environment and the people you surround yourself with. Knowing your values can guide you in the partner you choose, the lifestyle you develop, select work that you love, the culture of your team at work, and must match with the overall culture of your organization to feel engaging.

If one of your values is "excellence," working on a team that is sloppy rather than paying attention to the details, will drive you crazy! Look for signs that your strengths and values are aligned with those of your leader and your team (as well as the overall organization). If you have not already done so from previous sections, I recommend taking the short (free) online VIA assessment to learn your character strengths now.[130]

Your character strengths and values are the primary anchors that will determine fit with the organizational culture, and guide you to creating more a meaningful life, with more purposeful work.

Alison Donaghey, host of the Think Opposite Radio Show, says "Confidence comes from within. The more we can know ourselves, the more confident we can be. As I have accepted more of myself, trusted myself more (and my intuition and seeing it works) my confidence grows. When we are able to acknowledge that we made a mistake and we are owning it and holding ourselves accountable, we can show up more confidently."[131]

Feeling stressed at work can be caused by many things. However, not using your strengths, misalignment of work responsibilities and work-style preferences, overwork (a lack of personal boundaries, an urgent project issue, a workload imbalance, or outdated/dysfunctional processes), or not feeling you are able to speak up — are frequent stressors. One of the keys to feeling more confident is knowing how to articulate your value, by showcasing how you are adding value, both in your family and community, and in workplace contributions. Start noticing when others "thank you" for something, showing they appreciate you, and begin noting down specifically what they are thanking you for. Is it showing your generous heart, your drive and determination to finish something, your musical talent, your willingness to share insights or make connections for them, or for your culinary genius creating a delicious meal for a pot-luck lunch?

Knowing how you are making a contribution that is valued by others will fuel a feeling of inclusion, and encourage you to further develop that skill, increasing your sense of self-worth and confidence. Look for ways others are using their skills and what you value about them, and share your positive feedback, fuelling the circle of reciprocity.

You may have heard the phrase, "describing your unique sales position (USP)." In the workplace, think about your PVP — your "personal value proposition," and how to describe this so that it doesn't seem like blatant bragging. What do you complete or contribute in your work which you know you do far better than anyone else? If you perform the same job that several others in your department perform, how can you find a way to differentiate your approach? What enables you to be more efficient, more effective, to work faster or more accurately, to have better customer relations, or to be a stronger team leader? (Is it your sense of humour, customer-service orientation, empathy, or your discipline, attention to detail, influence, or your relationship building skills?)

Look at your values and character strengths list, and see how these characteristics intertwine with your skills (what you know how to do) your interests (what you like to do) and your talents (what you are very good at). If you draw four circles that overlap, you will start to see the commonalities between the lists. The S represents the 'sweet spot' where elements converge:

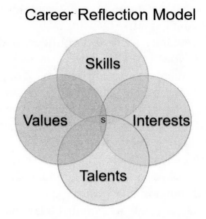

Career Reflection Model

Reflect on your accomplishments, the activities you completed in your role that had a specific *outcome*, and find ways to show a measurable result. If you are a leader responsible for HR, do you know your department metrics? (How do you track and measure: cost per new hire, the number of employees with over three years of service, the cost of staff turnover, or percentage/dollar value for training granted to each employee.) Knowing these metrics enables you to be more efficient with your time and leverage the organization's budget. If you find out the cost per hire is 1,878 dollars (including the cost of a job posting, interview time with a manager, completing references, preparing an offer of employment letter, etc.) how you can add value to your role by reducing this cost? What steps can you eliminate, do more efficiently, more creatively, or can you automate repetitive tasks to reduce costs, or save managers' time?

If your role is answering the telephone in the reception area of your organization, you can answer the phone consistently and quickly, or on the second ring. You can take ownership of transferring a caller to the correct person to answer their question every time, instead of passing the caller around various departments, creating frustrated callers. Can you develop a system to ensure that you remember a returning visitors name every time, or eight out of ten times, or the names of their family members for regular callers? Where and how are you adding value for your organization (or for your clients)?

Be proud of your accomplishments! Describe the unique way that you use your natural strengths and abilities to deliver value. Articulate your expertise by using statistics and quantifiable numbers — it is much easier to feel confident and to blow your own horn! (Did you save X dollars in expenses, increase production by Y percent, increase revenue by Z dollar — how can your value stand out or be showcased?) Often in succession planning meetings I have observed that women are identified for a promotion based on their past contributions rather than their potential, so articulating your value clearly and numerically will support your career advancement.

Be known as a team player, and engage others with powerful forward-thinking and positive questions, inviting them into the conversation, into action, to collaborate, or consider challenges or ideas in a new and more efficient way. Business and technology evolve quickly, and by showcasing how a small shift in efficiency can make a huge difference to profit levels, you garner additional recognition.

Amplify other women especially on your team who share great ideas, fostering your team spirit. If you are suggesting a new idea, first engage those impacted the most by your proposed change, to build buy-in and gain early adoption supporters. In HR, I learned how important early engagement was for the overall success of a project, rather than moving forward with an idea developed in isolation without consultation (which is rarely adopted and integrated smoothly). By investing time at the beginning of a project to understand the full scope and impact, you will have an easier implementation phase later. Understand *their* issues first, as Stephen Covey shares in his book *The 7 Habits of Highly Effective People* "Seek first to understand". [132]

Powerful questions start with...

ASK vs. TELL

ACTION STEPS:

Clearly identify, where are you adding value currently in your job or community? If you are not currently volunteering, consider what you are passionate about — an injustice that you get upset about — and find an organization where your skills and talents could contribute and make an impact for that cause. Does one of your children have a school volunteer committee or joint charity project you could work on together, increasing your bonding time together with your child in a meaningful way while role-modelling the importance of having a social conscience and contribution?

1 — What causes or topics do you care deeply about?

2 — How you are demonstrating value in your current job, in one of these ways: Saving the organization money (reducing waste, unnecessary costs or expenses, etc.)? Ensure your leader knows this!

3 — Increasing efficiency? How can you quantify the improvements you are making at work or with your team: reducing down-time, increasing research and development time to help new products get to market faster or quicker than the competition, aiding a first-to-market advantage?

4 — Increasing revenues? (Are you adding new clients — even if you are not in a direct sales role — encouraging staff referrals, creating new products or upsell opportunities, creating new lines of business for existing clients to buy, adding new markets or geographies, identifying new industry uses for your product with slight tweaks to packaging?)

5 — Helping to retain existing clients? (Engaging clients in community projects or fundraising with them or their favourite charity, dropping off seasonal gift baskets, organizing a "customer appreciations day," creating special offers for key clients, etc.)

6 — Helping to retain critical staff? (Engaging staff in community projects or organizing fundraising for their favourite charity, suggesting a rewards and recognition program, identifying "plum" projects or volunteer activities to increase their visibility with the executive, helping them find a mentor inside the organization, etc.)

7 — How can you summarize and highlight your most valuable contributions? You are extremely valuable!

6.5

How

Three small letters, yet a word with so many uses . . . I love using words (and questions) that open possibilities and encourage creativity and innovation. Hence, I frequently use *how*. Any question that contains the curiosity gem word *how* is intriguing, and holds a warm invitation for creative input. If you ask someone directly if they can do something for you, you have a 50 percent chance that they will say *yes*. When using *how* in your question, such as: *"How can you ensure achieving top marks in your new class subject?"* it takes the focus off whether or not the person *will* achieve top marks, to refocus on *how* to make it happen. Using the word How offers encouragement instead of doubt.

Asking: *How can I have an exceptional performance review that shows I am ready for a promotion?* Will increase your chances of receiving what you are asking for. By using an open-ended question, your mind then creatively seeks out possible options. *How* questions are powerful when used in many situations, at home or at work: *"How* can we move the needle on this initiative?" — you are not asking for permission, you are sharing optimism — of course it will happen as it is implied in your question (by using HOW).

Asking *how* places the emphasis on action and creatively making something work. *How* invites others to brainstorm ideas, to explore, to gather new perspectives and understand issues, to decide on potential actions to achieve the chosen goal. If you want to engage your team, "How soon can we get started?" is an encouraging question, which may also flesh out any concerns to explore before they can begin, so that these can be addressed before moving forwards.

How — an excellent action word, supporting change. Change begins with awareness. If you are totally unaware of an issue, it has to first catch your attention, to move you from being unconscious to being conscious about the topic. Often the news or social media grabs your attention with something that will trigger an emotional reaction — a horrific crash, a group of children stuck in a cave tunnel, an uprising of women standing in solidarity at the Golden Globes or ESPY Awards . . . Our body reacts to pain faster than it does to pleasure, experienced if you accidentally put your hand on the scorching stove before the burner has cooled. *How* can we leverage this natural pain *reaction* and turn it into positive action?

Several social media platforms have been showcasing strong women, and garnering our attention by putting the spotlight on events and unacceptable behaviour that appears unjust, out of integrity or unfair. To help women elevate their confidence, I believe we need to focus energy on this from two angles, from the bottom upwards and from the top downwards, and eventually we will meet in the middle. In organizations, a grassroots initiative triggered by staff can bolster support for change and action, yet unless the top executives are willing to acknowledge or endorse the actions or cause by putting focus and resources towards moving it forward, mostly in my experiences in HR, I have seen these initiatives rarely gain traction.

Women speaking up about mistreatment and injustices are equivalent to the grassroots innovators, and women in the media (female leaders, politicians, founders and business owners, and most recently actresses with a fan base, following or platform) are equivalent to the executive, as they have the support and resources (the media attention, money or sponsorship supporters, relationships and staff) to make powerful change happen. Are you ready to speak out about an issue? To put the spotlight on it and help others rally around a powerful cause? *How* can you use your increased, blossoming confidence for the greater good of your community? What are you willing to take a stand for? (Journal this!) Once you have identified your cause, who are several leaders already publicly supporting this important initiative, and how can you creatively connect with one or two of these champions? Teresa de Grosbois, author of book *Mass Influence: The Habits of the Highly Influential* has excellent lessons to share (in her book as well as her blog, talks and interviews) on evolving your influence and increasing your relationships with influential people.[133]

Developing a win-win reason to connect with an influencer, where there is a clear potential opportunity for collaboration, to be more effective together for the cause than working individually, takes creativity and knowing what is important for them. Put on your Sherlock Holmes hat and invest the time to be a detective, to learn more about them, their public profile, key messages and statements, their background, interests, education, events hosted or attended, where they live and who they spend time with. Identify who you already know that is connected to them, and begin there, finding common ground to lead eventually to a conversation.

Relationships take time to develop (as covered in 4.4 Trust) and trying to push to an outcome will cause unnecessary resistance. I will often ask, "if I could connect you with one particular person who could help you with XYZ (depending on what you have learned is a focus area for your conversation partner), who would that be?" While I may not know the ideal connection personally, I often know someone who does. In addition to your personal network, LinkedIn is a great resource to trigger reminders about who may be a valuable connection in this instance. Once you begin to gather a large number of colleagues, LinkedIn has your first and second level connections shown on the screen, as well as groups that each person follows, offering clues to their interests. The world is connected some say by six degrees of separation[134], how can you leverage this by offering a gift of connection to someone else. They will remember your generosity, and be more than happy to reciprocate. If you are committed to making progress and change happen, connect with others with a similar vision, and move forward leveraging the power of collaboration.

Change happens slowly, especially women's equality, although many examples exist. For example, historically, women's magazines showed extremely slim female models, with some bordering on an unhealthy skinny figure, mostly with Caucasian skin (Twiggy in the 1960s). Today, we are seeing more acceptance and adversity, including models with exotic looks, all skin colours and ages, and models who are closer to the body sizes of real women. In the September 30, 2016, *Forbes* featured an article — "The 'Average' Woman Is Now Size 16 Or 18. Why Do Retailers Keep Failing Her?"[135] sharing that the average women's clothing size stated has now moved from size 14 to size 16. As a full-figured woman myself, I am hoping that retailers will eventually realize that stocking a size 16 (without me seeking out specialty Plus Size stores) will soon be a new norm. The world is changing, and thank you to plus-size model Ashley Graham for taking a stand and developing a lingerie company for more curvy women. (She recently launched a plus-size line with lingerie company Addition Elle at Nordstrom.)

Confidence is felt when you are living authentically and purposefully and your energy resonates. Your clothing is only one way to share more of who you are. When you know that you have well-fitting clothes, and how you can have clothing choices no matter what size you wear (especially foundational underwear) the feeling of stepping out confidently is much easier. Squeezing yourself into a size that does not fit well or flatter your body shape, will only feel good momentarily, and your confidence will wane if you are fidgeting and constantly adjusting your clothing. Find a more flattering fit, as the size label inside the garment will not be noticed by others, while the style and fit will.

With the support of messages on social media, many women are now feeling more confident overall when speaking up about sexual misconduct at work. Where some men in positions of power are still abusing it by asking for sexual favours, *how* can we use the social media revolution to advance the rights of women in the workplace?

How can we encourage more male CEOs and executives to consider women more often for senior roles? *How* can we leverage the statistics we have available to showcase the potential of women to increase profitability? The stated findings of The Peterson Institute showed that having a 30 percent female share in corporate leadership is associated with a one-percentage-point increase in net margin—which translates to a 15 percent increase in profitability for a typical firm. [136] What are some of the numerical evidence factors, measurable results, statistics or percentages that showcase your personal impact, and *how* can you leverage this demonstrated success?

Knowing *how* to quantify your personal productivity results, in clear percentage increases, is important (as outlined in the previous *ACTION STEPS* for the word *value*). Find ways to bring these results into conversations that matter (with your supervisor, team, or sponsor) and include these on your resume and LinkedIn profile (a popular recruiter choice for sourcing qualified candidates). *How* can your resume or profile stand out — with your accomplishments and measurable results showcased? You may not be looking for a new opportunity or job today, however, business changes quickly and keeping your resume current including your successes is a benefit. Technology is evolving and several platforms now search proactively for qualified candidates, and can bring new opportunities to you (passively), so updating your online profile after your career plan review (mentioned in 6.2) will keep your accomplishments fresh.

How can you help other women to advance in their career? According to Catalyst, in their "High Potentials in The Pipeline: Leaders Pay It Forward" report, "women develop other women at higher rates than men do." It was reported that 65 percent of women who received career development support are developing new talent — particularly other women (73 percent) compared to 56 percent of men, of which only 30 percent are developing female talent. [137] Decide today that you will help another woman, either through mentorship or informally in the workplace, or join a women's organization that is advocating for change or bringing women together around a common cause.

Questions beginning with or including *how* are so powerful. HOW can you leverage your success for more purposeful work and fruitful advancement in your career or life? HOW can you help other women advance? I have been a protégée and regularly mentor other women to success, as well as designing and hosting group sessions as Program Chair for several women's Mentorship Group programs. The individual conversations are rich in content and extremely rewarding for both parties. I frequently receive program participant feedback from mentors who thought they would do most of the sharing, then found simplicity in viewing a topic with younger eyes and themselves learned far more than anticipated.

How? A small yet incredibly powerful word!

ACTION STEPS:

1 — Pay attention today to your language and frequency of the word "how". What happens when you use "how" rather than asking for permission — how are your results different? Note observations in your journal.
2 — What are you willing to take a stand for, and how can you build support for this issue tapping into the power of social media?
3 — How can you help other women become more confident?
4 — How can you step into a more confident version of yourself?
5 — From the words highlighted or word concepts shared in this book, which one or two words have been the most impactful for you so far, and what will you do with this knowledge?

Buy another copy of this book and help another woman become more confident, by gifting one to her. Encourage her to download the special report on "Top 10 Tips to Elevate your Confidence at Work", and the What's My Confidence Level Quiz (www. WordsWomenAndWisdom.com) and brainstorm HOW you can support each other.

Join the **WordsWomenAndWisdom.com** movement for more on the Modern Art of Confident Conversations through the Facebook Group (listed in About the Author), and watch for further tips and insights on the topic of confidence. New programs evolving and current learning opportunities are listed on: www.WordsWomenAndWisdom.com

6.6

Just

An interesting word, used more frequently than you might initially realize. In relation to the justice system, often *just* is used when viewing something as fair, or someone "got what they deserved." However, in everyday conversation, the word *just* seems to be used more commonly to excuse a behaviour, or be apologetic. "I *just* wanted to say something, I will do that in *just* a minute, I was *just* wondering . . ." If you want to take back your word power, first you need to be aware if you are using the word *just* in this manner, and ask yourself *why?*

In her article, "Just' Say No," author of The Happiness Hack and speaker Ellen Petry Leanse did an informal experiment which showed that women entrepreneurs use the word *just* five to six times more often than men when introducing their business to another person. As women entrepreneurs who could possibly be fairly confident already, and passionate when explaining their business, using the word *just* in this example was staggering to me! Imagine how frequently it is used in general by women every day? In a recent conversation with Ellen she also shared that "in the years since that article was published, hundreds of women have sent in notes and LinkedIn comments, to share how once they were aware of their language patterns, they became much more confident when they felt they belonged in the room." [138]

If you want to tell another person something, by adding the word *just* into the sentence, it sounds weaker, as though you are unsure of what you are saying, and creates doubt whether what you have to say is worth listening to at all. If you say "I was just wondering . . ." by adding *just* in the middle of the sentence, it makes it sound as though you are apologizing for even asking the question. Asking is how we learn. No one can know every detail about everything, so asking questions is a natural way to learn and grow. An afternoon with young curious children will often be a game of, "why?," "why?," "but why?" (One word to use sparingly is *wondering* when you are speaking with senior leaders, especially men, who may interpret your uncertainty as a weakness.)

Asking the *right* question for the situation is a key way to learn, and an opportunity to showcase the depth of your knowledge, especially in business. To share your wisdom without bragging, ask a relevant question that shows you have considerable depth in that topic. "I understand that one of the critical industry trends currently is XYZ, and I am curious to hear your viewpoint on the possible impact of this trend for our organization?" By sharing that you are aware of the issues and gathering insights, it gives you a better opportunity to bring innovative ideas forth, and invite engaging open conversation.

Posing a relevant question shows insight and when combined with your desire to add value, your chances increase that you will be heard, or asked to lead the "special project" raising your visibility (and credibility). If you complete a successful, innovative project at work — you may be asked to speak at an executive or board meeting about your results, at an industry conference, win an innovation award — all because you showcased your knowledge by asking a *strategic* question. Confidence is like a muscle, it needs to be exercised and developed. Learning to ask strategic questions is an art, to be developed.

Listening carefully to the words that you use can show you so much about your own confidence level. A fully grounded confident woman wouldn't include the extra word *just* in her sentence — she is not apologizing for asking, she is clearly asking. She is not meekly saying something ("I just wanted to say . . ."), she is clearly stating her opinion or concisely making a request. At home, you will have less arguments when you leave the word *just* out of your request, showing strength in your parental authority.

Sometimes uncertainty and doubt show up in the language you use, even when sharing a passion, with extra explanations which dilute your conviction, or show up in your intonation. When I first moved from England to Canada, I was aware instantly of the intonation and sentence structure differences between the two countries. Although Canadians speak English, the same overall language as I did in England (some of the object names are different) *how* we speak is quite different. Listening to a Canadian talking, at the end of their sentence, the last word or two is normally spoken with their voice pitch rising, and the sentence sounds like a question. Whereas "It looks like it will be sunny today" — said with your pitch lowering on the last word (*today)* makes a statement rather than a question. Lowering your pitch signals the end of the sentence. (This could be an unconscious cultural habit, as Canadians are a country of peacemakers who do not go directly to war, we support other countries war efforts globally as peacekeepers. The raised pitch could be heard and interpreted as a willingness to explore opportunities and remain open to discussion.)

In England, the common use of tone is to dip down at the end, signalling that sentence is complete — it is not open for debate or discussion. This was a cultural difference I adjusted to when I first arrived in Canada, as most people here sounded almost apologetic in all their communications. If you are new to your country, or another part of the country, pay close attention to how the "locals" speak, and within your organization. If you want to be a leader in your family, community or organization, learn how the leaders express themselves, and find strong local female role models who inspire you. Watch *how* they communicate their ideas, their tone and the language they use, then decide what you can leverage, while staying true to your authenticity and your personal values. Listen for one or two particular words that you can repeat back to them in conversation to show that you heard their ideas and willingly endorse them.

My aforementioned interview with Jenny Gulamani-Abdulla — BPW Canada President (2016-2018), highlighted one of the words she shared: meritocratic — relating to a meritocracy (a social system in which people's success or power is related to their abilities). [139] BPW advocates for women's equality and empowerment through awareness endeavours, as well as making progressive recommendations to various levels of government, and seeking legislative changes to remove barriers to women's success.

When filling a position, often women are passed over for consideration for senior roles, or as I have also observed in my HR experiences, women are still sometimes considered a risk for leadership position. Seasoned male executives often seek a successor who is like them, to minimize any risk, yet in doing so miss out on developing highly talented women with excellent potential. Minimizing any obvious potential objection by demonstrating measurable success and being aware of jargon, acronyms, speech patterns, and communication styles, does matter. Be "seen" as already in the role by speaking in a similar manner, speaking about critical trends, and dressing for the role that you want (rather than the one you currently have), all helps others endorse you. If your leaders typically wear a jacket in a meeting rather than dressy shirts, begin also wearing a jacket. There are so many flattering styles of women's jackets available today, the main professional guidance is to pick one that has a collar, which creates a formal and <u>authoritative</u> image. Dress for the success you desire! When you look and sound ready to belong in the role, it is easier for you to be selected or promoted.[140]

In a previous organization, a colleague had a very high-pitched voice. When she answered her home telephone, the caller would frequently ask to "talk to her mom," thinking from her pitch that she was a young child. This was her normal high pitch, yet as a supervisor this didn't endorse her as an authority figure at work or reinforce her strength as a leader. Her voice did not resonate deeply and express authority. Although she was very technically competent, she had to work much harder to be recognized as a leader. New team members and clients who interacted with her had to *see* her wisdom and knowledge being applied, they did not simply take her word for it. Once this blind spot was shared with her, and coaching given to practise speaking in a deeper tone, I observed a major shift in how people around her perceived her authority level.

The unmistakable influence of voice pitch on our perception of a speaker suggests that this trait may play a role not only in social interactions, but how we perceive and select political leaders (as printed in *The American Scientist* magazine). The first study to test this proposition, conducted by Cara Tigue and her colleagues at McMaster University, consisted of two experiments. In the first, recordings of spoken remarks by nine US presidents were manipulated digitally to yield higher- and lower-pitched versions of the original remarks. A total of 125 research subjects (sixty women and sixty-four men) were asked to "vote" for the higher- or lower-pitched version of each of the nine pairs. On average, the subjects voted for the lower-pitched voices sixty-seven percent of the time.

In a second experiment, Tigue and her colleagues manipulated six novel male voices, rather than those of known leaders. The forty subjects (twenty women and twenty men) were again presented with pairs of voices and asked to vote for either the higher- or lower-pitched voice of each pair. As in the presidential voices experiment, the subjects preferred candidates with lower-pitched voices; this time the candidates with lower voices were selected sixty-nine percent of the time. [141]

Your pitch matters!

ACTION STEPS:

Much has been written about the Law of Attraction and manifesting. I believe The Universe also knows exactly how to help you determine your purpose, and who to bring into your life to help you on your journey, when you are specific and clear with your words. Notice your confidence level (score yourself one to five) when you use the word just. Pay attention to how others treat you after you add just, into a sentence, and focus on deleting just from your conversations. Bring power back into your sentences: speak confidently in a lower pitch, stating clearly what you want.

Be prepared to give your opinion and take a stand for it. Use fewer and more precise words, to get your point across with more clarity. Speaking fast often indicates being nervous. "Less is more" — in all aspects of life — leveraging the concept of "quality rather than quantity". When there is "space" around your words it invites collaboration rather than leaving no room for others to join the conversation. Raise your vibrational energy with powerful and descriptive language. Others will more often give you what you want because you were clear in your question, and showed the energy of resolution and commitment, using concise and passionate language.

Pay attention to your intonation, especially when you are speaking publicly or want to convey your opinion with strength. Deepen your tone and see how others respond differently.

Note in your journal:

1 — When I noticed and stopped using just, here is what I observed in how others treated me:

2 — When I lowered my voice pitch to resonate deeply, this is how I felt about my confidence:

CHAPTER 7:

Powerful Words at Work — Be Heard!

A male voice is neutral, a female voice is defined as

female — we are seen as a subcategory . . .

— Sally Hogshead, brand strategist, author of

Fascination* and *You are Fascinating

Many of us have created lives that are way too busy. We support everyone else, and have no time or energy left for ourselves, and then wonder why we are exhausted! Many of my clients have found themselves in work roles or organizations that are a mismatch for their skills and abilities, or where their personal values are not in alignment with those of their chosen organization — which is draining their energy! Does this sound familiar? If you are feeling low energy or looking for more insights on this topic, view the resources available which are online at: www.WordsWomenAndWisdom.com Let's explore some key words relating to elevating your confidence at work:

7.1

Focus

Using focus we gain traction towards reaching a result, a work project or a creative endeavour, leveraging a concentration of energy. While writing this book and expanding my creative genius, I find my best writing time is between 5:20 and 6:30 am, after twenty minutes of meditation (and a few minutes of journaling), then from eight to ten am daily. By journaling what occurred the day before, being grateful and reflecting on what has surfaced during my meditation, my writing seems to flow effortlessly, to be grounded in truth, and feels energetically aligned. Most likely I feel the connection to universal energy that was made in my meditation being drawn into this writing. I feel "in flow" and fully focused when I am writing early in the morning before anyone else is awake, or prior to opening email and being distracted with external messages.

When you focus a magnifying glass onto dried grass, the combination of the sun angled with the lens has the power to create a fire. When an earthquake begins, a powerful eruption is called the "focus point" in geology. Where light rays converge with the sun, a rainbow appears — all powerful examples of what happens during a concentration of energy or *focus* — creating powerful results. In business especially, by sharing with others where you are putting your focus, you help them understand your priorities. By sharing with a colleague, "my focus is building a trusted relationship with you," it helps others understand what to expect — learn how you will take action and appreciate your behaviour — based on what you consider to be important. With the awareness that you are focussing your attention on a special project, they will be less likely to ask you to take on other tasks, as they anticipate you will likely decline, as your stated focus is currently elsewhere. By sharing your focus areas, you naturally have to say *no* to other things less frequently, as others appreciate your dedication, and often don't even ask . . .

Today we have messages coming through so many mediums: our cell phones, email and intranet options, social media and Twitter, text messages, and Facebook Messenger alerts. With so many potential distractions everywhere, having the resilience to retain our focus is increasingly challenging. Everywhere we look we are bombarded with advertising, and messages clamouring for our attention. To complete something, you need an exceptionally strong purpose and clear focus, *why* the completion of your project or task is critical, which imitates a tractor beam of light pulling you in. This book has been my focus project over the past year, compelling me to share my learnings from working with thousands of women over a period of many years. While it was originally conceived in January 2017, I believe the world is now ready to embrace a new wave of change — helping women have the words and language concepts to fuel their desire to be heard, and build the confidence to refuse to accept anything less than respect.

Helping women flourish in business is a passion for me. Every day I hear from women asking for guidance through the mentorship programs which I chair, after my talks and public speaking, when coaching (in groups and one on one with VIP clients). Women want to "be more confident, to know how to ask for what they want and get it, and be recognized for achieving clearly articulated, positive results." Their gratitude after a coaching conversation has shown how important it is for more women to understand how to leverage their words, which guided the selection of the forty words and concepts shared in this book. I have seen hundreds of women gain enough confidence through using more powerful language to ask for a raise, request an assistant, quit their job and follow their dreams, leave an unsatisfying relationship, secure a promotion, or articulate their business vision with clarity — the ripple effect is massive!

That impact, a bigger *why*, is fuelling my desire to "uplift the spirit of humanity," creating the compelling reason for my focus when writing this book. With a big project, allow a reasonable timeline to complete it, and then add 25 percent extra time (to allow for unexpected surprises to come up, to learn new technology or industry quirks, to allow time for completing your best work), especially if you need to engage others around you, and work your request into their calendars. Having sub-categories of concurrent activities running at the same time, all coming together is similar to operating different trains on lines that all eventually merge and lead to one central station.

All these elements are channelling your energy to a central point, to create success. (I realize now that I am at the end of this book-writing project that my preferred writing style is to tap into early morning downloads of thoughts that are important to include, and yet adding 25 percent extra time did not allow for the creativity I needed for this book to feel "complete." It also did not take into consideration that without a firm completion timeline it would be harder to reserve time with an editor, for formatting help, and the various other elements to move to the finished publication point.)

Concentrated energy is required to launch a rocket into space, a powerful thrust in order to burst through the earth's gravity field. What is the rocket fuel, the powerful purpose that will support *your focus* to finish a project, and what does the finished outcome look like? How will you measure your success? Invest time at the beginning of the idea, to figure out why anyone would care about it, what they will do when they know about it, and how will you know when it is finished? (Many of the questions I asked myself as I embarked on the journey of writing this book.)

When we say we are "focused" on something, our brains also shut off new thoughts, and allow the purity of the creative energy to flow. Mihaly Csikszentmihalyi a Hungarian-American psychologist (distinguished professor of psychology and management at Claremont Graduate University) recognized and named the psychological concept of "flow, a highly focused mental state." Csikszentmihalyi (pronounced "Cheeks send me high!") describes "8 Characteristics of Flow":

1. Complete concentration on the task.
2. Clarity of goals and reward in mind and immediate feedback.
3. Transformation of time (speeding up/slowing down of time).
4. The experience is intrinsically rewarding, has an end itself.
5. Effortlessness and ease.
6. There is a balance between challenge and skills.
7. Actions and awareness are merged, losing self-conscious rumination.
8. There is a feeling of control over the task.[142]

The best moments in our lives are not the passive,

receptive, relaxing times . . .

The best moments usually occur if a person's body or

mind is stretched

to its limits in a voluntary effort to accomplish

something difficult and worthwhile.

— Mihaly Csikszentmihalyi

In his book *DRIVE: The Surprising Truth About What Motivates Us,* author Daniel H. Pink shares research which shows that people need three things to flourish at work: autonomy, mastery, and purpose. Doing your best work will be easier if you can be *in flow* for large portions of your day. If you feel you are being micromanaged, don't understand how your role contributes to the broader organizational purpose, or lack interesting and challenging work, this will drain your energy. Constant interruptions drain energy while you struggle to get back to where you were before the loss of your concentration. Pink shares how happy employees who are engaged with their organization, eagerly contribute new ideas, which is often the missing value an organization cannot tap into — *innovation energy.*

Competition is rampant in business, hence having employees who are strongly aligned with the values of the organization, who willingly work overtime or bring a new idea forth, is an important competitive advantage. When employees leave an organization of their own accord, whether they are disengaged or unhappy (with the overall fit, their leader, with their role or disrespect of their values) or when their contribution is not appreciated, "turnover" costs are significant. Often a staff resignation often comes as a surprise creating chaos. Rarely is a replacement fully trained and waiting in the wings ready to step into the role of the incumbent immediately.

When employees leave, they take their insights with them about how internal processes worked, valuable customer relationships, trusted connections with colleagues — all information that could possibility be shared with their next organization, impacting the competitive advantage for the previous firm. Their departure causes a flurry of unexpected activity, to find a replacement worker to fill that gap; to advertise the position, short-list and interview candidates, host reference checks, to prepare an offer of employment (or a contract for a temporary worker) to orient them to the culture and operational processes, to integrate with other staff or clients. All that wasted energy is part of the cost of turnover! Employee retention is a success strategy regardless of economic factors and business cycles.

As mentioned, when I worked with a compensation consulting firm back in the 1990s, each year their salary survey data identified that out of a list of ten topics, there were two items that staff wanted the most: to be paid a fair salary, and have interesting and challenging work.[143] When employees are paid fair wages, they move from the mindset of scarcity to one of abundance — they do not spend hours each day stressing about being underpaid — they are freed up to be as creative as possible.[144] This engaged state fosters creativity and the willingness to share ideas, as there is a sense of reciprocity — I work hard for you and I am fairly rewarded. You provide me with interesting and challenging work, and in my moments of being *in flow* brilliant ideas often surface, which you encourage me to bring forth, sharing innovation through some of my greatest ideas.

While working in a flow state often taps into your brilliance, it is worth stopping to take time to smell the roses in life by taking regular breaks of concentration. After a sixty-minute period of focus, take a short break and clear your mind, as Mark Waldman, author of *NeuroWisdom*, suggests.[145] If you are a baby boomer you may remember back in the early 1960s when the toy Etch A Sketch was introduced, with the red border and looking like a television screen with a dial knob on each lower corner? It was like magic to have the opportunity to draw with lines through the black aluminum powder coated screen, with a stylus controlled by two knobs, seeing your artwork come to life.

When you were finished with that picture, you simply shook it and erased it, generating a fresh drawing screen, which created endless fun without pencils and paper. [146] It was an intriguing toy for a young artistic mind, also to teach that anything is possible, if you don't like the picture of your life, shake it up and change it! Create a new picture.

Women have frequently been featured as effective at multitasking, cradling a baby balanced on one hip, stirring a pot on the stove with one hand and a phone cradled in the neck, juggling multiple tasks at once. However, author of *Your Brain At Work*, David Rock, director of the NeuroLeadership Institute, has a different view of multitasking, based on brain science. After interviews with thirty leading neuroscientists from all over the world and reviewing more than three hundred research papers, he shares that making decisions and solving problems relies heavily on a region of the brain called the prefrontal cortex.

According to Rock, there are five main mental processes relevant to getting work done: understanding, decision-making, recalling, memorizing, and inhibiting. Each process involves manipulations of billions of neurological circuits, and here's the key: one operation must finish before another can begin.[147] Queens of multitasking take note! Focus is a powerful tool when we use it well. When you split your focus, everything is diluted, similar to adding cranberry juice to a glass of soda, it shifts from deep red to pale pink, creating a watered-down lame drink. Focus on one task at a time for full-strength results.

ACTION STEPS:

Invest time on a Sunday evening to plan out your week, and determine your priorities or focus areas for the coming week, so that you are ready to begin work as soon as you arrive on Monday — with your plan already prepared.[148] Put those high priority areas that require a block of "focus time" in your calendar first, so everything else has to fit around your items already in there. Sounds easy so far, right? Your priorities and focus areas go in first. (Stephen Coveys "Big Rocks" concept.)[149]

Plan your concentrated time around when you work the best, your peak energy cycles. If you are an early riser, put your most important priority item in the calendar first. If that is your health, block that time for a run, a walk or heading to the gym, depending on your goals. On Monday morning, arriving at your office or place of work, do not open up your email as the first thing you do, if you have planned for your project time from eight to ten am. Your full focus is on your priority project, with your cell phone on "airplane mode," and your office telephone on "Do Not Disturb" — dedicate time towards your focus area — no excuses! Which do you choose: excuses or results?

After ten am, open your email. You may find multiple requests for your time from different people requiring something from you, which would have distracted you from your prioritized tasks, yet these are generally not urgent. If it was truly an urgent request, they would likely have sent a text message, telephoned you, or simply walked down the hall and asked you in person. (Different organizations each have different cultures and expectations for acceptable "response time" to a request sent via email.)

To ensure that your requests are responded to in a timely manner, choose your request method to fit your urgency level. Email is a one-way communication. If you want to ensure the other person received it (and read it) always include a question they need to respond to, and indicate when you need their reply by in the email subject line. For urgent matters, say "URGENT, reply requested" in the email subject line and mark it with a priority flag when you send it, for tracking your sent messages. If your technology allows, include a "read receipt" to encourage your recipient to confirm they have received and read your note. Most importantly, pose a question requiring a response, to see how quickly the recipient replies. Remember to update the subject line so that it clearly identifies the current status or action required (vs. forwarding and replying with no updates).

Identify one project that has a bigger impact than solely your own benefit — something you want to take a stand for, or an injustice you see in the world that you can no longer ignore. Step into solving an important issue that has a massive ripple effect, and watch what happens to your focus. If you are working on your passion project, you will easily slip into "the flow state" which Csikszentmihalyi describes. What critical task deserves your full focus right now, to complete it?

Whether you are learning, writing, or researching, set a "break alarm" between activities, to catch your breath and help your brain switch gears, so that you can give the next item your full focus. With larger projects, break it down into manageable chunks and take regular breaks to give your billions of neurological circuits' room to breathe before moving to the next piece. If focus is a challenge, find yourself an "accountability partner" to help keep you (and her) on track with encouragement and regular progress updates.

What actions can you develop new habits around, which will increase your focus? Commit to these in your journal, because putting your own needs first matters.

7.2

Prioritize

I found it interesting exploring this word and finding it was first recorded in 1965 to 1970, not that long ago. In Latin history the word *pre* (*meaning earlier, before, in front of*) is a root of many words including *prefer, prepare, preliminary, prejudice*, and *premium* — all things that come first. Also, we have *pro* (Greek and Latin history: meaning *before, in front of, for*, or *forward*) a prediction of what will happen; *prologue* — a passage before the main part; *prophet* — a person who foretells the future. Words beginning with *pro* include *program, proposal, provoke, propose*, and *proceed* — all words looking at a future event or idea. The word *prioritize* combines both of these in a modern way — as you put *first* on your list of action items that which is most important for you (the *i* in prioritize).

If you have trouble prioritizing, reflect and explore the deeper "why." Are you doing something because it is important to you, or because it is important to someone else? Sit quietly and take a few deep breaths, then check in with your gut (and your body) and feel if this is a heart-based decision, or made from your head from "thinking things through." How you feel about the activity is an important indicator. Does the activity make you feel alive, or give you knots in your stomach — pay attention to those messages from your body.

For any potential applicants and job seekers, it is especially important to listen to your gut, and understand your personal character strengths and values first, and then look for organizations and roles that align with your values. Find a role where you bring your natural gifts to light, and receive a fair wage for doing what you naturally love to do anyway. When job-hunting, *prioritize* your job search by finding organizations which demonstrate your values. When you feel pushed into a situation where your actions don't align with your personal values, that's when you will feel out of sorts — things feel wrong, unsettled, and you cannot specifically put your finger on why — causing a feeling of unease or unhappiness.

If you base decision making on your personal values and your priorities, your confidence level will significantly increase. Making decisions becomes easier, as you have a sense of inner peace and knowing that you have made the best choice possible for yourself in that situation, with your important projects and activities identified first, before anyone else tries to add items to your calendar.

Women often tend to want to please everyone, so saying *no* or putting ourselves first can be a challenge. At the beginning of this book I shared the importance of creating space, so that you can take back control of your time. Yes — there, I said it . . . "Take back control of your calendar and your time!" For some of you it may seem like an insurmountable task, and yet I know it is possible. How? I have done it myself!

When I gave birth to our son Alex in 1995, immediately he was treated for bilirubin (newborn jaundice) and at age six-months we learned that he would experience developmental delays that later evolved into health challenges, which placed additional stress on our lives. At one year old, he began having grand-mal seizures, and after a discovery MRI (magnetic resonance imaging) his family doctor began referring him to pediatric specialists. (His five experts ensured the best treatment options were identified to take into account the complex overlaps with his health issues.)

With his unusual developmental issues, using a values-based prioritizing approach supports decisions to help Alex (age twenty-three at time of writing) access the best programs available to him, and provide access to extra-curricular activities for a robust life. Alex has support workers from several special needs agencies and programs who expand his development and ensure his safety. Similar to a student's annual individual progression plan, Alex also has priority areas for his adult programming, measuring both development and life enjoyment, with clear outcome measures (aligned to funding his programs).

As his mum, one of my goals is to have him both happy and healthy, as well as being a contributing member of society, despite his special needs status. In early 2016, an event happened which made my heart sing. Alex saw an Operation Smile advertisement on television, showing the results of volunteer surgeons who had transformed the faces of children with cleft lip (or palate) surgery, so they could smile again. He came running into the kitchen to ask me to "get a credit card for him." I asked him what he needed it for. "I want to buy a child a smile!" he shared eagerly.

Confused, I asked him to tell me more. He took my hand and pulled me into the living room to show me the fundraising telethon he had been watching. I was extremely touched, surprised, and delighted at his response and desire to help another child. He was impatient waiting to receive a credit card of his own, as applications seemed to take a long time for processing. So he decided to sell a few of his paintings to raise money to "buy a smile" instead. Helping others even less fortunate than himself was a priority in alignment with his value of *generosity*.

So far Alex has helped four children to have new smiles, with surgery transforming their lives (as they are often teased or hidden away and not accepted by others). I am so proud of his generous soul, his ideas and his hard work, giving selflessly. Helping others is his priority and overcoming obstacles has been a recurring theme for Alex. After being told by a medical specialist he would likely never walk, he persevered until he was two and a half years old and could walk slowly on his own. Overcoming his disabilities and walking independently was his focus and a priority for me too, to watch him flourish.

A few years after divorcing Alex's father in 2000, I fell in love with a wonderful, kind man who had three teenagers (then ages fifteen, seventeen, and nineteen), and two years later we married. When we combined our families together in our new home, my world got a lot more complex co-managing a household of six (plus the shared parenting arrangements coordinating Alex's time spent at his Dad's house). During that era I was also operating my own HR consulting firm for five of those years, while volunteering with the local HR Association . . . *I had nothing going on in my world!*

Today, I have a better appreciation of Alex's special needs, liaising with his five adult specialists and various appointments to help him have the best medical options and lifestyle. Now operating two business ventures (Alex's Amazing Art and my own business Flourish!) and now Women & Wisdom Media, I continue to juggle multiple calendar needs and evolve my skills to effectively *prioritize* my important activities and co-parenting responsibilities.

As Alex grew, he required extra supports, and I was his primary special-needs advocate. I learned how language plays an integral role in asking for what we want, and how this helps us prioritize our needs while working around the perceptions of others. Often, I experienced concern and confusion when exploring enrolling Alex into regular extra-curricular classes. On one occasion I enrolled him in a children's music class, which he eagerly attended. The instructor was unfortunately not trained in managing special needs students. Even though I attended the class to help him engage with the content and practise the instructions being shared, clearly she found his needs too disruptive for the rest of the small group. (Later when we connected with Special Olympics Calgary and enrolled in programs and activities that are designed to accommodate all types of disabilities, he was accepted and welcomed.)

One of my priorities is to ensure that no matter what Alex's capabilities are, he achieves his potential to the maximum possible. This year he enrolled in special needs Toastmasters training, with a plan to share his compassionate message with younger children that "anyone can make a difference, no matter what their circumstances are". Way to go, Alex! Things take more time with a special-needs son. To enroll Alex in a class required talking personally to the instructor to confirm a supportive environment for him. To have an MRI, he needed the anesthesiologist for sedation, as he couldn't lie still enough for a clear image. Rebooking a client meeting following an impromptu seizure and hospital visit — all needed moment-by-moment reprioritization. My best anchors guiding my prioritization decisions are my values.

My values are *evolution* (a love of learning) *creativity* (expanding through possibility and potential) and *compassion* (a strong service orientation) combined with *excellence* (high quality and visually balanced) in all things. When you have clear values, you can prioritize more effectively, have less mind chatter (the story of what you could have done differently) and be more purposeful in harmony with your environment.

One of my favourite previous jobs was working with Minerva Technology, where I happily worked for fifteen years of my career. My values aligned nicely with the mission of that high-tech start-up organization, where I gradually advanced from administration and office manager to director of HR (while they grew from six staff members to 250 in multiple locations). Minerva was an information technology firm, in an industry that was constantly evolving (IT and software development in the mid-1980s changed rapidly) which meant constant expansion and growth (meeting my *evolution* value). The team created custom computer software and later moved into outsourced IT services, and as the organization grew each new internal process required developing and building (meeting my value of *creativity*). The services of the team involved helping clients automate their work using technology solutions to capture and process data. This creative and service-oriented environment was an excellent match for my values — with an energy of momentum and growth. (Minerva also won a Canada Award for Business Excellence in the Small Business Category in 1991, another alignment with my value of *excellence*).

My values of *compassion* (hiring a talented team with a strong service orientation) combined with *excellence* (delivering high quality and practical programs and HR solutions) all connected for a purposeful and impactful role. Eventually Minerva was purchased by a much larger organization, which didn't have the same focus on being nimble and innovative. It felt as though any change initiative moved like molasses . . . Sticky, thick and slow — not a match for me any longer.

When you are clear on your values, it is so much easier to prioritize and see new opportunities emerging. Ask yourself how this new task, activity or request fits for you — how it either connects with your values — or takes you further away from them.

One of my leading values is also *freedom*. For me to be working within a larger organization where innovation was slow and cumbersome was not a good fit. Working in an organization where layers of bureaucracy existed, I slowly felt stifled and the energy around me at work was heavy and uninspiring.

Hence my HR consulting firm was born, giving me the *freedom* to work with customers with similar values, who enjoyed high service levels and *excellence* in our projects together. It became much easier to prioritize, to start building a new venture that nourished my soul. I attracted clients who valued my creativity and HR problem-solving, and my ability to build talent management and staff development programs, leading to my current expertise areas: coaching and mentoring female leaders, professionals, and entrepreneurial women.

Often women have difficulty saying *no* to a boss who has unreasonable deadlines. I recommend not sharing that thought exactly with your boss, using the word "unreasonable," since this is subjective . . . Your supervisor may have different priorities and no plans after work when they dump a task on your desk at five pm, demanding it "must be done today." You may have a family event planned that evening, or as I had, a regular pick-up time for daycare to collect my son before the facility closed. So how can you remain assertive politely and stand your ground when your priorities are in conflict?

Here is what I have said, which was received as respectful. "Hmmm . . . That new last-minute request will be a challenge to fully complete, and I already have an appointment this evening. If I am unable to complete it in full by the deadline you originally requested, what are *your* other choices?" By phrasing it in this manner, you have not refused to do the task, merely shared that the fact is the request is "last minute," and indicated your lack of availability. Often I have counselled a stressed employee on conversations to have with their manager, yet rarely have I heard about a manager (except one who had a passive-aggressive personality) insisting that the project be completed or the employee would be fired. Speak up regarding your needs!

If your priority is your family time, it makes it easier by visualizing enjoying time that evening and how that nourishes your soul, rather than agreeing (with feelings of frustration) to staying at work late. The caveat here is to keep the conversation open. Your boss may then share their reason why it is an emergency request. If it is connected to a death or accident for example, the circumstances may change your viewpoint or your willingness to stay late.

If you choose to stay late, you are setting a dangerous precedent that you will likely always be available, if you simply accepted the request without using the statement above. If you are having a performance review the next week and your top priority is getting promoted, that value for career advancement over family will help you align your priorities. I recommend that you have a conversation with your supervisor regarding workload and priorities for the entire team or department and inquire "how can something like this be handled differently in the future?" once the immediate request has been fulfilled. If you make an exception by staying late, you don't want a lack of conversation about this request being an issue to be assumed as a new acceptable norm. Silence is seen as acceptance in most cases — so speak up!

If the company has a mission statement on the reception wall stating that "we value our employees and their family time" (or something similar) the after-hours work request is in conflict with the mission and values for the organization if you are treated without respect. Those values need to be upheld in all actions, processes, systems, and decisions, in order to be lived authentically. Company values are the guide posts for all decisions made at work, just as your personal values guide your decisions.

If you are a supervisor who is reading this and setting your team's priorities, be willing to accept a longer delivery timeline, or a scaled back element of the project, or recognize you may need to add more staff or resources to get the task or project completed urgently. You may choose to use a version of the statement I recommended with your leader, who may have delegated you the task. Help her or him stay focused on aligning work tasks with your company values too, by using respectful ways to realign requests with the values the organization has identified. When senior leaders in the organization role model the values of the firm, it helps staff see how to live those values by their own example.

Or you may say "based on the data needed for a solid decision on this matter, it will take a little longer to deliver the desired results. When is the latest that I can have this back to you?" Often a report is not going actually to be looked at until a meeting the following week, giving you a little more time to work on providing an excellent outcome rather than one that may be rushed, or include errors leading to a bad decision being made. "When is it *really* needed by?" is also a direct and specific question that you can follow the first request with if the answer to it has come back "ASAP!" I have often secured a later delivery date for a task with that last question . . .

Remember, you always have a choice in how you prioritize your time. Having three to four big goals for the year certainly helps calendar in YOUR priority areas FIRST in your home calendar. Fill in blocks of time for those activities that are important to you first, before the smaller and less important tasks fill up your plate. You have likely heard the expression, "the tasks will expand to fill the time available" — so set your available time blocks for priority areas first. As the airline safety demonstration shares, "put your own oxygen mask on first BEFORE helping others." If you have no air, or are trying to give from an empty fuel tank, your journey will be hard work and draining, rather than joyful and feeling alive. Your priorities matter!

ACTION STEPS:

Do you know your values yet? As mentioned previously, I highly recommend taking Dr. Martin Seligman's VIA assessment. The Happiness Institute has a well-researched and validated free (for the online assessment) tool identifying Character Strengths. When I explore these with my clients after they take the assessment, the results are very much worded like values. [150] *(Click the gold button to begin the assessment, and see your top twenty-four strengths pop up online for you to save and refer to.) Print your results and use these to anchor your actions and decisions in life (much like a ship anchor stops a boat floating away with the tide). Live these values in all that you do, and step into a higher level of alignment with your "why." Reflect back over the past few weeks on things that have annoyed you, or when you felt in a conflict. Consider each circumstance, and determine how "living in alignment with your values" can guide you to making a better choice next time.*

Prepare several phrases in advance that you can use at work for those short timeline requests, and practise saying them in your home environment first, until they roll off your tongue easily. If last-minute requests from your boss are a common occurrence, proactively schedule a meeting to review your workload and business priorities to ensure what is being requested can fit into a regular workday.

If there is too much work for one person, discuss the extra resources needed to support you (additional temporary support, a laptop to be able to work remotely, longer timelines or a smaller project scope, etc.). Scale back the project by advising what is possible, or if your skills or knowledge need deepening to be efficient, ask for the training, coaching or mentoring needed at that meeting.

What resources or changes do you need, in order to prioritize and complete your workload more effectively? What benefit would your company receive also by funding these resources? What additional value could you bring if they invested in your requests? List your ASKs and ACTIONS in your journal to prepare for this discussion, developing the Return on Investment (ROI) they will receive when you are working more effectively.

7.3

Delegate — Verb (used with object) Delegated, delegating

While this word is also used as a noun — to describe "a person designated to act for or represent another or others; deputy; representative, as in a political convention," this chapter explores its use as a verb: "To appoint (a person) as deputy or representative, to commit (powers, functions, etc.) to another as agent or deputy."[151]

Whether you are a newly promoted supervisor, a parent, or volunteer leader, or simply feeling overwhelmed, one of your most powerful words and principles to use effectively is to *delegate*. I have known many leaders who are reluctant to delegate activities to their team members. In order for you to move up your own career ladder into a more senior role, you need to delegate effectively. When you have learned the art of completing the work through other people, you can more easily see which of your team members is ready to move into your role next. Having your successor ready enables you to move up . . .

Through my years in HR, I learned that no one gets promoted if they have not already proven that they are capable of doing their current job proficiently. In succession planning conversations in larger firms, typically leaders consider if the person is "ready, willing, and able" to move up. Ready — because they have proven themselves to be capable. Willing — they are already volunteering for special projects, are asking about the additional skills needed to be promoted. Able — they are showing clear measurable results, and have the skills or knowledge for success — people visualize the successor already in the new role.

Assert your authority at work with a strong first impression, before you begin delegating. Understand the purpose and impact of completing the job, and the successful outcome or measure for each project or key task. When delegating, share the "ideal end-state" and any critical steps that must be followed, then open the conversation with your team member/s to see how she/he can work independently to achieve the desired outcome, using their knowledge and creativity. Micromanaging diminishes an empowered employee. Give them the opportunity to show you they are capable and independent. Describe clear and concise outcomes and the timeline for completion, then step back and empower your staff member, rather than hovering over his or her shoulder or asking for a daily update.

Decide if you are the only one who can attend every meeting. According to an article in *The Muse*, 35 percent of time is spent in meetings, and if you are in upper management it could be as high as 50 percent, while 67 percent of executives consider meetings to be "unproductive." The reasons for this vary, including remote connections lacking engagement, multitasking and a lack of planned structure. To leverage your time more effectively and efficiently, ensure your meetings do not have these issues. Using video conference reduces the likelihood of multitasking from 57 percent to just 4 percent. [152] A *Harvard Business Review* article reports that "On average, senior executives devote more than two days every week to meetings involving three or more coworkers, and 15 percent of an organization's collective time is spent in meetings—a percentage that has increased every year since 2008." [153]

Identify someone on your team who could attend on your behalf and bring back the notes or highlights of action items. Select the meetings that you feel you have a critical and valuable contribution to make or offer the best opportunity to showcase your knowledge. Prioritizing and delegating go hand-in-hand for new leaders to master, in order to focus on moving from the urgent activities to the important and strategic ones that have long term positive impact.

If you are newly promoted, ask your leader to announce your promotion. It is important for peers to hear the announcement directly from her or him and share what responsibility your role now includes. When your leader sets you up for success as the new team leader or manager, it makes it easier for you to delegate to someone who was previously a peer at the same level. (The "baton of authority" is officially passed to you.) Ensure that you clearly understand your new position metrics, which key measures show that your team is on track and meeting expectations, and how will your success in the new role be personally measured. When you have clarity on the specific expectations your leader has, it provides an end-state for you to work backwards from, to determine the individual steps needed to achieve the desired results.

Many of my client-coaching conversations involve women who were blind-sided during a performance review, by finding out they did not have clarity and agreement on what success looked like from the outset. Ask your leader for guidance (or confirmation if you develop the metrics) as you engage in your new role. It is also important to shift from completing tasks to investing in relationships, as you will often have cross-functional team projects and each department's actions impact another, requiring a collaborative approach. Which relationships do you need to build first with your new peer group, who are the early adopters of change, or those who are the informal leaders or influencers?

As you move from being an individual contributor to leading a small group or team, the skills for effective management may be new for you, and the middle-manager role can be a challenging one. When you are asked to implement a change by the executive team, you may not have been involved in any of the discussions about the issues or had any input on the solutions that may work best, yet now you are expected to deliver the update to your team and rally the troops around the new process.

Be prepared for your team to be hesitant about any change. As mentioned, the amygdala in the brain resists change! As a new process or program is shared with you, ensure you fully understand the business rationale or the "why" behind the change, for easier explanation and adoption by your team. Find out if the leaders are open to receiving feedback as the new process or program is designed or implemented. If this is the defined new norm, avoid making any promises to your team that you may be able to sway the decision whether or not to adopt the new way, to avoid getting caught in the middle of the two groups (your leadership team and your staff).

When delegating to your team, one of the most powerful perspectives is customer centricity. This term is used to describe putting the customer first in every decision made about how the organization or team will operate. When customers are placed as prime importance and the organizational values are clear and being lived, it is easier for your team (especially if they are front line staff directly in contact with the customer) to decide how to resolve an issue quickly themselves. Asking for your advice on small issues can often create bottlenecks, so give your staff the accountability and the authority to determine the best customer solution.

If your new staff are coming to you with small issues for guidance, gradually empower them to come to you with potential solutions, not only problems they experience. At one time in my career, I led a team of thirteen staff. As a new manager, I was initially frustrated by feeling that my office had a revolving door, with a constant flow of problems to deal with. I gradually helped my team think creatively and identify a few potential solutions before they came to me for advice, and encouraged each of them to share their ideas first. "Mary, what you have shared is an issue if not dealt with now. What are some of your ideas to address it?" After Mary shares her ideas, if one seems feasible, commend her! "That is a good idea of yours — let me know how it works." She will be more accountable for implementing and monitoring the success of *her* idea than if you had told her how to fix the issue . . .

Give Mary three opportunities to make suggestions for solutions, to cultivate creativity. If you feel the action she is suggesting will be unsafe or extremely costly, or might aggravate the client situation further, make your suggestion, without any judgement of her ideas. "Thank you for sharing your ideas, it's very valuable to understand your thinking on this. Have we considered the option of X (share your solution) as it offers (share why your idea would work) as an outcome? Can we try this first, and let me know how it works." She will likely feel her ideas were validated and heard, and she knows she can bring forth future ideas as you are creating a safe environment for discussion.

Women leaders have an advantage as we foster a nurturing and collaborative work environment, which often enables innovation and better solutions for the long-term success of the team. In my experience, female leaders frequently seek consensus or agreement while carefully considering the impact of change on the related parties before moving forwards, which often ends up with an easier implementation (as others have already bought-in to the idea).

As a new team leader, having a monthly staff meeting (or weekly if you are working on large projects with tight or critical timelines) has the benefit for sharing information once with the entire team, rather than individual discussions and repetitive one-on-one time-consuming conversations. In your regular meetings, focus on the positive topics first, to leverage the positive energy of accomplishment. Ask "What is working really well on this project right now?" then, "How could things be even better?" to leverage an Appreciative Inquiry style approach *(developed by David Cooperrider and his associates at Case Western Reserve University School of Management)*.[154]Ensure that the time together in meetings is lively and is used wisely, by providing any update that does not require discussion or brainstorming to be shared via email ahead of time, and only list the collaborative topics requiring group thinking and discussion to appear on the agenda.

Always have a written meeting agenda or a clear outcome identified, one shared in advance with the attendees, or do not have a meeting! Everyone's time is precious, so only invite those to attend who have an essential contribution to make, or you wish to build a strong relationship with. When a one-way communication works, share the message via email and include a question that requires a reply (to demonstrate the recipient has read it). When you anticipate a mood of conflict or upset on a particular topic, ask your team to send you their questions before the meeting, so that you can be as prepared as possible to address issues or concerns while thinking calmly prior to the meeting. This approach also gives you an idea who are your supporters and early adopters and who may be upset or may challenge the topic in the meeting.

Set your meetings for just fifteen minutes and have them standing up whenever possible. Melissa Dahl of *New York Magazine* recently wrote that standing-up meetings can reduce meeting time by 34 percent.[155] This concept encourages everyone to be brief and on their toes with concise sharing of their ideas. It keeps the energy up and sets the tone that you are leading your team in a new way. You are action oriented and getting things done! (Watch how people fidget in long meetings, get really comfortable and relaxed in their chairs and do not contribute except with a complaint, or yawning starts . . .) If you want to stand out and be noticed for a promotion, achieving results and being innovative and productive are the best ways to do so. Create some buzz about how your team achieves their results while having fun too, and then showcase your results to your leader.

If a discussion is getting emotionally sidetracked in a meeting, take charge as the leader and direct a question to the person getting upset. Our brains switch gears and stop when considering the answer to a new question posed. This technique can create an opportunity for a deep breath and create a space for you to reassert leadership of the meeting. Upsets or in-fighting in group meetings is awkward for everyone, and a sure way to lose the respect of your team — fast. If the heat continues with one particular individual, let them know that, "Clearly, we have touched on something that is important to you, and I do want to hear your perspective. However, so that we can honour everyone's time and our agenda, let's book a separate one-on-one meeting where I can *fully* understand your thoughts on this topic." Take the discussion offline and outside the bigger meeting, so one person's view does not inflame the entire team, while demonstrating your leadership strength and focus. Having a standard set of agenda items that specifically link back to your team's top three priorities will reduce meeting preparation time and maintain everyone's focus on the most important discussion points.

Empower yourself by delegating — to free up your time. Empower your team by giving them the authority to solve a customer issue or complaint by jointly identifying a few relevant options, clearly identifying first when you would like an issue escalated to you. Once you are comfortable in the role and showing success at the new level, ask your leader which of your particular skills and abilities most contributed to your promotion. Understand which new skills are the most important to enhance next to continue your growth and development. Delegating enables growth while empowering others — a win-win!

You may initially think you need a gentler style of delegating a task to your five-year old than to a staff member. Perhaps or perhaps not . . . One of the best methods I learned managing a household with four children was not to even say the word "delegate". Being factual about the importance of completing the task by the time required, while explaining how it would contribute to the good of the whole household and other family members, worked well. Your request is more readily received if the person understands why it needs to be done. Giving an instruction in isolation without any context makes it more challenging for the recipient to get excited about completing the task, depending whether they see it as a learning opportunity, or a chore . . . *Chore* is another word I encourage you to eliminate and instead use *activity* (*chore definition: a hard or unpleasant task, a small routine task*[156]). Rarely does anyone want to do anything labelled *a chore*.

For your five-year old, your request may sound like this: "Mary, I see that you love your dog and like seeing her happy and playful, which makes you feel happy too. Having clean food bowls is important, and I am sure she would be much happier if they were clean, which only takes a few minutes to wash. Let's clean them now and help her be happy." For busy parents, I know that took a few more sentences to explain *what* we needed, *why* it needs to occur, the *impact* it makes, and *how* you will feel — however, it is worth investing the extra few minutes! It takes considerably more time to soothe an upset five-year old, than it does to ask with clarity and purpose the first time. The second time you can ask a shorter question: "Are your dog's bowls clean and making her happy?" is all that is needed.

Household maintenance impacts everyone, and I believe it is a shared responsibility. In Sheryl Sandberg's research for her book *Lean In*, she found that when a husband and wife both work — the mother does 40 percent more childcare and 30 percent more housework. Ladies, it is time for change! You will receive help if you ask for it, and start early by asking each child to contribute to necessary household tasks, and recognize this is an important part of being a family. We show love in many ways, and Mum having time alone in the bathtub with candles and music for relaxation time (or time for meditation in peace) is a delicious treat. Showing respect for each other using assertive yet inclusive conversation promotes a family atmosphere. One good reason for spouses to contribute (according to Sandberg's findings) is her statistic showing that divorce rates drop 50 percent when the wife earns half the income and the other spouse does <u>half</u> the housework.

ACTION STEPS:

To get promoted, you have to do an excellent job of your current responsibilities, so track and measure your successes. Request a quarterly meeting with your leader to share your results. Create space to learn the skills you will need for the next role on your career ladder, by practising the art of delegating. If you have children, practise delegation with them first and get comfortable asking for help, creating some space for yourself — room for personal growth. Children who are taught early on to contribute to a clean and tidy home are learning valuable life lessons, while helping out with shared responsibility of an inclusive family lifestyle.

Find ways to create more productive time in your calendar by asking a colleague to attend some meetings on your behalf and provide a brief update afterwards on the key outcomes or any contentious issues discussed. Decide if the topic is one that you have a strong opinion about before you RSVP and be strategic with your time. Choose the relationships you specifically want to develop, then attend those relevant meetings which offer the opportunity for discussion. Let your leader know the next time you are on a critical deadline that you have arranged with a colleague for them to take meeting notes and share with you afterwards. Begin by planting a seed that you are not attending every meeting . . . When attending in person, showcase your wisdom by preparing relevant and insightful questions that align with the purpose for the discussion. Be proactive and prepared to contribute with at least three ideas showing how progress could be made, linking these back to the agenda items or discussion.

If you are a new team lead or manager, plan your meetings to be the most effective, by deciding the contributors who MUST be participating, and share your agenda and target outcomes ahead of time. Describe the context, and prepare questions that foster discussion, so that you are leading an informed group for discussion and efficient decision making during the meeting. Wrap up the meeting with a summary of the major items agreed to and completion dates (and who is accountable).

Many meetings are poorly run, ineffective, and quite frankly — boring! How can you enliven yours? With the various technology options available today (ZOOM teleconferencing with video, Skype and others) often attending a meeting online is equally productive for home-based staff or entrepreneurs while saving driving time and reducing greenhouse gas. Insist the video camera is on to help prevent multitasking . . . How much more you could accomplish one day a week by working out of the office (and all of those in-person distractions)? If you are not in a supervisor or manager role, you can develop your delegation skills by volunteering as a team leader for a not-for-profit charity, where they are typically glad to accept your help, while you develop your skills, ready to accelerate in your career.

Note down your actions to enhance your delegation abilities in your journal.

7.4

Negotiate

Almost every day, women are required to negotiate, whether in preparation of a treaty or contract, or with a spouse over who is taking the children to after school activities. We often feel required to negotiate for things that we are actually entitled to, such as leaving the office at five pm (or your agreed employment contract for regular office hours). We negotiate with another family member to pick up the children from hockey or ballet enabling us to attend a special event, or to have time to go to the spa for peaceful relaxation. What did you already *negotiate* today?

One of the most important beliefs that comes up frequently in my client coaching work is the belief that we are *worthy* — worthy of receiving. When you speak up, negotiate and ask for your needs to be fulfilled, you are role modelling assertiveness for your children, especially your daughters, nieces or female co-workers or your team members, hence negotiating successfully is a key to confident conversations.

Each time you attend a meeting and share a new idea, invite a potential client to a meeting, even going on a first date — you are selling yourself or selling an idea. Women are generally community-oriented and collaborative, often hoping that the other person will like us enough to want to hear what we have to say, appreciate our ideas, or want to build a relationship. (I use the word *relationship* generally here, referring to your client relationships.)

In order for a strong relationship to evolve (or for a sale to take place) your potential friend (or client) must know, like, and trust you. In *The Go-Giver*, authors Bob Burg and John David Mann share: "All things being equal people will do business with, and refer business to, those people they know, like, and trust." An interesting statement, as often for women in business all things are generally *not* equal . . . and this enables an easier decision regarding who to do business with — other women business owners!

You can increase the likelihood of building strong meaningful relationships by finding common values. *The Go-Giver* is a highly recommended read, as it tells the story of an ambitious young man who yearns for success, a "go-getter." It often feels as if the harder and faster he works, the further away his goals seem to be. One day, at the end of a bad quarter, he seeks advice and learns from other successful business owners how to open himself up to the power of giving, through observing what Burg and Mann describe as the *Five Laws of Stratospheric Success*, and magical results happen.

In our fast-paced world, making confident decisions in a timely manner is much easier when we can anchor our decisions to what is important to us — our *values*. A ship with an anchor firmly planted in the sea bed will not be swept to an unknown destination by the waves and current, it remains firmly in position. When we have clearly identified values, these become our anchors by which to ground ourselves, and help us make decisions which feel right. When you are running in circles of indecision, in essence "stirring up the mud at the bottom of the pond" with your activity, you create cloudy water and cannot see the obvious solution. When you stop, let the water settle, you can see clearly at how the decision you need to make connects with your values. It becomes far easier to make a choice and see what is important to you and what is non-negotiable in any situation.

Negotiation is a critical skill for women to develop. Data shows that women in many countries earn less than men for doing the same work. In Canada (at the time of this writing) statistics show that Canadian women earn eighty-two cents to every dollar earned by men. According to Catalyst Canada, a non-profit organization that focuses on expanding opportunities for women and business, this number is shifting at a snail's pace. Canada's numbers are marginally better than the US's seventy-eight cents for every dollar, but sets the gap in Canada at 18 percent — much higher than in other countries: "The global pay gap was about four thousand two hundred dollars on average between men and women, and the Canadian pay gap was just over eight thousand two hundred dollars" shares Alex Johnston, executive director of Catalyst Canada.[157]

Improvement in the wage gap has been minor since 1997 (77.2 percent to 83.0 percent for full-time workers). In North America, several other organizations track this statistic, including the American Association of University Women (AAUW). AAUW advances equity for women and girls through advocacy, education, and philanthropy, and proposes that "pay equity will not occur until around 2059." [158] Do we really want to wait that long? Women have an opportunity to move closer to receiving equal pay for equal work, especially when we have the belief we can negotiate successfully.

In 2012, the U.S. National Bureau of Economic Business Study explored a hypothesis that women avoid salary negotiation. The study showed that when a job advert was placed stating that an hourly salary rate was negotiable, women negotiated 9 percent more than men. However, men negotiated the salary (when the wage was fixed) 29 percent of the time. The report authors (Andreas Leibbrandt and John A. List of the Department of

Economics, Monash University) conducted a natural field experiment with 2,500 job-seekers. Their findings showed that "when there is no explicit statement that wages are negotiable, men are more likely to negotiate than women. However, when we explicitly mention the possibility that wages are negotiable, this difference disappears, and even tends to reverse." [159]

In their book *Ask For It*, Linda Babcock and Sara Laschever explore this further. Babcock and Laschever report survey evidence from 2003 that shows men are four times more likely to negotiate on first salaries, and that individuals who do not negotiate first salaries lose more than five hundred thousand dollars by age sixty. WOW — half a million dollars of lost wages by not negotiating![160]

When I worked in HR for many years and made job offers to men and women, I also observed a pattern that less women negotiated a salary offer. How can we change this? Simply by being given permission to negotiate? In our desire to be liked as women, do we go along with other people's ideas in order to keep the peace? At what cost do these beliefs keep us stuck and undervalued? What impact could five hundred thousand dollars more in earnings have on providing for your family?

In my prenatal class many years ago, I remember an approach the facilitator used to identify priorities around the birth experience. She asked us to list the top ten things that were important to us when we delivered our baby. Participants discussed their list, and almost everyone had listed things including: my doctor delivers my baby rather than an intern or strange doctor being present, that I have a pain-free experience, that I have my own private room, that my baby arrives within a few days of the identified due date. However, when asked to gradually compare items on our list in order of importance, it became clear that the absolute top priority for each of the women was to deliver a healthy baby. At the end of the day, nothing else mattered. Let your values, your inner compass, guide your decisions and your priorities, especially when negotiating.

One of my values is compassion, which guides how I treat others, how I offer help and support, and who I build relationships with. If I know that the person I am interacting with has a compassionate and generous heart (demonstrated by regularly volunteering, support a charity, donating intellect and time sitting on a board), I will feel a connection with their compassion value, and quickly build a deeper relationship. Look for others who share your values. You are more likely to have less friction in a relationship, and especially in your negotiations, when you both innately care about the same underlying principles.

If you are negotiating something straightforward, asking clearly for what you want and offering something in exchange is simple. You find a dress you like, you ask for a fitting room, find that it fits like a glove, you pay for it and leave the store with your purchase. A simple one-time transaction does not require a match in values or building a relationship.

When you receive a job offer you *can* negotiate the terms, the total rewards offered in exchange for the work you are being asked to complete. It is called a job "offer" because it is exactly that – an offer that is negotiable. Even though many companies have a specific salary range identified, often the elements of the total compensation can be repackaged to meet your needs. For example, if you are a seasoned professional with twenty years of industry experience, being offered a standard of two weeks of paid vacation per year might feel insulting after all your years of dedication to building your career and industry knowledge (while it may be that firm's normal practice and in line with legislated Employment Standards). In your previous role, you may have been entitled to four to six weeks of vacation, and your family time is an important value for you. Negotiating to have two to three weeks of unpaid leave may be an option if the hiring manager is willing to recognize your skills are necessary for the team, and therefore may offer a higher starting wage (which will offset the unpaid vacation time). You never know unless you ask!

Catherine Brownlee, founder of CBI, who leads a global job placement company, shares the importance of asking for clarity before accepting a position. She recommends asking at the end of an interview, "What is the most important measure of success for this position?" (Ask before an employment offer is made.) This question enables you to find out what to showcase in your skills, your experience and perspective, which clearly demonstrates you are the best candidate for the job, why you are worth a little time negotiating with. This knowledge will also confirm that the role is clearly thought through, and you know how your success will be specifically measured once you accept the position. It can also identify a leader who is overwhelmed and anxious to have an extra pair of hands on board, yet has not clearly thought through how the new hire can help alleviate their stress, and you may be walking into chaos . . . When you feel good, your body supports your decisions, and moves you closer to living authentically with your values.

If you move too quickly in evolving the relationship, by asking for too much too soon, it will often feel forced or fake, and you will often end up pushing the other person away. Relationship evolution is individual and may not be an exact science, however there are lessons we can learn from nature in this topic. Courtship in the animal kingdom leaves us clues. Birds exhibit some of the most spectacular courtship rituals. In a competitive jungle, males need to compete for female attention in order to secure mating rights. A mating dance between birds may be displayed for hours. Take the red-capped manakin, a fruit-eating bird native to Central America. The males of the species stand out with their dark black plumage and contrasting head of vivid red. But the plumage isn't enough to capture the attention of the ladies. The males also must have some impressive courtship dance moves.[161]

Negotiating a job offer can feel like a courting dance. Connect your values to those of the organization as you show how you can add value to the team — as your common starting point. Find something that brings you together first. Mirror the other person's body language to send unconscious signals that you are on the same wavelength as them. If they are leaning forward, lean forward yourself. If they are stepping back, step back yourself — to show that you are also willing to give them some personal space as well, and not rush into conversation elements that are deeply personal or potentially risky too early in the conversation. In job interviews or other negotiations that involve monetary value, find ways to gauge how willing they are explore a salary range or elements of a total rewards package, by listening to words like "perhaps we could" rather than "already set or non-negotiable." Even though their words may identify a predetermined pay rate, look at how your skills and abilities can add value to their organization, ask for what you want clearly, and then stop talking while you wait for their reply. Let the silence do the heavy lifting for you . . . Eventually they will need to reply, however, do not let the discomfort of the silence lead you into speaking first. Let them initiate their salary offer after you have confidently showcased your skills and demonstrated how you are a great fit.

Look at the bigger picture. Instead of identifying a list of individual things that contribute to you accepting what is being offered, state what the total package would need to look like in order for it to be accepted. "In our discussions I see that your organization values XYZ (connect back to their stated values). I can help you achieve your business objectives in this role by leveraging my values of XYZ" (show how your values align with theirs). When asked, "What did you make in your previous salary?" consider that giving a specific number can eliminate you from consideration. (Too high and you appear overpriced, too low and your efficiency is doubted.)

An alternate reply is to indicate that you "trust they pay competitively in the market, and you are looking for a company with similar values and offers interesting and challenging work." If pressed for a specific salary expectation, expand with: "Based on my industry research, for a position with the level of responsibility detailed, a total compensation package of X is appropriate." (Avoid the words "I need" or "I want," simply state your position, then stop talking and wait for their reply, without feeling a need to fill the empty silence while they reflect on your statement.) It is irrelevant to share your past salary as each organization has different benefit packages, hours of work, bonuses, vacation allotment, short or long-term incentives or stock options, RRSP or IRA matching etc., so the total package is the only valid number to consider — for an apples to apples comparison.

According to an article in *USA Today* (April 27, 2017) several states now have a ban on asking the question, "What's your current, or most recent, salary?" including Philadelphia, New York City, and Massachusetts, where legislation was passed[162]. At least eight other states are considering similar measures — Illinois, Maine, Maryland, New Jersey, New York, Pennsylvania, Rhode Island, and Vermont (at time of writing) according to law firm Fisher & Phillips. The bills are aimed at closing a long-standing gender-based pay gap that, according to the Census Bureau, has (US) women earning about eighty cents for every dollar earned by men. Studies that compare men and women in similar occupations and control for other factors, such as experience, find much narrower pay disparities. By basing future salaries on previous wages, employers can perpetuate the earnings divide, advocates for women say.

For hiring managers reading this article, my advice based on over fifteen years in HR interviewing thousands of candidates, is to determine the value of the job, and the readiness of the candidate to be competent from day one. In a 2017 *Harvard Business Review* article. "Why Banning Questions About Salary History May Not Improve Pay Equity," the writer recommends:

> A candidate's current salary should have no bearing on what an employer is willing to pay for a particular position. Compensation should be a data-driven decision based on the current value of a given position in the talent market. Certainly, a candidate's unique skills may place them lower or higher in the pre-determined range, but their current salary shouldn't be the basis for determining their pay. [163]

Agreed! While it is early to say how this US legislation has impacted pay equity, do your own research first before heading into an interview. Practise saying out lout what you have learned is an appropriate salary range for the role, and if you feel that is still lower than you are willing to accept in the role (if you know your last company paid above market average) be willing to negotiate on the total compensation package, and be ready once an offer is made to confirm that you "are interested in the role, and the organization is an excellent fit for your values, so you would like the opportunity to review their overall offer in order to make a final decision."

When you receive a job offer is the best time, when you have the most leverage to ask for appropriate compensation. Your future organization wants you to join them, or they would not be making you an offer . . . Once you are on the team, internal salary bands and levels will often determine the maximum increase percentage you will be eligible for, more on salary structure and less on what a fantastic job you are doing (unless you are paid on a commission or in a sales role). The larger the organization, in my experience, the more structure is in place regarding salary increases.

In interviews and internal performance reviews, find ways to naturally showcase your success, in status meetings or performance review conversations. Be factual using the following format: WHAT you did (the project or context) HOW (you used your skills/values) the RESULT (your achievement — shown in measurable outcomes or percentages) and the BENEFITS (to the team or organization). The statement of your achievements could look like this: "I used my leadership, industry connections and compassion to lead my team to develop a community partnership that secured fifty dollars in funding, which will enable us to meet our impact goals."

I know from hosting over six thousand career interviews that many women are uncomfortable talking about themselves, blowing their own horn or bragging. However, with focus placed on serving and service first, speaking about your achievements becomes a matter of pride, and simply stating the facts. Put your needs first, because of you don't do it, you risk no one else doing it for you . . . ask! What action can you take today to increase your earnings?

ACTION STEPS:

Begin each day with a mantra, repeating a powerful acknowledgement to yourself in your bathroom mirror, "I am worthy, I am worthy, I am worthy." "I AM" is a powerful daily statement to make. The positive energy created by your intention will support your motivation to take a stand for what you really want. When you say what you want out loud, as with writing it down — it takes your commitment to a new level. You may have heard about an urban legend or study conducted with Harvard MBA students? Only 3 percent of the group had written goals, with 84 percent who had no goals. Ten years later, the 3 percent group with written goals had earned ten times as much as those with no written goals. Interestingly the 13 percent who had goals identified but had not written them down still earned twice the amount of those who had no goals at all. Whether legend or not, I have personally found writing down my goals to be extremely beneficial to achieving them, including one "bucket list" goal to "write a best-selling book" — time will tell on this one!

Track your results in your journal and note what "showed up" today to support you achieve your goals. When you look back at previous years of journaling, it is amazing to see how your mind has expanded and your goals have become more expansive.

Practise negotiating — starting today! Find one small thing each day to request and hone your negotiating skills. In everyday situations, find something in common with the other person first before making a request. If you meet another mother at a children's sporting event, your children playing on the same team, or enjoying the same sport, create a natural first connection in the conversation. If you have a colleague who has introduced you to each other, that may be the bridge over a gap and starts the connection. Women will often notice another lady's shoes or purse, creating a point of opening conversation, a compliment or comparison if you also have a purse of the same brand name. Look for something you both share in common first, then expand your conversation.

If you are at a networking event, find a way to be "memorable. Offer to be the event MC. Being on the event stage, wearing brightly coloured clothing or funky glasses, or sharing an insightful perspective in a conversation and actually following this up with an article in an email, will create a stronger connection. Many people lack follow-up skills or commitment, show yourself to be reliable and trustworthy from your first conversation. Be memorable by offering to make a connection with another person that your conversation partner wanted to meet (either at the event, or someone in your connections circle) and showcase your generosity and willingness to be "trusted" first by making an introduction between them. If someone has helped you first, you are more inclined to agree to their request afterwards — the power of reciprocity.

Do your own salary research before heading into an interview. Practise saying what you have learned is an appropriate salary range for the role, and if you feel that is still lower than you are willing to accept in the role (if you know your last company paid above market average) practise saying a higher number. Keep saying a higher number: forty thousand dollars, sixty thousand dollars, eighty thousand dollars, until you begin to feel discomfort in your body — which is sharing its natural value point with you, and know this number before the interview. Be willing to negotiate on the total compensation package, and be ready once an offer is made to confirm that you "are interested in the role, and the organization is an excellent fit for your values, so you would like the opportunity to review their overall offer in order to make a final decision.

What can you negotiate, simply by asking? Ask — "Is that the very best that you can do?" Practise using direct eye contact as you ask and let the silence after the question fill the air, encouraging your conversation partner to reply with their best offer.

7.5

Amplify

When you find other supporters to amplify your message and funnel opportunities to you which may provide growth and leverage your skills and talents, you will achieve greater career success much faster. While training and coaching provide excellent ways to expand your knowledge, in some economies you will need to get creative when there is no funding for your development available. Focus on zero or low-cost development options — find a mentor and a sponsor to support your development.

Building your support network is critical for your growth. Access to deeper expertise when you need it reduces self-doubt and contributes to feeling confident. You might not know how to do something, but you know someone who does! When you first start in a new organization or a new role is the best time to ask your leader "who might be a good mentor for me?" A mentor helps you learn from their real-life experiences and can speed up your learning time significantly by introducing you to the things that you did not even realize were important or would not know to even ask about. You don't know what you don't know.

Select a person holding a role which you are hoping to be promoted into — one level up from the one you hold right now. In small organizations there is no great mentor for you, seek out other organizations where your current role (or an equivalent one) exists, and find an industry-wide mentor. Agree that the conversations that take place between you will be in confidence to reduce any concern about sharing any information during your discussions. Keep the discussions focused on what you can be learning and developing, the skills that you can hone which contribute to having more confidence in your role. Here are some guidelines in selecting a mentor:

<u>Mentor:</u>

- **Someone you admire.**

- **Who is respected and influential.**

- **One level higher in the organization.**

- **Someone with a strength in your area of need.**

Once you have identified your prospective mentor, request to "meet to discuss industry insights." Gather their wisdom in this area first, then before the end of the meeting directly relate what they have shared to your specific role and situation. Ask if you can reconnect in a few months rather than specifically asking if they would be your mentor (unless you were assigned to them as part of a corporate program). Develop good rapport first, then ask if they are open to an occasional email or call with any specific questions, then evolve to a regular meeting, possibly monthly or quarterly as your relationship deepens.

Prepare in advance by keeping a log of questions to ask your mentor, so each focused conversation is as meaningful for them sharing knowledge as your learnings are. Your development is a *priority* not a last-minute item squeezed in (while advance scheduling is likely easier for them too). Having a fan and supporter with more life experience for guidance can be a great way to maintain or boost your confidence at work. Often your mentor can introduce you to people in a new influence level or to resources (books, conferences, or articles) you may not know about.

I also encourage finding a *sponsor* inside your organization. This is a senior person who can recommend you for a promotion, who knows the quality of the work that you do, and some of your strengths and interests. Here are some guidelines for selecting a sponsor:

<u>Champion/Sponsor:</u>

*   **Someone you admire, who is respected and influential.**

*   **Two levels higher in your current organization.**

*   **Is an advocate and a fan of your work (or could be).**

Once you have identified your top choice, look them up on LinkedIn to see where they have worked previously, their education, which groups they are a member of, organizations or charities that they volunteer with, and where you can connect with them. Identify upcoming company events that they are attending, or charity events based on your research, and be strategic in connecting. If you have good rapport, ask if they are aware of any special project opportunities internally, or if they would be willing to meet with you periodically (once or twice a year) to discuss industry trends. Asking for a "research interview" with your desired sponsor is outdated and sounds like you are fishing for a job. A sponsor will be able to suggest you for consideration for roles that you may not even hear about . . .

Cultivate mentor and sponsor relationships. The more others know about your perspective or work accomplishments and personal growth, the more likely they are to recommend you when an opening for a promotion arises. Keep track of your PVP contributions (personal value proposition) and your proudest accomplishments to share at these meetings, and casually mention your results in the last five minutes of your meeting together. Keep your summary short with measurable results.

Volunteering on a committee is a great way to make a contribution to your company or community, and to build some excellent relationships. Upon conclusion of each project, ask others to share what contribution each person made to the success of the project, while discovering what others value about your skills and your personal contribution. Volunteer contributions mentioned on your resume showcase your social conscience and build your support network. When you need encouragement, knowledge, or an introduction, you will be amazed how supportive your volunteer committee members will be. It is humbling helping others who are less fortunate than yourself, another reminder of how capable you are, another confidence booster.

ACTION STEPS:

Build out your Career Circle, to include supporters in several categories:

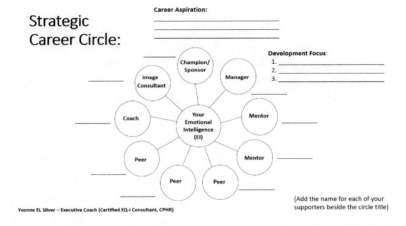

Peers (who can support you, amplify your ideas, talk about your successes, share promotional postings or new job prospects as

they are familiar with your work. Mentors (as described above). A coach. A supportive manager or Supervisor (who knows what your career goals are and how your current role and responsibilities align with your aspirations and growth targets. A sponsor (per the description above) or champion who can help you to be considered for more responsible roles or special projects (or volunteer committee roles) to provide you with visibility inside your organization or within your industry.

> *1 — List a minimum of three peers to book a conversation with to discuss how you could help each other, by understanding each other's career aspirations and talents.*
> *2 — Identify two to three potential mentors to approach.*
> *3 — Source two to three potential sponsors or champions to approach.*
> *4 — Find a quiet place to reflect on your career aspirations — in a year, what changes you would like to see that would help your role to be more purposeful, more rewarding, align more closely with your skills and interests as well as being challenging enough to peak your curiosity.*
> *5 — Define three development focus goals that you could expand into with the help of a coach, then seek out a coach skilled in this specific area (confidence coaching is my expertise, for example).*
> *6 — Discover your Emotional Intelligence strengths by completing an EQ-i Assessment, and incorporate these fifteen scales and subscales into your personal development plan. (Email <u>Admin@we-flourish.org</u> for instructions and how to access an EQ-i Workplace Report, and receiving/interpreting your results with a Certified Consultant such as myself.)*

7.6

Confident

Using the phrase "I am confident . . ." describes your current state of certainty, and endorses your language as powerful, especially in the workplace. When working in a male-dominated environment, stating your opinion with the words "I feel . . ." is often received with less strength. The more senior your position, the more you benefit from using clear, concise, and powerful language. When we are acutely aware of our language and how we can use our words to our advantage, leadership authenticity is easy to see. Clear, confident and resonant energy can be felt, and shows up in unwavering clarity, clear decision making, and looking forward outlining the greater goal, with the most community impact.

Our challenge as women is often to navigate between being our masculine and feminine energy, between our authentic self and leveraging the skills that help us become respected leaders (displaying high integrity, developing and empowering others, collaboration, and teamwork) as referenced in Zenger Folkman's Leadership Competencies research. [164] If you are a professional woman looking to move into a more senior role, it is important to use powerful language that is authentic and effective, and radiates confidence. Using "I think" or "I may" will often be interpreted that you have not yet made a final decision, you are still negotiable. Be clear in your position, where you are in the process of deciding, and state that accordingly. Business moves at a fast pace, is volatile and uncertain, so even though you may end up needing to change strategy (pivot) in the future, taking a confident stand for today's decision is important for your credibility as a leader. Your team is looking for fairness and strength in leadership rather than indecisiveness.

Research shows that women are looking for three key specific leadership qualities to "build trust in the workplace." Leaders need to show competence, consistency and caring. [165] Women leaders do not have to be liked in order to be successful, however, building trust is a core element of leadership respect. My own experiences gathered in 3 senior Human Resources roles echo other research which shows that women are often evaluated for a promotion based upon past work (rather than the potential to be successful in the new role, which is often the measure for men). Hence clearly showing your current abilities and capacity to moderate your emotions at work are important. Employees respect a leader who is reliable, stays calm in a crisis and gathers input from their team before making decisions, not surprising them with unexpected changes without clear rationale.

Reflect upon the last time you were in a building when the fire alarm went off. The fire marshal (or designated emergency leader) did not say, "please, if everyone could possibly start heading to the fire escapes, when you have a moment . . ." While very polite and warm, the instructions needed in this situation required a clear directive: "The Fire Alarm requires everyone exit the building using the stairwell immediately. Pick up your coat and purse now, and clear the floor, to ensure everyone's safety. Follow me and leave the building now." Use distinctive, clear language, and you will see a shift in how others respond. Additional words and phrases to avoid using include: *forgot, almost, lazy, however, but, deserve,* and *try.* Stop using filler words (not required, unnecessary, and padding a sentence): *such as, hmmm/um/er, anyway, okay, you know, perfect, awesome, that may be — but in my experience, basically, what's-her-name, thing-a-majig,"* or using excessive swear words — regardless of your organization's culture.

Avoid any remarks that are non-descriptive, such as *busy, supported/helped, administered,* or *good* — what do those words really mean? *Good* is a subjective term. If the outcome is *exceptional, appropriate, insightful, innovative, phenomenal, or outrageous* — say so!

Keep your language positive without gossip: although you may be tempted to refer to others, especially other women (as *bitchy, bossy, cranky, pushy, stubborn, PMS-ing*), rise above the crowd and keep your opinions to yourself. After all, they are your opinions, they are not the other person's truth. If you want to know why someone is coming across in a certain manner, ask them. "I am curious if you are upset about something, as your behaviour is not showing your typical happy self?"

Likewise, if you are upset about something I am sure you would not want others talking about you behind your back, so role model how you want others to treat you. Anna Maria Chávez, CEO of The Girl Scouts of the USA says that

> girls are listening and watching, and for girls — words matter! So as adults, what are the messages we are sending girls every day, whether we are a

parent, a teacher or a peer?" Saying "I don't like the way you lead, why are you being so bossy?" We need to take that out of our vocabulary and start using other positive words for girls. The Girl Scouts has a research Institute that studies girls and boys, which shows that girls understand the opportunity to lead but they opt out of leadership by middle school, they know it is a negative stereotype to be seen as a leader.[166]

The "Ban Bossy" movement (combining together the goals of *Lean In* and Girl Scouts) aims to encourage girls to lead. "There are powerful things that every single one of us can do, every day, to change the equation for leadership in our world," added Sheryl Sandberg in an interview with Anna and Joanne Po with *The Wall Street Journal*, when talking about eliminating the word "bossy."[167] There are other words women benefit from eliminating. International Stylist Leslie Davies says:

> I think the word *fat* needs to be eliminated from our vocabulary, there is nothing positive about using that word, it undermines our confidence, and is not empowering. Let's focus instead on the pieces of ourselves that we are happy with, that we like. (Even replacing *fat* with *curvy* still has a feeling of being overweight). Being healthy and beautiful is important as we are so much more than our body shape.[168]

Be thoughtful when using: *I imagine, perhaps, spent, wish/hope, may/might*, and watch how others respond when you use these words. Using *I imagine* when coming out of a meditation and writing in your journal works well, yet used at work may indicate uncertainty and doubt.

Phrases and words to incorporate in your conversations that convey your role in leading the team to take action include: *mobilized, implemented, catalyzed, created, innovated, launched, mandated, instigated, established, triggered, negotiated, won, initiated, cultivated, organized, ignited, advocated, led, optimized, mentored, coached, refreshed, revitalized, invested,* or *initiated.*

(Powerful descriptors to also use in your reports or on your resume.)

For women working with teams of women, avoid these words: *spear-headed, drove, driven, pushed, strived, contrived, fought, drop-dead* (find other language to describe a deadline such as a *critical date* or *key delivery timeline*). These are the *hard-driving power words* that women often use when trying to act like men at work, instead of leveraging our own capabilities and collaborative advantages and cultivating our authentic female leadership style. If we want the workplace to be supporting our career goals and encouraging more women leaders, we need to build an environment which attracts and retains women.

Building a strong culture of inclusion, acceptance, diversity, recognition and validation will require more women to take a stand for the type of workplaces we want to create, not just tolerate.

In Sheryl Sandberg's book *Lean In*, she also writes about the conundrum of "being liked" for women. Most of us want to be liked. If our success means that others don't like us, how motivated are we to do well? Sheryl tells a concise story of her first performance review with Mark Zuckerberg (co-Founder of Facebook), six months into her job at Facebook. He told her that her desire to be liked by everyone was holding her back. "If you please everyone, he said, you won't change anything. Mark was right," she shares.

While you may feel the sting and painful emotions that come with any form of rejection, practise acknowledging those feelings and shift from activities "to be liked," to be seen as "fair." Not everyone will like you, however, it is better that they respect you, which results from them feeling as though you treated them fairly and with respect. Show them respect first and see what happens.

Each word explored in this book has **Action Steps** leading to developing more confidence, using powerful language, collaborative yet direct communication to empower others while building relationships and respect. There is so much more to being confident, it is much more than our words, the external expression of how grounded we feel. When you are living authentically, fully grounded and showing up living into your values, confident words will flow more easily. This book is a journey, looking at your values and how you live into them each day, how you show up authentically and confidently. When you resonate positive energy and your spirit is comfortable with who you are, you resist the need to be liked by everyone — because YOU are the only one that YOU need to be liked by, actually LOVED by.

ACTION STEPS:

Confidence is embodied when we know we are capable. It evolves by struggling through something and achieving it, through surviving adversity. Courage is not developed doing the everyday things, it is in reaching for something more and through challenge and accomplishment. Confidence is an inner knowing that "you've got this!" and that you have enough knowledge, skill, support, and resources to make it happen.

Knowing how you will be measured by others is important, so that you know what external success looks like. Understanding your own motivation, WHY you are doing something impactful and how it feels in your heart and soul (intrinsically) is critical. Begin today by understanding what your intrinsic success feels like, at work, at home, in your volunteer activities, in your business or role as a leader. How will you absolutely KNOW that you have achieved success? Is it a numerical measure, how it will feel, how others respond or engage, the impact it will have in the community, the response from your spouse or children? What are you doing when you feel most proud? Get clear on those measures.

If you are working outside the home, or in a professional capacity, look at your current job description, identify areas where you excel, such as activities that generate revenue for your company, helping to decrease costs or improve productivity, innovate new products, and detail your achievements in writing. Start keeping an "accomplishments" file in your desk, with all of your wins and successes, ready to take into your next performance review discussion with your leader. (If you are a professional who needs to track activities for future accreditation, this comes in handy to keep a register or log of these activities, rather than a last minute scramble to try to remember when your renewal date is looming . . .) When a disappointing event occurs, having a way to remember all the other successes you have had in the past will keep you going. Your resilience will be bolstered by remembering your past achievements rather than getting stuck or upset with one recent poor outcome, and not letting this one instance derail your day.

CHAPTER 8

When No Words are Required . . .

I always tell young girls, surround yourself with goodness.

I learned early on how to get the haters out of my life.

— Michelle Obama

8.1

Silence and The Power Pause

Silence — one of the most powerful communication concepts is often not the words that you use, it is your use of silence. As a coach, I have heard the expression said many times "let the silence do the heavy lifting." When asking a question, let the silence following your question draw out a reply from the other person. By not saying anything, by letting the energy of possibility hang in the air until the best answer appears, an open invitation pulls the other person to stay in connection, even though no words are spoken. The question keeps the opening there, while the longer the silence stretches, the more it invites a deeper response.

Melinda Wittstock, founder of technology firm Verifeed and founder of Wings of Inspired Business podcast shared in a recent interview with me, how "important it is for women not to feel the need to fill conversational gaps." Yes! Get comfortable with the sometimes awkward silence between the conversation elements. "In any of these things we are confronted with a choice, to give into the fear and give up, or push through them and get out of your comfort zone, and that is where real personal growth happens."

She also shared:

> I remember doing a pitch competition (there were ten of us) in the technology world with three women and seven men. I did my pitch identifying what traction we already had in the marketplace and talked about specific customers and the activities and value that was driven. At the end one of the investors said, "I really wished that someone had talked about their customers." Really? I thought I just did that! As a broadcaster, I know that my delivery was my "pitch-perfect." Women tend to be more conservative about their numbers, they are more accurate about forecasting and tend to be downgraded by the venture capitalists.[169]

Ladies — it is time to examine and be proud of your numbers! Confidently point to your revenue and the strategies you devised that achieved that success, and let the results speak for themselves. Then stop talking, and let the silence draw out any questions your venture capitalists may have.

At work, if an event occurs where something goes wrong, you may pose a question to the person who has the responsibility to fix the issue: "The current approach is not working. What are some alternative ways we can handle this situation?" Then stop talking and wait. Uncomfortable as that silence is, wait and endure what may seem like an eternity before the other person replies. Let the energy do the heaving lifting — drawing out their response like a silken thread. If it is their responsibility, let them figure out how to fix it, they will be more committed to implementing their own idea anyway.

Yes, it is uncomfortable, and you will likely feel a prickly energy in your body by not talking and filling the silence with potential options, and letting the other person come forward. Practise it, as silence can be a powerful ally. With practice, you can let go of needing to know all the answers, becoming comfortable letting others make suggestions or recommendation.

Be assertive without being aggressive, and let the silence speak.[170] When I sit in meditation each morning, it is the silence that allows thoughts to gently bubble up from my inner self, from my heart not my head. I am allowing the ideas to flow, not forcing them into thoughts with my brain, simply letting them flow from my heart — flow through me. Silence is just as powerful as our words can be, in allowing space for the emergence of ideas. Space between ideas is as important as the value of space overall. You will pay more for a five thousand square foot home than a one thousand square foot home, as space is valued. Space to grow into, opening up potential for energy to flow . . . A corner office is generally bigger than a mid-row one — and if offered a corner — take it!

You can also use silence to your advantage in other ways. Recognize when *not* to leave silence hanging. If you are in conversation and are inviting a reply from the other person, leave space at the end of a sentence for them to respond. (Different cultures have different norms of acceptance for turn-taking in conversation.) Turn-taking in a conversation encourages the ebb and flow, builds reciprocity, and shows that you value the opinion and input from your conversation partner. Hogging the conversation by talking only about yourself, your needs, and what is happening in your life leaves no open space for the other person to be included. One-sided relationships usually do not survive, as each person is looking to have their needs met, and when there is an unequal amount of give and take, someone typically opts out.

Use the power of a pause . . . Developing your pause statement has been covered already. If you are in sales and are feeling unsure if a potential client will say *yes* to your offer, your uncertainty may show up almost unconsciously. When you pause at the end of your sentence it signals a reply from the other person. However, if unconsciously you are expecting them to speak up with an objection, your pausing may actually create the space for them to jump in. A self-fulfilling prophecy! Instead of inviting an objection, pause in the middle of your sentence to take a breath. At the end of your sentence, do not stop talking, simply dip your tone down to indicate you have concluded that sentence, then roll right into the beginning of the next sentence. Your conversation partner would likely not be rude by jumping into the conversation in the middle of your sentence, so the likelihood of you completing your sentence without any interruption or objection is much higher.

A well-constructed sales conversation leads to a natural outcome, when you understand the challenges in their business, and how purchasing your product or service provides a solution. "Objections" are simply requests for more information, as they seek more reassurance that the risk for them to engage with you is low. Be thorough in asking purposeful questions at the beginning of the relationship-building process, so you know enough about your prospective client to appreciate how they can benefit the most from your offering. Then align your benefits with their problems, for a clear solution in how your product can help them transform from where they are today to a positive future outcome. I have eliminated the word *objections* when talking with a new prospective client, by setting my intention to discover if they are an ideal client for me or not. When starting a conversation with an intentional energy seeking fit, there is no room for objections, as that would mean I am trying to force someone else to be wrong and they then need to defend themselves. Invite your clients and conversation partners, drawing them in with appreciation, collaboration, and innovation.

Sometimes an answer is not required. I have noticed an increase of the word *really,* posed as a question. It is one word that is often used for pushing back, causing the speaker to re-examine what they just said, inquiring within to explain what was meant by their comment. Or to continue the conversation if the speaker wants to take a stand for what they said, to show disapproval without a rebuke . . . One word can say so much, or be misinterpreted in so many different ways . . . (Or it can be a complete sentence with no extra words required: *No, yes, never, agreed, stop, true*). In a world where texting and Messenger are more frequent communication methods, the shorter the sentence often the more likelihood of a miscommunication.

8.2

Intentional Energy

Be clear in your intention and your desired outcome, and choose your words accordingly. We may think we do that automatically anyway, that we don't need to focus on our language — *really*? As this book has shown, placing emphasis on specific words, or avoiding others, can shift how you are accepted (or not) by others and how you are treated by them. By taking back your word power, you take back your self-esteem which is an incredible feeling of inner confidence!

 <u>Be intentional about sounds.</u> If you are hosting an event, carefully select the music for your event room, as walking into a silent room for a workshop where you came alone does not feel very inviting . . . Select music that correlates with your intention for the room. Elevator music is often selected to be calming, yet if you want to stir up creativity or excitement, a higher energy music choice can prepare your audience for your talk.

 <u>Tapping into your flow.</u> Momentum arising from being inspired has a very different energy than "pushing or striving." Push energy creates unnecessary resistance, rather than "finding flow" and the purposeful things that are working well for you and doing more of those. Pushing is often what causes resistance and objections from others rather than an intention to invite someone into conversation or to a relationship with you. The energy of positive intention, collaboration, and "serving rather than selling" is shared in your body language and resonance before you speak. When your intention shifts, your energy shifts. On a larger scale, I have seen public speakers who shift from educating their audience to ending their talk with a "closing sale offer," and as their intention shifts so does their energy. This often results in "losing their audience" who can pick up subtle signals that something has now shifted, and it now feels different and uncomfortable.

8.3

Leverage the Silence

When in conversation, listen also for what is *not* being said. If you tell your new boyfriend "I love you" and get nothing back in return, the silence tells you something . . . If you meet a work colleague in the hall and say "Hello, how are you today?" without a response, their silence tells you something. However, deciphering the silence is what stirs up mind chatter, as we imagine all sorts of things that are often untrue, when we assume something from the silence. Ask for clarification, yet own your discomfort in doing so. "Hmmmm, when I shared that I love you just now, there was a long silence that felt very uncomfortable for me. I don't want to misinterpret your silence. I am curious, what you are thinking since I shared that?"

It is equally important to reflect: "What are the questions I avoid asking myself (or asking deeply of my soul)?" Sometimes we are stuck in a rut, feeling comfortable, and not tapping into our full potential because we are afraid to open the door of possibility, we are afraid of uncertainty and change . . . While staying comfortable is nice, the confidence gained from stretching yourself, trying new things that you never dreamed possible, is where you will enhance your resilience. Confidence comes through surviving adversity and knowing you will land on your feet — you did before in previous situations. Recognize how the brain works (the amygdala) and how it responds to situations it deems as dangerous, or reacts to trigger a feeling of fear.

In David Rock's book *Your Brain at Work*, he describes a how our brain responds when we are insecure, or scared of losing our status, with his SCARF model. As the director for the Neuroscience Institute, his studies show that the human brain is wired to move us faster from danger than to move us towards pleasure. Remember the small almond shaped structure within the brain — the amygdala — is part of the limbic system, which is responsible for regulating emotions.

His SCARF model explores five domains of human social experience: *status, certainty, autonomy, relatedness*, and *fairness*. Our desire for community with others translates to a feeling of fear if our "status" is threatened, or we may "lose face" or be publicly humiliated. A job loss may cause a loss of status for those who strongly identify in public with their job authority rather than who they are as a person. As Rock shares, even a small amount of uncertainty to predict the future can cause fear. Autonomy is related to feeling independent and in control of our own environment, which is impacted significantly with a sudden job loss for example. Relatedness is the feeling of security we have when we belong to a group. Fairness is created when we experience transparency and have clear expectations. [171] Since there are so many ways that fear can crop up, clarity in our communications is important, to create certainty and not assume something creating mind chatter. If you are curious, ask — and see if you can create your sentence without using the words *why* or *you* — which are two trigger words which often cause the other person to be defensive.

8.4

Presence and Body Language

Your presence speaks volumes, even before you say a word. Your presence creates a whole message with your body language, your clothing, your eye contact or smile, how you walk into a room, even before a single word is shared. We all have energy, chakras (energetic power centres) that are part of the universal energetic field, as quantum physics has shown. Your personal "energy" can permeate up to four feet from your body, as I discovered when taking my reiki training with reiki master Dixie Bennett. Your seven chakras control energy flow within your body, and auras vibrate outside your body at varied energy frequencies that mirror our emotions, feelings, and thoughts. Each of us has several aura layers (physical, etheric, emotional/astral, mental, causal, spiritual, and divine/intuitive), each with a different vibration.

Since we are all made up of energy, we can feel each other's energy when we are in close range (someone's personal space) which will either attract us or repel us. When we have harmonious vibrational levels, we attract (much like a magnet attracts metal particles), and when our vibrational levels are widely different they act like polar opposites and move us away from each other. If you have been to an event and shaken someone's hand and felt a wet-fishy handshake that caused you to pull away, you know how that felt, not very appealing! Seek out people who are on a similar vibrational frequency to you for alignment rather than resistance, by feeling into the energy around you.

Strong body language. What does your body language say to others about how you are feeling?   Can your co-workers, your leader, your customers, (as well as your friends and family) tell when you are upset, embarrassed, elated, sad, disappointed, or proud? How will you know if they are reading your body language correctly? Watch for their reactions . . . How they treat you will provide clues to how your actions and your non-verbal communication is being observed and received. If you are feeling shy or lack confidence, you may withdraw inwards to make yourself seem smaller (so that others do not notice you), and your shoulders may droop, your chin will drop, your eyes may not look straight at another person, or you may show a lack of engagement by sitting back in your chair with your hands in your lap. Learn how to show confidence, even if you are not feeling it that moment!

Social psychologist Amy Cuddy, associate professor at Harvard Business School, uses experimental methods to investigate how people judge and influence each other. If you act powerfully, you will begin to think more powerfully. We can take up a small amount of space in a room, or be expansive using bigger hand gestures and take up more space by extending our arms in a wide stretch, having our hands on our hips or standing with our feet further apart creating a wider foundation. [172] If you are meeting to be interviewed for a new job, one of the most stressful situations for many people, use her bathroom preparation technique shared in the video, and see how different you feel. To learn more on this topic, and how cortisol makes a difference to confidence levels, watch this informative video, then practise some of her suggested poses and see how your temperature decreases and your confidence level rises.

Mirror their body language. Even if your conversation partner is doing all the talking, you can still be communicating your interest in what they are sharing, with your body language. If they are excited and leaning into the conversation, lean in too. If they are sitting back with their arms extended taking up all the space around them, mirror their pose and do the same. When your body language shows you are on the same wavelength as your communication partner, the conversation flows more readily. If they are excited and talking at a fast pace, do the same in your reply. You are likely already doing this — if someone smiles at you, even a complete stranger — you smile back! A smile speaks volumes.

Listen to yourself . . . This may sound strange and yet it is so valuable to hear how you are coming across to others. At age seventeen I was working in a tele-sales role, arranging appointments for sales representatives, and one training exercise included recording a call and listening to yourself. What a valuable activity! When you listen, really listen to how you sound, you can either slow or speed up your pace, enunciate your words more clearly, stop using slang words or acronyms the other person many not understand, and elevate your professionalism. (When I first moved from England to Canada, I had to slow down and change my speech patterns significantly in order for my broad English accent to be understood.)

More recently, as a speaker, watching myself on video after several events has been significant in evolving my presence, my speaking style and content delivery. I encourage you to try recording yourself, or making a video of yourself, even if you are in a role without much public interaction, and see what you learn about yourself, and if your vision for how you want to be perceived matches what you see on your video.

8.5

Wardrobe and Image for Career Advancement

Your image speaks volumes, as your first impression will be judged in the first few seconds of meeting someone new. As my international stylist colleague, Leslie Davies with The Stylish Insider, shares, being thoughtful and planning your visual image to align with your personality and purpose can create a sense of calm in your dress. Wearing a third piece (a jacket, vest, scarf, etc.) can transform the impact you make, as each layer adds an element of formality and interest to your outfit. Layering your clothing with an intention of the *feeling* you want to create is fun, expressive, and provides visual interest. This draws people to you like a magnet, when they also value your personality through your intentional dressing. Careful selection of colours and styles helps you show up confidently, and be able to take advantage of the opportunities in front of you. It is so important to show up authentically, be expressive and confident. Feeling a sense of ease around what we are projecting allows you to show up confidently.[173]

Clothes can change the shape of your body, by emphasizing parts you want to draw attention to, and minimizing areas you do not like about yourself. In the same interview Leslie shared that one of her clients calls the work she does "image voodoo." She recommends creating a "style recipe — a unique combination of words that convey how you want to feel when you step out into the world." Clothing can change your authority level, simply by adding a jacket you step into a leadership mindset. Think about a president or politician who has a high contrasting blue suit and white shirt — that contrast creates a formal look. An invitation to a "black and white tie ball" is a formal affair requiring a specific style of dress. Crisp fabrics, tailored, and structured outfits say formal.

Align your clothing style and external image with your personality, the impact you make as you walk into an event, and how you want to feel need to fit together. Feeling confident is about alignment of values and feelings inside, and personality and polish on the outside. Even the colours we wear speak volumes about us — depending on our skin tone and hair colour. Selecting black or navy is the most formal choice, followed by jewel tones (burgundy, forest green, royal blue, or purple) whereas a pastel (pale pink, yellow, or baby blue) will not have the same high impact. A polished person on the outside, but feeling frazzled inside will reflect a disconnection, and that energy will be felt by others . . .

How do you want to feel, and what do you want to project with your image? If you are leading a staff team-building session, you will likely want to show up in different attire than attending a meeting at the bank applying for a loan. Applying for a loan is a more formal meeting to have a conversation with an important impact (whether that is a home purchase or a business loan). Showing up as though you already have received the loan approval, "as if" you already have been approved, creates a level of assured certainty in the meeting. "Dress for success" is a good phrase to remember, as it will raise your own energy level if you know you have already stepped into the role of home owner or business expansion expert. Dressing for the situation is important, so that you show up in an energy of "ease and flow."

8.6

First Impressions Matter

Banking institutions have very distinct lending criteria and standard practices to stay within the banking legislation, so showing a flamboyant first impression may not support your loan request. The bank loans officer will certainly need the formality of checking your five C's of Credit, and not solely be making a decision based on your attire, however, first impressions count. The five C's of credit is a system used by lenders to gauge the creditworthiness of potential borrowers.

The system weighs five characteristics of the borrower and conditions of the loan, attempting to estimate the chance of default, and lower their risk of investing in you or your idea. (The five C's are: character, capacity, capital, collateral and conditions. [174] Wearing more traditional darker colours aligns with a more traditional institution such as a bank. Select solid colours without crazy patterns, or pick pin-stripes that convey linear thinking, a moderate length skirt rather than wearing a bright pink leather mini-skirt. Think about the event, the purpose of being there, your desired outcome, and then select your wardrobe accordingly. Alternatively, if you want to browse around a furniture store without being trailed by a sales associate, dress down for the occasion, wearing your ripped jeans and un-ironed shirt, carrying a phone and no shoulder purse, and most will leave you alone, assuming you do not have the money to buy anything in their store. Select your clothing with intention, using it to create the impact you desire.

Assert your authority at work with your first impression, before you begin delegating. If you are promoted, or getting ready for a promotion, one simple addition to elevate your new authority level is to wear a jacket. Wearing a jacket elevates your wardrobe and expresses a sense of authority instantly. There are so many styles of jackets available for women, and the crisper or heavier the fabric the more it conveys a sense of competence and consistency (lined jackets are more formal than unlined and hang differently on your body). Select your clothing to fit the role that you want next when you receive the promotion, then dress as though you were already in that role.

We can influence others with our wardrobe choices too. My stylist also taught me that if we want to be perceived as more influential, wearing straight lines (pin-stripes) and high contrast combinations, we exude authority. (For example, a white shirt is in high contrast to a navy blazer.) If we want to be inviting, wearing a tie or a blouse with a curved pattern is softer and creates a more approachable feel. Try some of these concepts as you prepare your wardrobe for the day (unless you are in a uniformed environment or role where safety clothing is mandatory) and see how others respond to you. The more formal your attire (a matching suit rather than a coordinating jacket and pants), the more authority your overall image creates.

For a team-building meeting, if you are in an offsite setting (such as an outdoor agility course for a physical team event), you can still dress in a comfortable manner and show leadership by wearing dark coloured casual pants, and a third piece — for the reasons stated earlier. Dress in a way that you can be part of the team for the event, yet add a jacket for any portions of the event where you have to speak to kick it off or link the event to business strategic goals, or the wrap-up segment for a conclusion and next steps. Wearing a shirt that has a collar also adds more formality than a crew-necked T-shirt. Depending on your objective, you may want to select the same shirts as your team. (Think about your local golf club, collars are required rather than collarless T-shirts.)

8.7

Choices and Timing: Leveraging Resources

Your choice of venues communicates your values. For one-on-one or smaller meetings, arranging a coffee shop connection rather than a formal boardroom brings a more collaborative energy to the conversation. Having a meeting where you are exerting your authority in your office (your territory) will extend an air of confidence and authority, just as taking a seat at the head of the table puts you in command of the room without a word being spoken.

If you are meeting a potential client for lunch, I usually let them choose the venue, which gives me an indicator of their preferences (both in food: vegan, vegetarian, cultural, etc.) as well as style and taste. If they pick a local café, it may be because it is close to their offices and no travel is required, or if a higher priced steak house — that sends another subtle message regarding their lifestyle level. In reverse, if you are selecting the venue, why does this particular venue resonate with you? Is it the variety of food, the fine cuisine, the location, the ambiance, or the overall experience you want to share with your meal guest? Pay attention to restaurant noise levels when you first visit each one, so that you know whether or not the loud music from the frequently positioned speakers will allow you to hear your partner's conversation without raising your voice. Restaurants with carpet rather than stone or marble floors generally baffle some of the sound, as popular restaurants are frequently busy at lunchtime making it difficult to have a meaningful conversation. Sometimes it is not even your words that send a clear message . . . Selecting the right venue matters.

Your timing communicates what you value. Do you always arrive for appointments, meetings, or events early? If you arrive thirty minutes early for an event, unless you are at a football game or a concert which will often cause large crowds vying for a parking space, arriving excessively early may not be beneficial. Pace your day so that you have enough space in your calendar for travel time if needed, so that you can aim to arrive fifteen minutes before your appointment time. This gives you time to find a parking spot, check your image in the mirror or touch up your lip gloss, and gather your thoughts for the upcoming conversation.

Your communications method matters. If you are broadcasting an update to the entire organization, a one-way message such as a company-wide email may be efficient, yet it does not invite what I call "feel-back." Delivering a "state-of-the-union" address in a town-hall meeting verbally will provide information and still open up conversation with a question period after the event, allowing you to feel the pulse of your group and their engagement level. Always have a team member ready with a question or two, to break the ice for less confident employees to add their question once the flow has already started. Asking for employee feedback via an electronic survey administered by a third-party organization will enable you to collect opinions while still remaining confidential to the individual who provided their input. Having the quantifiable statistics of response percentages and a scoring system is valuable, yet so are the individual comments and questions, which tell you so much more.

What would be an ideal outcome from the connection? Picture the outcome, and feel yourself smiling and having a warm glow in your belly of satisfaction or love, or a sense of accomplishment that you capitalized on your time for a meaningful connection. If you make every conversation count, you will be amazed when you reflect in your journal just how much has been achieved in the past few days.

Leverage technology. Sometimes a face-to-face meeting is not required. If you have already met in person, following up with a video call or telephone call is an efficient way to build the relationship as you deepen your conversation, while carefully managing your calendar. I learned this when I purchased my first real estate rental property, with four tenants occupying different apartments. It was close to my home, with a fifteen-minute drive to reach it, yet I soon realized that any time a tenant called with an issue (such as locking themselves out or a noise complaint), I lost an hour of my time. Driving there and back took fifteen to twenty minutes each way (depending on the time of day), plus the fifteen to twenty minutes sorting out their issue. Another hour of time gone!

Value your time. Today with the options of ZOOM teleconference, Skype, and other video conference options, shaving your travel time can give you a big advantage, as well as helping with our carbon footprint by not driving and adding pollution to the air . . . My meetings under thirty minutes are now almost always via telephone, which also allows me to serve English-speaking clients around the world wherever there is internet service, while helping the planet overall by not elevating my carbon footprint.

Always choose a gift. Your conversation could be with your mother-in-law, or a prospective client or alliance partner, so your offer will vary appropriately. As you head into the conversation, think about your desired outcome. If you know their hobbies or interests, industry or profession, consider what you can offer them that would be a valuable ending to the meeting. It could be an invitation to an event with you, a potential client connection for them, a recipe, an interesting article or TED Talk you recently saw, or buying lunch — always have something you can give the other person. Your generosity will be remembered, and the next time that you need something, you have already paved the path with that person, and will be more likely to have your request granted.

Choose reciprocity . . . Always have "an ask": While you want to give your gift freely, often the power of reciprocity will cause your conversation partner to ask how they can help you also. Be ready to leverage this opportunity! They may have a circle of connections that you would like to meet, a referral or recommendation to a specific service you need, an association or trade magazine for trend insights — always have something you can readily respond with that is a strategic request or moves the relationship deeper in some way.

Let others know you are ready for business. In a restaurant, closing your menu signals to the server that you are ready to order your meal. Be prepared is a common theme that came up in many of the interviews in my Confident and Influential Women interview series. [175] (A complete interview list is shown on www.WordsWomenAndWisdom.com) By being clear in your intention before a meeting or event, you can ensure you are ready for the next step (have a gift, have your order form, have your performance results to share, have your "ask" prepared, or well thought through innovative ideas). In a business meeting, build rapport for a few minutes first before whipping open your binder or notepad, building relationships is like a conversational dance, it takes time to evolve and move in synchronicity in a graceful way. If you are having a restaurant conversation, build rapport until your server has brought your meal, as wait staff generally will then leave you uninterrupted until your meal is finished, enabling you to have the most important conversation together without a waiter buzzing around constantly.

Select the time of day — for your best energy cycle. If you are a night owl, agreeing to an early morning call or meeting will not give you the best advantage. Pay attention to what times of day you have your highest energy, and tap into this to do your most important work. If you are working on a strategic project requiring your brightest mind, book your time to work on it when you will be uninterrupted and at your sharpest. Close your door, put your phone on Do Not Disturb, turn off any computer "pop-up" windows and do your best work. Every interruption costs you up to twelve minutes of time lost getting back into the flow state you were previously in. How can you step further into the most confident version of yourself, by embracing a few of the concepts included?

Be **flawsome!**
(Flawsome: <u>Something</u> that is <u>totally awesome</u>,

but not <u>without</u> its flaws.)

Urban Dictionary.com

ACTION STEPS:

Practise bringing silence into your life. *In business, resist the urge to have an opinion about everything, unless you are invited into the conversation. Nervous people who want others to like them have a tendency to keep talking, hoping that something they say will hit the mark and connect with others. Pay attention to where you need to simply be silent. A nod of understanding goes a long way towards acknowledging that you heard the other person, and you are considering the point they are making.*

 Learn how to use silence to your advantage. *"I appreciate you sharing your opinion, and I will give this some further thought." Period. You do not need to explain your thought process further, nor start defending your thinking right now, let the silence hang, and only when you are ready with a fully developed reply step back into that conversation and give your opinion.*

 Try mirroring another person's body language *and pace of speaking, and watch what happens to the connection forming between you both, and if they are leaning into the conversation.*

 Dress purposefully. *As you visit your closet, consider what will you wear today that is purposeful for the events you are attending, and helps you FEEL confident and at ease? Check-in with yourself in the mirror to confirm your chosen outfit works, and at the end of the day to note your observations and how others treated you today.*

CONCLUSION

Confidence is experienced when you are comfortable in your own skin. When you know that no matter what events and circumstances come your way, you have the ability to survive them, with grace and humility. When you are independent of the NEED to be with others, you can CHOOSE who to include in your life. Be with others because you want to or because you enjoy their company, not because you HAVE to be with them, or you are dependent on them for your safety and happiness.

Confident women recognize that they need to energetically refuel periodically in order to be strong enough to support others, by gearing up for a high energy run, choosing to be with others or to quietly indulge in a book. Know what recharges you. More choices equals freedom! Freedom supports confident living.

While this book shows you how to have more confident conversations with others, I hope you are also enjoying the journey towards having warm and compassionate "I am . . ." conversations with yourself.

Stepping into a more confident version of yourself is an evolution. Recognizing your areas for self-development (your shadow side), and purposefully choosing to deepen your relationship with the most important person in your life – YOU – will enable your confidence to deepen as you evolve and resonate at a higher energetic vibration.

While I wrote this book to help you to begin shifting your awareness with individual disempowering words that women use, your language reflects how you feel inside about yourself. When you are confident in your accomplishments, are proud of your abilities, know your values (and your value to others) and how to assertively hold a conversation, you flourish. Your body language is different, you will hold your head up a little higher, lift your chin with determination to take your place in a society that now recognizes, and is more welcoming, for strong women. Others will notice your inner strength, and treat you differently, with more respect.

When your internal sense of who you are and the contribution you make in the world are clear, your passion and energetic resonance shines. Use that positive energy to shine brightly, to encourage other women to step into the best version of themselves. Support them by amplifying their ideas, and encouraging them to achieve their dreams. The ripple effect that one woman can make on this planet is powerful. The ripples we can make together to leverage our natural, nurturing, and collaborative community spirit will make a massive positive difference – and most importantly, role modeling feminine strength for our children is one of the greatest gifts we have to share.

When women band together in wisdom, recognizing that we are stronger in numbers, we are a powerful force of feminine energy. What difference will you choose to make today, elevating yourself and elevating another woman along the way?

The Modern Art of Confident Conversations is about

loving yourself FIRST.

Be bold! Be confident!

ABOUT THE AUTHOR

Speaker, coach, mentor, writer, business owner, mother, wife and growth catalyst.

Yvonne E. L. Silver is a Catalyst for Women's growth. She teaches women to flourish in business, by elevating more confident conversations, to enable women to have more success and fun in business! Yvonne is passionate about supporting women entrepreneurs and leaders, especially those with a social enterprise business, or women ready to step up into leadership. When women can elevate in their career, ask for what they want, negotiate successfully, connect with clients, increase sales, and engage staff more authentically, their confidence blossoms.

Dedicated to changing lives, Yvonne currently serves on the board for The Nest Foundation, sharing expertise in helping women rebuild after divorce and flourish. She develops programs for women who need to rebuild their confidence, build up their resources, elevate their career and become the best version of themselves. Yvonne brings together her twenty-five plus years helping people develop, combined with past board experience with The International Coach Federation – Calgary Chapter.

An innovative advocate for women, she is a BPW Canada ambassador and active member. (BPW has forty thousand women advocates and members globally, and consults to the UN on women's issues.) Yvonne is an experienced speaker and program developer, who chairs mentorship programs for multiple groups, including BPW (Business and Professional Women Calgary (2016-2018) and Canadian Business Chicks BOSS Chicks

Authentic Mentorship program, which launched in 2017. She is a member of the Evolutionary Business Institute & HR Institute of Alberta, and was recognized with a Women of Inspiration 2018 Award for Mentorship.

Yvonne leverages her core values of **creativity, compassion, inspiration,** and **possibility** to help women develop extreme clarity — achieving purposeful success while reducing stress. Her clients have more confidence, success in life and business, more joy, work-life balance, and more quality family time. She incorporates over twenty-five years of success (working with eight start-ups plus a corporate VP role in a global firm) to coach others to their maximum potential. Professionally, Yvonne holds an executive Coaching Certificate from Royal Roads University, a Chartered Professional in HR designation (HR Institute of Alberta) and has completed a Business Management Certificate at the University of Calgary. She is also a Certified Reiki Practitioner, integrating energetic presence and resonance into her work, and Certified EQ-i Consultant (helping women leverage their Emotional Intelligence).

Happily married with four grown children (ranging from twenty-three to thirty-three at time of writing), Yvonne enjoys reading, writing, entrepreneurship, nature, design, travel, and supporting women with a massive vision to achieve it. Yvonne attended a first-round pitch on Dragon's Den with her son Alex — a special-needs artist who is raising money for Operation Smile (Alex's Amazing Art) and changing children's lives with his art. https://www.facebook.com/alexgorskiart/

Yvonne is an "in-demand" speaker for conferences and corporate events, women's groups and tele-summit/radio show interviews — sharing wisdom with audiences up to five hundred women to date (at the Fearless Women's Summit in March 2018). Her "Words, Women and Wisdom Show" launched in July 2018, to expand her teachings (with guest speakers) to larger audiences via radio, with upcoming show information at: https://bbsradio.com/wordswomenandwisdomshow

Yvonne's mentorship and group coaching programs offer custom opportunities for clients to access seasoned coaching for women, at varied price-points, to enable any woman who wants to elevate her confidence to step into action. Yvonne's latest programs, events, courses, and blog information can be found at: www.WordsWomenAndWisdom.com

Book purchases and donations made, along with book launch related information is at: www.WordsWomenAndWisdom.com

Connect with Yvonne at:

Facebook — https://www.facebook.com/yvonne.silver33

LinkedIn — /yvonnesilver/

Twitter — Yvonne_ELSilver

<u>2017-2019 Keynotes and Talks —
Women's topics:</u>

WORD-POWER: 5 keys to being a confident woman using powerful language
* *How Women can Rock in Business: Authentic Leadership*
* *Emotional Intelligence for Women*
* *STOP BURNING OUT: Living with Purpose and Joy!*

To book Yvonne as your Speaker, email mailto:admin@WordsWomenAndWisdom.com for availability for your event date or call 403.999.4749. Talks can be tailored to your particular audience and time-block desired. More at: http://speakers.ebcouncil.com/speaker/yvonne-el-silver?b=s

I welcome receiving your comments via email directly. I am curious to hear how your world changes after shifting your language to have more Confident Conversations. You can connect with me through my "Contact" page at: www.WordsWomenAndWisdom.com or send me a message via LinkedIn or Facebook.

Please buy an extra copy and gift it to another woman who could benefit from having more confidence.

For every copy sold, one copy will be donated to a women's shelter, foundation, or not-for-profit.

END NOTES

1 United Nations, "Sustainable Development Goals, United Nations Development Programme".
http://www.undp.org/content/undp/en/home/sustainable-development-goals.html (accessed August 20, 2018).

[2] "Women Leaders Launch "TIME'S UP" Campaign to Eradicate Abuse of Power, Shift Leadership Imbalances, and Promote Equality", Yahoo Finance, PR Newswire January 1, 2018.   https://finance.yahoo.com/news/women-leaders-launch-times-campaign-133000452.html (accessed August 20, 2018).

[3] The International Federation of Business and Professional Women (BPW) http://www.bpw-international.org/ National Business and Professional Women's Clubs https://www.bpw-international.org/about-us/4-benefits-of-membership (accessed September 14, 2018)

[4] More on the history of feminism at:
https://en.wikipedia.org/wiki/Feminist_movement (accessed August 20, 2018); Rampton, Martha, "Four Waves of Feminism". (October 25, 2015) http://www.pacificu.edu/about-us/news-events/four-waves-feminism www.pacificu.edu. Archived from the original on 2015-11-19; Humm, Maggie "wave (definition)", *The Dictionary of Feminist Theory* (Columbus: Ohio State University Press, 1990), 251. ISBN 9780814205075; Walker, Rebecca, "Becoming the Third Wave". *Ms. Magazine* (January 1992). (New York: Liberty Media for Women: 39–41). ISSN 0047-8318. OCLC 194419734. (accessed September 14, 2018)

[5] Further history about the Famous Five at: http://www.famou5.ca/the-famous-five-women/ (accessed August 20, 2018).

[6] This Day In History: https://www.history.com/this-day-in-history/equal-rights-amendment-passed-by-congress History.com Editors, A&E Television Networks (accessed August 20, 2018).

[7] Canada, Ontario, *Fair Employment Practices Act, 1951 (S.). 1951, c.24* and *the Female Employees Fair Remuneration Act*, S.O. 1951, c.26 (Ref: opentextbc.ca/postconfederation - Robert Rutherdale, Department of Philosophy & History, Algoma University. (accessed August 20, 2018).

Further History of women's rights in Canada:
https://www.canada.ca/en/canadian-heritage/services/rights-women.html

(accessed August 20, 2018).

[8] Reference* https://www.reference.com/technology/many-tvs-world-9b0c2005f3b30c1c# (accessed September 14, 2018)

[9] Women in the Workplace 2017 is a comprehensive study of the state of women in corporate America. This research is part of a long-term partnership between LeanIn.Org and McKinsey & Company. Further information: https://womenintheworkplace.com/ (accessed September 14, 2018)

[10] United Nations Entity for Gender Equality and the Empowerment of Women (UN Women) Women's Empowerment Principles — Equality Means Business http://www.unwomen.org/en/digital-library/publications/2011/10/women-s-empowerment-principles-equality-means-business#view (accessed August 20, 2018).

[11] Marcus Noland and Tyler Moran, "Firms with More Women in the C-Suite Are More Profitable", *Harvard Business Review*, (February 08, 2016); Peterson Institute for International Economics survey - https://hbr.org/2016/02/study-firms-with-more-women-in-the-c-suite-are-more-profitable (accessed August 20, 2018).

[12] "Why Diversity Matters", (Catalyst, July 2013). More at: http://www.catalyst.org/system/files/why_diversity_matters_catalyst_0.pdf

[13] Vivian Hunt, Sara Prince, Sundiatu Dixon-Fryle, and Lareina Yee, *Delivering Through Diversity* (McKinsey & Company, 2018). McKinsey & Company's global study of more than 1,000 companies in 12 countries (accessed August 20, 2018).

[14] Nancy M. Carter and Harvey M. Wagner, *The Bottom Line: Corporate Performance and Women's Representation on Boards (2004–2008)* (Catalyst, 2011).

[15] Lindsay Fortado, "Hedge funds run by women outperform", Financial Times (March 10, 2017).

[16] Jenny Gulamani-Abdulla – BPW Canada President 2016-2018, Founder - Gulamani-Abdulla & Co., Immigration Consulting, ZOOM Interview - December 1st, 2017 https://youtu.be/uxPwuJtW4aw

[17] Sarah Cobarrubias, instructor, *Intro to Psychology: Help and Review* / Psychology Courses (Study.com).

[18] Jon Gordon, Dan Britton, and Jimmy Page, *"One Word That Will Change Your Life",* (Wiley, 2013).

[19] Margarita Mayo, *"To Seem Confident, Women Have to Be Seen as Warm"*, Harvard Business Review, (July 08, 2016). https://hbr.org/2016/07/to-seem-confident-women-have-to-be-seen-as-warm

[20] Dictionary.com, "Confidence".

[21] Jayne Warrilow, *"The Secret Language of Resonance"*.

[22] Interview with Karen McGregor - CEO, International Speaker and Author - Speaker Success Formula. ZOOM Interview - Nov. 21, 2017 https://youtu.be/QPSsoRJssBU

[23] Samantha Olson, *"Your Gut Feeling Is Way More Than Just A Feeling: The Science Of Intuition"*, Medicaldaily.com. More at: https://www.medicaldaily.com/your-gut-feeling-way-more-just-feeling-science-intuition-325338

[24] Brené Brown, *"Daring Greatly"*, (Avery, 2012).

[25] Viktor Frankl, *"Man's Search For Meaning"*, (1946).

[26] Viktor Frankl, *"Man's Search For Meaning"*, (1946).

[27] Jack Canfield, Mark Victor Hansen, and Les Hewitt, *"The Power of Focus"*, (Health Communications, Inc., 2000).

[28] Wikipedia, Japanese Buddhist Mikao Usui. More at https://en.wikipedia.org/wiki/Mikao_Usui

[29] Mark Waldman, *"NeuroTips for Money, Happiness & Success: 21 Productivity Tips for your Brain"*. Mark is on the faculty of the executive MBA at Loyola Marymount University.

[30] "Positivity", Go Strengths, By Neutrino on April 4, 2012. For more: https://www.gostrengths.com/positivity/

[31] Ellie Lisitsa, "The Positive Perspective: More on the 5:1 Ratio" (December 5, 2012). For further information on the work of Dr. John Gottman, go to: https://www.gottman.com/blog/the-positive-perspective-more-on-the-51-ratio/

[32] Simon Sinek, "Starting with Why", (TED Talk). Video at: https://youtu.be/ZKyf7eeMzdY?t=10

[33] Pam Stone, "Crying and Comforting, The Attached Family", *The Journal of API* (December 23, 2008). Originally published in the Non-AP Issue of The Journal of API (Summer 2008). To read the article:

http://theattachedfamily.com/membersonly/?p=1255 (accessed September 14, 2018)

[34] Louise Hay, *"You can heal your life"*, (Hay House, 1984).

[35] Dr. Martin E.P. Seligman and Christopher Peterson, "The VIA Survey of Character Strengths", validated by Robert McGrath, PhD. To access the survey, go to: https://www.viacharacter.org/www/Character-Strengths-Survey

[36] "Words to use with caution: 'But', But, however, nevertheless, still, and yet." Pegasus NLP. For further information: https://nlp-now.co.uk/be-careful-with-but/ (accessed September 14, 2018)

[37] Dictionary.com https://www.dictionary.com/browse/but?s=t

[38] Zoom interview of Teresa de Grosbois, *"Mass Influence: The Habits of the Highly Influential"*, ZOOM Interview, (Oct. 10th, 2017). https://youtu.be/BCDriBNTwLk

[39] Daniel Pink, *"DRIVE: The surprising truth about what really motivates us"*, (New York: Riverhead Books, 2009).

[40] Van Vliet, V. *Henri Fayol.* (2010) (accessed September 14, 2018) at https://www.toolshero.com/toolsheroes/henri-fayol/

[41] *Henri Fayol's 14 Principles of Management - Functions and Principles of Management, Management Study Guide.* Further information: https://www.managementstudyguide.com/management_principles.htm

[42] Michael Losier, *The Law of Attraction*, (Victoria, B.C.: Warner Wellness, 2003).

[43] Sarah Stawiski, Jennifer Deal, and Marian Ruderman, "Building trust in the workplace – A key to retaining women" Centre for Creative Leadership. (August 2010). To read the article: https://www.ccl.org/articles/quickview-leadership-articles/building-trust-in-the-workplace-a-key-to-retaining-women/ (accessed September 14, 2018)

[44] Daniel Pink, *"DRIVE: The surprising truth about what really motivates us"*, (New York: Riverhead Books, 2009).

[45] The Wynford Group *"Salary Survey and Recommended Best Practices Report"*. More on their customized reports at: https://www.wynfordgroup.com/wynfordsurveys/

[46] Alison Donaghey – Founder – Domino Thinking, Speaker, Think Opposite Radio Show Host, author *of Think Opposite: Using The Domino Effect To Change Your Business, Change The World.* ZOOM Interview – Apr. 3rd, 2018 https://youtu.be/_YXKZ7HF6tI

[47] Michael Bernard Beckwith, New Thought Minister, Author, Founder of the Agape International Spiritual Center: *"Believe in What You Don't See"*. Watch the full segment: http://www.oprah.com/own-supersoulsessions/michael-bernard-beckwith-believe-in-what-you-dont-see

[48] *Dr. Wayne Dyer,* "When you change the way you look at things…*"* YouTube: https://youtu.be/urQPraeeY0w?t=10

[49] Lisa Mundell-Lawrence, Executive Vice President - Western Canada PMA-Brethour Realty Group, and co-owner of the Cheap Smokes & Cigars Franchise. ZOOM Interview - Feb. 27th, 2018 https://youtu.be/BzEDwOjZUGo

[50] Dr. Robert Emmons, *Thanks! How the New Science of Gratitude Can Make You Happier* (Boston: Houghton-Mifflin, 2007).

[51] Louise Hay, *"You can Heal your Life"*

[52] Amy Morin, (contributor), "7 Scientifically Proven Benefits Of Gratitude That Will Motivate You To Give Thanks Year-Round", Forbes (November 23, 2014). Article at: https://www.forbes.com/sites/amymorin/2014/11/23/7-scientifically-proven-benefits-of-gratitude-that-will-motivate-you-to-give-thanks-year-round/#26715924183c

[53] Amy Morin, "7 Scientifically Proven Benefits Of Gratitude That Will Motivate You To Give Thanks Year-Round", Psychology Today (April 3, 2015); Dr. Robert Emmons, *Thanks! How The New Science of Gratitude Can Make You Happier"* (Boston: Houghton-Mifflin, 2007). More at: https://www.psychologytoday.com/us/blog/what-mentally-strong-people-dont-do/201504/7-scientifically-proven-benefits-gratitude

[54] Dr. Robert Emmons, "Why Gratitude Is Good", the Greater Good Science Center at UC Berkeley, The Greater Good Magazine, (The Greater Good Science Center, UC Berkeley, November 16, 2010). To read this article: https://greatergood.berkeley.edu/article/item/why_gratitude_is_good

[55] Amy Morin, contributor, "7 Scientifically Proven Benefits Of Gratitude That Will Motivate You To Give Thanks Year-Round", Forbes (November 23, 2014). Article at:https://www.forbes.com/sites/amymorin/2014/11/23/7-scientifically-proven-benefits-of-gratitude-that-will-motivate-you-to-give-thanks-year-round/#26715924183c

[56] Dr. Robert Emmons, "Why Gratitude Is Good", The Greater Good Magazine (The Greater Good Science Center, UC Berkeley, November 16, 2010). To read this article: https://greatergood.berkeley.edu/article/item/why_gratitude_is_good

[57] Melinda Wittstock – Founder Verifeed and the WINGS of Inspired Business Podcast, ZOOM Interview - Dec. 20th, 2017 https://youtu.be/AsenQD2Hk8M

[58] More on Verifeed's Return on Authenticity algorithm:
https://verifeed.com/return-on-authenticity/

[59] Wikipedia, Stephen Covey, *The 7 Habits of Highly Effective People*, first published in 1989. Full article:
https://en.wikipedia.org/wiki/The_7_Habits_of_Highly_Effective_People

[60] Gary D. Chapman, *"The Five Love Languages: How to Express Heartfelt Commitment to Your Mate"*, (Chicago: Northfield Pub., 2010).

[61] Fire Nation Podcast, John Lee Dumas interview, Episode 1259: "Create a massively successful word-of-mouth campaign" with Teresa de Grosbois (12.20). Listen here: https://www.eofire.com/podcast/teresadegrosbois/

[62] Daniel Pink, *"DRIVE: The surprising truth about what really motivates us"*, (New York: Riverhead Books, 2009).

[63] Mihaly Csikszentmihalyi, "Flow, the secret to happiness", TED2004 (February 2004). *More on the talk:*
https://www.ted.com/talks/mihaly_csikszentmihalyi_on_flow

[64] Tracy Williams, Personal Coaching Session conversation.

[65] Craig Elias, "How to Overcome the #1 Sales Objection", . *Article at:*
http://shiftselling.com/2018/01/17/how-to-overcome-the-1-sales-objection/

[66] Rabbi Steven Carr Reuben, Ph.D., *"What Baby Elephants Can Teach Us About Human Freedom,* Huffington Post, THE BLOG 01/11/2013 (Updated Mar 13, 2013). Further information: https://www.huffingtonpost.com/rabbi-steven-carr-reuben-phd/what-baby-elephants-can-teach-us-about-human-freedom_b_2452099.html

[67] Jan Fable, MS, LADC, "Dealing with Shame", posted on November 24, 2014 More at: http://janfable.com/dealing-with-shame/

[68] David Rock, "Managing with the Brain in Mind", Strategy+Business, August 27, 2009 / (Autumn 2009, Issue 56). Originally published by Booz & Company. Read the article: https://www.strategy-business.com/article/09306

[69] David Rock, "Managing with the Brain in Mind", Strategy+Business, August 27, 2009 / (Autumn 2009, Issue 56). Originally published by Booz & Company. Read the article: https://www.strategy-business.com/article/09306

[70] Mike Dooley, *"Manifesting Change: It Couldn't Be Easier"*, (Atria Books/Beyond Words, 2010).

[71] Wikipedia, Astington and colleagues (1993) More at:
https://en.wikipedia.org/wiki/Intention

[72] Monica Kretschmer – Founder, Canadian Business Chicks and Women of Inspiration, ZOOM Interview - Nov. 21, 2017 https://youtu.be/XKjNBqkteMY

[73] *The Bucket List*- Warner Bros. · Zadan / Meron Productions · Two Ton Films (2007).

[74] Rhonda Byrne, *The Secret* (New York: Atria Books; Hillsboro, OR: Beyond Words Publishing, 2016)*;* Rhonda Byrne, *The Power* (New York: Atria Books, 2010).

[75] Esther and Jerry Hicks, "Abraham – Laws of the Universe*", Money, and the Law of Attraction,* (Carlsbad, CA; Vancouver, B.C.: Hay House, 2008).

[76] Evelyn Lim, *Abundance Alchemy* (CreateSpace, 2010).

[77] Dixie Bennett, Reiki Master & Master Healer, Reiki Mentorship Program – 2017

[78] Mark Waldman, *NeuroWisdom: The New Brain Science of Money, Happiness, and Success*, shared in a recent interview on the Wings Business Summit, launched April 13, 2018.

[79] Michael Michalko, *"What Nature Teaches Us About How to Deal with Adversity"* and *"Thinkertoys: A Handbook of Creative Thinking Techniques"* (Ten Speed Press, 2010). *More at:* http://creativethinking.net/author/michael-michalko/

[80] Abraham Harold Maslow, *"Hierarchy of Needs", A Theory of Human Motivation",* (Psychological Review, 1943).
Note of Respect: Respectfully acknowledging Blackfoot people's teachings, Tsuu T'ina reserve, Alberta connects with the work of Abraham Harold Maslow, Psychologist*: "Maslow's Hierarchy of Needs".*

[81] Jeff Wise and Vladimir Zatsiorsky, "Yes, You Really Can Lift a Car Off a Trapped Child" and "The Science Behind Seemingly Impossible Feats of Strength Stealth Superpowers", Psychology Today. More at:
https://www.psychologytoday.com/us/blog/extreme-fear/201011/yes-you-really-can-lift-car-trapped-child

[82] Jeff Wise and Vladimir Zatsiorsky, *"Yes, You Really Can Lift a Car Off a Trapped Child"* and "The Science Behind Seemingly Impossible Feats of Strength Stealth Superpowers", Psychology Today. More at:
https://www.psychologytoday.com/us/blog/extreme-fear/201011/yes-you-really-can-lift-car-trapped-child

[83] Anne Kreamer, *"It's Always Personal: Navigating Emotion In The Workplace"* (Random House, 2011).

[84] Catherine Pearson, "What 15 Female Leaders Really Think About Crying At Work*"*, Huffington Post, WOMEN (05/28/2014 09:26 EDT) | Updated 12/06/2017, reference to Mika Brzezinski, Co-host - "Morning Joe" on MSNBC. More on this article: https://www.huffingtonpost.ca/entry/crying-at-work-women_n_5365872

[85] Sylvia Ann Hewlett, founder and CEO, *Center for Talent Innovation*, and author of *Executive Presence: The Missing Link Between Merit and Success* in Catherine Pearson, "What 15 Female Leaders Really Think About Crying At Work*"*, Huffington Post, WOMEN, (05/28/2014 09:26 EDT) | Updated 12/06/2017 More on this article: https://www.huffingtonpost.ca/entry/crying-at-work-women_n_5365872

[86] Dana Dovey, "How To Not Cry: 4 Ways To Stop Tears From Falling", The Grapevine – Medical Daily, Aug 1, 2016 quoting Dr. Sneh Khemka, Medical Director at Bupa International. More on this topic: https://www.medicaldaily.com/how-not-cry-393317

[87] Brigitte Lessard Deyell, Founder – Women Talk, ZOOM Interview - Mar. 6th, 2018. (Listen to full interview at: https://youtu.be/T5c0W2-t5Lo)

[88] Lisa Nicols, *"Abundance Now: Amplify Your Life & Achieve Prosperity Today"*, YouTube, at: https://www.youtube.com/watch?v=nKTAZAmJ_Js

[89] Christian D. Larson — a.k.a Christian Daa Larson (1866-1955) — an American New Thought leader and teacher, and a prolific author of metaphysical and New Thought books.

[90] Kimbel Musk, *"Trust is the new currency"*, Underground Seminar. More information about Underground Seminars at: https://undergroundonlineseminar.com/

[91] Robert T. Kiyosaki, *Rich Dad's Cashflow Quadrant* (Plata Publishing, 2011).

[92] K.J. McCorry, "Little Disruptions Can Steal The Whole Day Away", Boulder Business Report (August 10-23, 2001). *(Ref: Margin, Dr. Richard Swenson, 1992)*.Read the article with additional information: https://www.interruptions.net/literature/McCorry-BCBR01.pdf

[93] Jonathan Spira, *Overload! How Too Much Information Is Hazardous To Your Organization"*

[94] Markus MacGill, "What is the link between love and oxytocin?" *Medical News Today,* Last updated Mon 4 September 2017. Reviewed by Michael Weber, MD More at: https://www.medicalnewstoday.com/articles/275795.php

[95] Mark Waldman, *NeuroTips for Money, Happiness & Success: 21 Productivity Tips for your Brain.*

[96] Marci Shimoff, *"Happy for No Reason: 7 Steps to Being Happy from the Inside Out"*, ZOOM Interview – Jan. 2nd, 2018
https://youtu.be/0VK8554aoTM

[97] Connie Podesta — Motivational Speaker, *live Achievers Canada Talk organized by Les Hewett, Calgary, 1980-1990*

[98] Steven Shea (contributor), "The Characteristics of Sleep". Read the article (with videos):
http://healthysleep.med.harvard.edu/healthy/science/what/characteristics

[99] Wikipedia, "Adrenal gland". More at:
https://en.wikipedia.org/wiki/Adrenal_gland

[100] Julia Layton, "How Fear Works", How Stuff Works. Read the full article at:
https://science.howstuffworks.com/life/inside-the-mind/emotions/fear2.htm

[101] Jon Kabat-Zinn, *Full Catastrophe Living*, (New York: Dell Publishing, 1990). https://www.mindfulnesscds.com/

[102] Dr. Al Noor Mawani, "Mindfulness". A short article at:
http://drmawani.ca/general-information/mindfulness/

[103] Ruth Baer, (editor), "Mindfulness-based treatment approaches". (San Diego: Elsevier, 2006).

[104] Marci Shimoff – Global Transformational Leader and Best-Selling Author of *"Happy For No Reason: 7 Steps to Being Happy from the Inside Out"*, ZOOM Interview – Jan. 2nd, 2018 https://youtu.be/0VK8554aoTM

[105] "Greeting Adversity", PPOTECH 2012. YouTube:
https://youtu.be/YhnCNC6ROGc

[106] Christina Marlett, Founder - The Courageous Self-Care Movement ZOOM Interview - Nov. 15th, 2017. https://youtu.be/-i4mxp56AM8

[107] Christina Marlett, Founder - The Courageous Self-Care Movement ZOOM Interview - Nov. 15th, 2017. https://youtu.be/-i4mxp56AM8

[108] Amy Cuddy, "Your Body Language Shapes Who You Are", TEDGlobal 2012.
http://www.ted.com/talks/amy_cuddy_your_body_language_shapes_who_you_are#t-37436

[109] Wikipedia, "Post-It Note". More at: https://en.wikipedia.org/wiki/Post-it_Note

[110] Lou Dzierzak, "Factoring Fear: What Scares Us and Why - Scientists scan the brain in an attempt to explain the hows and whys of being afraid--very afraid" (Scientific America, October 27, 2008). Read the article: https://www.scientificamerican.com/article/factoring-fear-what-scares/

[111] Joy Hirsch as quoted in "Factoring Fear: What Scares Us and Why - Scientists scan the brain in an attempt to explain the hows and whys of being afraid--very afraid", by Lou Dzierzak (Scientific America, October 27, 2008). Read the article: https://www.scientificamerican.com/article/factoring-fear-what-scares/

[112] Wikipedia, "Amygdala". https://en.wikipedia.org/wiki/Amygdala

[113] Andrea Bonior, Ph.D., licensed clinical psychologist and speaker. She is the author of the upcoming *Psychology: Essential Thinkers, Classic Theories, and How They Inform Your World*, and *The Friendship Fix,* and serves on the faculty of Georgetown University.)

[114] Dictionary.com, "Striving".

[115] Wikipedia, "Shell money". https://en.wikipedia.org/wiki/Shell_money

[116] Wikipedia, "Wealth". https://en.wikipedia.org/wiki/Wealth

[117] Lisa Nicols, "*Abundance Now: Amplify Your Life & Achieve Prosperity Today"*. Talks at Google. Published on Jan 13, 2016. Listen at: https://www.youtube.com/watch?v=nKTAZAmJ_Js

[118] Douglas Harper, "Strive" (Dictionary.com, 2010).

[119] Dictionary.com, "Striving". https://www.dictionary.com/browse/striving?s=t

[120] Yanik Silver, *"Evolved Enterprise"* (Idea Press Publishing, 2017), including *"TOMS Shoes"* and *"Warby Parker".*

[121] Dr. Martin E.P. Seligman and Christopher Peterson, "The VIA Survey of Character Strengths", validated by Robert McGrath, PhD. To access the survey, go to: https://www.viacharacter.org/www/Character-Strengths-Survey

[122] Michael Brown, *"The Presence Process"* (Beaufort Books, 2010).

[123] Tasha Giroux, Regional Vice President – RBC (Royal Bank of Canada), Teleconference interview - July 31, 2017
To listen to the audio recording, go to: https://yvonne_5471e7.gr8.com/

[124] Mark Waldman, *"NeuroTips for Money, Happiness & Success: 21 Productivity Tips for your Brain".*

[125] *Etch-A-Sketch* – The Ohio Art Company, and Spin Master

[126] Gill Corkindale, "Overcoming Imposter Syndrome" Harvard Business Review (May 07, 2008). Read the full article: https://hbr.org/2008/05/overcoming-imposter-syndrome

[127] Carol Dweck, *Mindset: The New Psychology of Success* (New York: Ballantine Books, 2016).

[128] Sean Stephenson — https://www.youtube.com/watch?v=50vKBG4NTE8
Amy Purdy — https://ed.ted.com/on/EEqOvVLr
Nicholas James Vujicic — https://youtu.be/8jhcxOhIMAQ
Conjoined Twins Abby And Brittany — https://www.youtube.com/watch?v=VMzK6iz6uVs

[129] Catherine Brownlee – Founder, CBI (Catherine Brownlee International) and Prominent Personnel
ZOOM Interview –Dec. 28th, 2017 https://youtu.be/wLyvNzexAnY

[130] Dr. Martin E.P. Seligman and Christopher Peterson, "The VIA Survey of Character Strengths", validated by Robert McGrath, PhD. To access the survey, go to: https://www.viacharacter.org/www/Character-Strengths-Survey

[131] Alison Donaghey – Founder – Domino Thinking, Speaker, Think Opposite Radio Show Host, Author - *"Think Opposite: Using The Domino Effect To Change Your Business, Change The World"* ZOOM Interview – Apr. 3rd, 2018 https://youtu.be/_YXKZ7HF6tl

[132] Dr. Stephen R. Covey, "Seek first to understand", *The 7 Habits of Highly Effective People* (first published 1989). https://www.franklincovey.com/the-7-habits/habit-5.html

[133] Teresa de Grosbois, author of *Mass Influence: The Habits of the Highly Influential*. More on influence at: https://teresadegrosbois.com/

[134] Frigyes Karinthy in 1929 and popularized in an eponymous 1990 play written by John Guare, on Wikipedia. More at: https://en.wikipedia.org/wiki/Six_degrees_of_separation

[135] Didem Tali (contributor), "The 'Average' Woman Is Now Size 16 Or 18. Why Do Retailers Keep Failing Her?", Forbes, September 30, 2016. Read the

article at: https://www.forbes.com/sites/didemtali/2016/09/30/the-average-woman-size/#e079c1c27911

[136] Marcus Noland and Tyler Moran, "Firms with More Women in the C-Suite Are More Profitable", Harvard Business Review, February 08, 2016. Peterson Institute for International Economics survey - https://hbr.org/2016/02/study-firms-with-more-women-in-the-c-suite-are-more-profitable http://www.catalyst.org/system/files/why_diversity_matters_catalyst_0.pdf

[137] Sarah Dinolfo, Christine Silva and Nancy M. Carter, "High Potentials in The Pipeline: Leaders Pay It Forward", Catalyst Canada, June 1, 2012. Read the article: https://www.catalyst.org/system/files/High_Potentials_In_the_Pipeline_Leaders_Pay_It_Forward.pdf

[138] Ellen Petry Leanse, "'Just' Say No". Article at: https://www.linkedin.com/pulse/just-say-ellen-petry-leanse/)

[139] Cambridge Dictionary – English, "Meritocratic". https://dictionary.cambridge.org/dictionary/english/meritocratic

[140] Leslie Davies — The Stylish Insider – International Women's Day Conference 2012 co-chair with Yvonne E.L. Silver. Article at: https://www.winnipegfreepress.com/business/coaches-help-women-reach-for-heights-143034735.html

[141] Casey A. Klofstad, Stephen Nowicki, and Rindy C. Anderson, "How Voice Pitch Influences Our Choice of Leaders - Candidates' vocal characteristics influence voters' attitudes toward them", *The American Scientist*, Issue September-October 2016, Volume 104, Number 5, Page 282, DOI: 10.1511/2016.122.282 Read the article at: https://www.americanscientist.org/article/how-voice-pitch-influences-our-choice-of-leaders

[142] Mihaly Csikszentmihalyi, "All About Flow & Positive Psychology", Positive Psychology Program. More at: https://positivepsychologyprogram.com/mihaly-csikszentmihalyi-father-of-flow/

[143] The Wynford Group, *CANADIAN SALARY SURVEYS (IAT)*. Further information at: https://www.wynfordgroup.com/wynfordsurveys/surveymain.shtml

[144] Daniel Pink, *"DRIVE: The surprising truth about what really motivates us"*, (New York: Riverhead Books, 2009).

[145] Mark Waldman, author of *NeuroWisdom: The New Brain Science of Money, Happiness, and Success*

[146] Wikipedia, "Etch A Sketch". Information at:
https://en.wikipedia.org/wiki/Etch_A_Sketch

[147] David Rock, *Your Brain At Work*, (HarperCollins, 2009). More at:
https://blog.12min.com/your-brain-at-work-summary/

[148] Darren Hardy, Daily Success Mentoring

[149] Steven F. Covey, "Big Rocks Time Management". Watch the demonstration
at: https://youtu.be/fmV0gXpXwDU

[150] Dr. Martin E.P. Seligman and Christopher Peterson, "The VIA Survey of
Character Strengths", validated by Robert McGrath, PhD. To access the survey,
go to: https://www.viacharacter.org/www/Character-Strengths-Survey

[151] Dictionary.com Unabridged, based on the Random House Dictionary,
(Random House, 2018).

[152] Scott Dockweiler, "How Much Time Do We Spend in Meetings? (Hint: It's
Scary)", The Muse, The Daily Muse. Read more at:
https://www.themuse.com/advice/how-much-time-do-we-spend-in-meetings-
hint-its-scary

[153] Michael Mankins, Chris Brahm, and Greg Caimi, "Your Scarcest Resource",
Harvard Business Review - Meetings, From the May 2014 Issue. Read more at:
https://hbr.org/2014/05/your-scarcest-resource

[154] David Cooperrider and associates, "Appreciative Inquiry", Case Western
Reserve University School of Management. Study information at:
https://en.wikipedia.org/wiki/Appreciative_inquiry

[155] Neal Taparia, "Kick The Chair: How Standing Cut Our Meeting Times By
25 percent", Forbes, June 19, 2014ore at:
https://www.forbes.com/sites/groupthink/2014/06/19/kick-the-chair-how-
standing-cut-our-meeting-times-by-25/#12fa66e035fe

[156] Dictionary.com, "Chore".

[157] Status of Women Committee on April 30th, 2014. Comments by Alex
Johnston, executive director of Catalyst Canada. Read the meeting notes at:
https://openparliament.ca/committees/status-of-women/41-2/21/

[158] AAUW – reports have been updated since quote researched in March 2018.
More current information on wage gaps at:
https://www.aauw.org/resource/gender-pay-gap-by-state-and-congressional-

district/

[159] Teresa de Grosbois, *Mass Influence: The Habits of the Highly Influential (Wildfire Workshops, 2015)*. More at: https://teresadegrosbois.com/

[160] Babcock and Laschever (2003) reported survey evidence in "Do Women Avoid Salary Negotiations? Evidence from a Large Scale Natural Field Experiment". Andreas Leibbrandt and John A. List, NBER Working Paper No. 1851, November 2012, JEL No. C93, JO Abstract: http://www.nber.org/papers/w18511.pdf

[161] Jaymi Heimbuch, "*10 bizarre and beautiful bird courtship dances*", Mother Nature Network, November 16, 2015. More on this: https://www.mnn.com/earth-matters/animals/stories/10-bizarre-beautiful-bird-courtship-dances

[162] Paul Davidson, "What's your salary? becomes a no-no in job interviews", USA TODAY, April 27, 2017. Read the article: https://www.usatoday.com/story/money/2017/04/27/whats-your-salary-becomes-no-no-job-interviews/100933948/

[163] Lydia Frank, "Why Banning Questions About Salary History May Not Improve Pay Equity", Harvard Business Review, September 05, 2017. Read the article: https://hbr.org/2017/09/why-banning-questions-about-salary-history-may-not-improve-pay-equity

[164] Bob Sherwin (contributor), "Why Women Are More Effective Leaders Than Men", Business Insider, Jan. 24, 2014. Read the research: https://www.businessinsider.com/study-women-are-better-leaders-2014-1

[165] Sarah Stawiski, Ph.D., Jennifer Deal, Ph.D., and Marian Ruderman, Ph.D., *"Building trust in the workplace – A key to retaining women"* Centre for Creative Leadership, Published August 2010. To read the article: https://www.ccl.org/articles/quickview-leadership-articles/building-trust-in-the-workplace-a-key-to-retaining-women/ (accessed September 14, 2018)

[166] Sheryl Sandberg and Anna Maria Chávez, "'Bossy,' the Other B-word", The Wall Street Journal - Saturday Essay, Updated March 8, 2014. Article at: https://www.wsj.com/articles/sheryl-sandberg-and-anna-maria-chavez-on-bossy-the-other-b-word-1394236848

[167] 'Bossy,' the Other B-word, Wall Street Journal interview, Sheryl Sandberg and Anna Maria Chávez, embedded in article: https://www.wsj.com/articles/sheryl-sandberg-and-anna-maria-chavez-on-bossy-the-other-b-word-1394236848

[168] Leslie Davies, Internationally Certified Image Consultant, Stylist with The Stylish Insider. ZOOM Interview - November 13, 2017 https://youtu.be/__Ijcvyjrbk

[169] Melinda Wittstock – Founder Verifeed and the WINGS of Inspired Business Podcast, ZOOM Interview - Dec. 20th, 2017 http://bit.ly/2Fwlizd

[170] Eckhart Tolle, *Stillness Speaks* (New World Library, 2003).

[171] David Rock, *Your Brain At Work*, (HarperCollins, 2009).

[172] Amy Cuddy, "Your Body Language Shapes Who You Are", TEDGlobal 2012. Watch the video:http://www.ted.com/talks/amy_cuddy_your_body_language_shapes_who_you_are#t-37436

[173] Leslie Davies, Internationally Certified Image Consultant, Stylist with The Stylish Insider. ZOOM Interview - November 13, 2017 https://youtu.be/__Ijcvyjrbk

[173] "What are the 'Five Cs Of Credit", Investopedia. Article at: https://www.investopedia.com/terms/f/five-c-credit.asp

[175] Yvonne E.L. Silver, Confident and Influential Women interview series,, shared on YouTube at: Patty Farmer, International Speaker, Growth Strategist, co-author: *Make Your Connections Count: Top experts share strategies that work* https://youtu.be/DOwPImWq5xQ